THE SOVIET UNION AND THE YEMENS

STUDIES OF INFLUENCE IN INTERNATIONAL RELATIONS

Alvin Z. Rubinstein, General Editor

THE SOVIET UNION AND THE YEMENS

Influence in Asymmetrical Relationships

Stephen Page

PRAEGER SPECIAL STUDIES • PRAEGER SCIENTIFIC

New York • Philadelphia • Eastbourne, UK
Toronto • Hong Kong • Tokyo • Sydney

Library of Congress Cataloging in Publication Data

Page, Stephen.
  The Soviet Union and the Yemens.

  (Studies of influence in international relations)
  Bibliography: p.
  Includes index.
  1. Soviet Union – Foreign relations – Yemen. 2. Soviet Union – Foreign relations – Yemen (People's Democratic Republic) 3. Yemen – Foreign relations – Soviet Union. 4. Yemen (People's Democratic Republic) – Foreign relations – Soviet Union. 5. Soviet Union – Foreign relation – 1945-   I. Title. II. Series.
  DK68.7.Y4P.34 1985   327.47053'3   85-512
  ISBN 0-03-070738-2 (alk. paper)
  ISBN 0-03-070739-0 (pbk. : alk. paper)

Published and Distributed by the Praeger Publishers Division (ISBN Prefix 0-275) of Greenwood Press, Inc., Westport, Connecticut

Published in 1985 by Praeger Publishers
CBS Educational and Professional Publishing, a Division of CBS Inc.
521 Fifth Avenue, New York, NY 10175 USA

© 1985 by Praeger Publishers

All rights reserved

56789 052 987654321

Printed in the United States of America on acid-free paper

INTERNATIONAL OFFICES

Orders from outside the United States should be sent to the appropriate address listed below. Orders from areas not listed below should be placed through CBS International Publishing, 383 Madison Ave., New York, NY 10175 USA

Australia, New Zealand
Holt Saunders, Pty, Ltd., 9 Waltham St., Artarmon, N.S.W. 2064, Sydney, Australia

Canada
Holt, Rinehart & Winston of Canada, 55 Horner Ave., Toronto, Ontario, Canada M8Z 4X6

Europe, the Middle East, & Africa
Holt Saunders, Ltd., 1 St. Anne's Road, Eastbourne, East Sussex, England BN21 3UN

Japan
Holt Saunders, Ltd., Ichibancho Central Building, 22-1 Ichibancho, 3rd Floor, Chiyodaku, Tokyo, Japan

Hong Kong, Southeast Asia
Holt Saunders Asia, Ltd., 10 Fl, Intercontinental Plaza, 94 Granville Road, Tsim Sha Tsui East, Kowloon, Hong Kong

Manuscript submissions should be sent to the Editorial Director, Praeger Publishers, 521 Fifth Avenue, New York, NY 10175 USA

Dedicated to
the memory of my father
and to my mother
without whose support over the years
none of this would have been possible

CONTENTS

Editor's Preface ... ix

Preface ... xi

Acknowledgments ... xv

Glossary of Acronyms ... xvii

Glossary of Arabic Names ... xix

PART I: INTRODUCTION

1 Background and Setting ... 3

PART II: MOSCOW AND THE PDRY: THE DEVELOPMENT OF A LOYAL ALLY

2 Moscow: Hesitation and Commitment to the PDRY (1967-73) ... 15

3 The PDRY: *Zigzagy* in Its Relations with the USSR (1973-78) ... 49

4 The PDRY: A State of Socialist Orientation (1978-84) ... 86

5 Moscow, the PDRY, and Oman: The Limitations of Influence (1967-84) ... 125

PART III: MOSCOW AND THE YAR: THE PROGRESS OF RELATIONS AND THE YEMENI UNITY ISSUE

6 Moscow and the YAR: Relations at Low Ebb (1970-77) — 157

7 Moscow and the YAR: Disaster and Recovery (1978-84) — 179

PART IV: CONCLUSION

8 Conclusion — 205

Selected Bibliography — 215

Index — 219

About the Author — 227

EDITOR'S PREFACE

Soviet policy toward the Yemeni sector of the Arabian Peninsula has unfortunately received relatively little attention in the West, even though over the years it has loomed prominently in the Kremlin's "forward policy" of penetrating the Middle East, seeking military advantages, and affecting regional developments. The two Yemens — the Yemen Arab Republic (YAR) in the north and the People's Democratic Republic of Yemen (PDRY) in the south — occupy the strategic littoral of the Arabian Peninsula at the entrance to the Red Sea and astride the sea lanes to the Persian Gulf and South Asia. Their vulnerability to intrusion — and intrinsic strategic importance — was recognized by the USSR in the mid-1950s when the Kremlin's quest for clients among the anti-Western Arab countries began in earnest. Given the region's huge oil resources, Moscow's ultimate objective is presumed to be the subverting of the Saudi monarchy, most probably through aggravation of Saudi-Yemeni tensions and radicalization of the Yemeni rimland of the Arabian Peninsula. Courtship of the two Yemens has enabled the USSR to pursue a low level, low cost, and low risk, but high stake, foreign policy in a complex region where sudden turnabouts can have disproportionate impacts on the broader strategic environment, not only in the Arab world but in relations between the Soviet Union and the United States as well.

Soviet strategists sense that the Yemenis are a key to the future of the Arabian Peninsula. Forming the most numerous single Arabic-speaking group on the peninsula and constituting an essential component of Saudi Arabia's work force, the Yemenis have spread throughout the peninsula. Their emerging nationalism and political restlessness will have momentous consequences for future stability in the region. A rapidly multiplying, energetic, economically backward and socially depressed people, whom the Saudis fear, they are ever in the eye of Soviet diplomacy.

Dr. Stephen Page's study, *The Soviet Union and the Yemens*, is a signal contribution to our knowledge of the Middle East. A model of scholarship, it is the first book on the subject in the English language, and shows what can be done with existing materials. It is a mine of information, rich in insights and thoughtful speculations about Soviet-YAR and Soviet-PDRY influence relationships. The author skillfully probes the uneven layers of tenuous data that are available and relevant to illumine the tactile nature of these relationships, and amply documents the predominantly strategic-military character of Soviet aims and accomplishments. His assessment is as lucid as it is thoughtful.

The chronological approach seems well-suited for elucidating the often deliberately obscure meaning of Soviet and Arab writings and for suggesting plausible underlying patterns. It permits the reader to trace the evolution of Soviet policy, to consider the ways that domestic developments helped shape Soviet moves and were in turn affected by them, and to assess the multitiered levels of explanation offered by the author.

Dr. Page brings Yemeni politics alive — an impressive feat, given the relative isolation of the two countries from mainstream Western scholarship. In the process, he makes understandable the intricacies and interconnections of tribal, ideological, political, military, economic, and personal determinants. What we have is a cast of little-known actors who behave in varied, complicated, occasionally ruthless, yet invariably coherent, ways.

Though the main setting is the PDRY and the YAR, always in our purview are relevant developments in Saudi Arabia, Oman, the Arab nationalist movement, and across the Red Sea in the Horn of Africa. Also never far from view is the ongoing U.S.-Soviet rivalry in the region. Reluctant to conclude more from the episodic record than is substantively warranted, Dr. Page demonstrates the USSR's tenacious policy of exploiting, and sometimes fostering, regional instability and conflicts, and provides a clear analysis of the subtle nature — and limits — of Soviet influence. His study of Soviet-PDRY and Soviet-YAR relationships is a distinguished addition to the series, *Studies of Influence in International Relations*.

Alvin Z. Rubinstein
Series Editor

PREFACE

The two Yemens, the People's Democratic Republic of Yemen (also referred to as the PDRY, South Yemen, and until 1971, the People's Republic of South Yemen, or PRSY) and the Yemen Arab Republic (YAR, North Yemen) occupy important strategic positions on the southwestern edge of the Arabian Peninsula. Small and desperately poor, threatened at times in the 1970s by outside attack and internal subversion, they appear to be susceptible to influence exercised by global and regional powers ready to extend assistance. The disparity in resources and power in these relationships inevitably makes them heavily asymmetrical.

Neither country has suffered from inattention by outside powers. North Yemen, after being wooed by the Soviets and (more forcefully) by the Egyptians in the 1950s and 1960s, has been persistently and obtrusively courted by Saudi Arabia since then. Moscow did not abandon its suit, and by the end of the decade was again in pursuit of an influential position. However, the Soviets devoted greater effort to the PDRY; its location and military facilities were potentially of more substantial benefit to Soviet goals; in addition, the South Yemen regime was isolated from its conservative neighbors by its ideology and radical policies, and actively sought out Soviet assistance across the whole spectrum of its activities. This relationship was so one-sided that the comprehensive exercise of influence seemed inevitable.

"Influence" is a much-used word in international affairs, and it is usually used without much precision. Great powers are assumed to exercise a great deal of influence. In the United States it is often assumed that the Soviet Union influences, or even controls, the decisions of countries (particularly small, impoverished clients such as the PDRY) in which it has a significant military and political presence. (In the USSR the same assumptions are made about U.S. presence.) It is also often assumed that such influence is ever-increasing and permanent, and overrides any interests the client state might have. This however is too simplistic and dangerously misleading. All states do try to build influence — to induce other states to take actions or positions favorable to the interests of the influencer; superpowers are particularly intent on this. However, evidence indicates that even a substantial military, political, and economic presence in a client country does not translate automatically into influence, that even in such a situation it may be the client state that is the 'influencer,' the superpower the 'influencee.' Moreover, even when a superpower has established influence over the decisions of a client, it has been observed that such a relationship is rarely lasting without constant reinforcement.

Despite such difficulties, the prize of gaining some measure of control over the actions of strategically located states is sufficient to warrant considerable attention to influence-building by the superpowers and other countries. This has been evidenced by their activities in the southwest corner of the Arabian Peninsula.

It is the purpose of this study to discover the actual extent of Soviet influence in the PDRY and the YAR in the 1970s and early 1980s.

The concepts and methodology used have been adapted from Alvin Z. Rubinstein's *Red Star on the Nile: The Soviet-Egyptian Influence Relationship since the June War* (Princeton, N.J.: Princeton University Press, 1977), the flagship of this series. Thus 'influence' is said to be manifested "when A affects, through non-military means, directly or indirectly, the behavior of B so that it redounds to the policy advantage of A" (p. xiv). Two categories of influence may be construed from Professor Rubinstein's study: that in which A acts to change B's behavior, and that in which A provides the resources enabling B to pursue its goals (which are in concert with A's). I have added a third category: that in which A acts to change the regional political environment so that B's policy options are significantly limited or even restricted to policies favored by A. Influence is assumed not to be constant and to reveal itself most readily in a close examination of the parties' interaction on 'issue areas'; one of the main instruments of such an examination is the visiting (particularly of political and military delegations) that occurs between the countries, and the communiqués of and media reaction to these visits. Another underlying assumption is that the exercise of influence (and the limitations on that exercise) becomes evident in the behavior of the country influenced, and thus it is crucial to pay close attention to its political process and decisions.

This methodology raises certain problems in a study of Soviet influence in the Yemens. The difficulties in analyzing Moscow's aims and political decisions in its relations with other countries are well known; they are compounded in this case by the secretive nature of the political systems in the two Yemens (and in neighboring states, whose actions and reactions have been an important factor in Soviet activities in the Yemens), and the difficulty of getting nonofficial interpretations of events there (especially in the PDRY). This forces an analyst to deal in more speculation than he or she may be comfortable with. In addition, the relatively small number of visits (only two by YAR leaders in the 14 years under study; many more by PDRY leaders and delegations, but still not a large number) has meant that other instruments of analysis have been extensively used as well.

Finally, there have been few significant on-going but limited issues between these countries on which to concentrate. One, the Soviet interaction with the PDRY over the Dhofar rebellion and PDRY-Omani relations, I have treated on its own (Chapter 5). Another, the Soviet reaction to the Yemeni unity issue, I have analyzed in conjunction with the developments of Soviet-YAR relations (Chapters 6 and 7) on the grounds that Moscow is only interested in seeing unity achieved if the YAR will agree to the PDRY's conditions. The centrality of the PDRY-Soviet relationship to the other issue areas, and indeed to Soviet objectives in the Indian Ocean/Red Sea region, led me to designate its development as a third, very broad, issue area (Chapters 2-4). Inevitably the first two areas are overlapped by the third and must be read in close conjunction with it.

ACKNOWLEDGMENTS

I do not have words to express the gratitude I feel toward Albert and Roberta Wohlstetter who, on the strength of a ten-year old book encouraged and stimulated me to resume research into Soviet-Arabian Peninsula relations, and made it possible for me to find funding, and toward J.B. Kelly, who backed them up. To Alvin Rubinstein, who on similarly tenuous grounds invited me to write this book, and whose infectious enthusiasm kept me at it, I owe an equally large debt.

Many people, American, Israeli, Yemeni, and English have been very generous in sharing their time and ideas with me; in Washington, D.C. where I did most of the research, officials, former officials, and academics readily made themselves available. They were too numerous to mention here, but I would like to thank specifically Oles Smolansky of Lehigh University, Bernard Reich of George Washington University, John Peterson of the College of William and Mary, Joseph Kostiner of Tel Aviv University, and Karen Dawisha of the University of Southampton, and to acknowledge a special debt to Fred Halliday of the London School of Economics for his patience in answering my many requests for information and interpretation. All of the above, named and unnamed, have helped with the preparation of this book; I alone am responsible for any errors or omissions of factual material and for its interpretation.

I wish to thank the Social Sciences and Humanities Research Council of Canada, which provided generous funding for the writing of this book, and for the research on Soviet-Arabian peninsula relations of which it represents one part. I also want to thank Sheridan College for the remainder of the funding and for the time to do the research and writing, and the Library of Congress for the provision of study facilities. My thanks also to those involved in the production of the book, especially to Heather Leshuk, who coped valiantly with the typing of the manuscript and the many last-minute revisions, and to Fran Wilson for her constant help and support in these and other matters.

Finally, I can express only inadequately my gratitude to my family — my two boys, Geoff and Ian, for their acceptance of the importance of this work to me, and most of all to my wife, Joanne, who for the past three years put aside much that was important to her in order that I might accomplish this.

GLOSSARY OF ACRONYMS

CMEA	Council of Mutual Economic Assistance
CPSU	Communist Party of the Soviet Union
DLF	Dhofar Liberation Front
FLOSY	Front for the Liberation of South Yemen
GCC	Gulf Cooperation Council
NDF	National Democratic Front (YAR)
NF	National Front (PDRY)
NLF	National Liberation Front (PDRY)
PDRY	People's Democratic Republic of Yemen
PDU	Popular Democratic Union (PDRY)
PFLO	Popular Front for the Liberation of Oman
PFLOAG	Popular Front for the Liberation of the Occupied Arab Gulf
PFLOAG	Popular Front for the Liberation of Oman and the Arab Gulf
PRSY	People's Republic of South Yemen
PVP	People's Vanguard Party (PDRY)
RDF	Rapid Deployment Force (U.S.)
UPONF	United Political Organization-National Front (PDRY)
YAR	Yemen Arab Republic
YSP	Yemeni Socialist Party

GLOSSARY OF ARABIC NAMES

PDRY

Ali, Salim Rubay	President June 1969 - June 1978
Antar, Ali	Defense Minister 1977 - 1981
Ismail, Abd al-Fattah	General Secretary of the NF and YSP June 1969 - April 1980; President December 1978 - April 1980
Muhammad, Ali Nasir	Prime Minister August 1971 - present; President April 1980 - present; General Secretary of the YSP April 1980 - present
Muti, Muhammad Salih	Foreign Minister May 1973 - August 1980
Qasim, Salih Muslih	Interior Minister 1973 - 1977; Defense Minister 1981 - present
as-Shaabi, Qahtan	President 1967 - June 1969

YAR

Abd al-Alim, Abdullah	Commander of the Paratroops until he led them in rebellion April 1978
al-Ahmar, Abdullah	Leader of the Hashid tribal federation
al-Asnaj, Abdullah	Leader of FLOSY; Foreign Minister 1971 - March 1979
al-Ayni, Muhsin	Prime Minister September 1971 - December 1972, June 1974 - January 1975
al-Ghashmi, Ahmad	Chief of Staff 1974 - October 1977; President October 1977 - June 1978
al-Hamdi Ibrahim	President June 1974 - October 1977
al-Iryani, Abd al-Rahman	Leader of the Presidential Council 1970 - 1974
Salih, Ali Abdullah	President July 1978 - present
Umar, Sultan Ahmad	Leader of the NDF

OMAN

Al Said, Qabus bin Said	Sultan July 1970 - present

THE SOVIET UNION
AND THE YEMENS

PART I

INTRODUCTION

1
BACKGROUND AND SETTING

Isolated historically in its location on the periphery of the periphery of the Middle East and further cut off by its division into hundreds of tribal areas, possessing few natural resources, the southwest corner of the Arabian Peninsula might seem at first glance an improbable region for a superpower's quest for influence and advantage.[1] In fact, South Arabia has continually been the object of intense interest of powerful countries, primarily because of its location adjacent to major communications and trading routes. Thus, for example, the British took Aden in 1839 as part of their strategy to protect the western approaches to India. After the opening of the Suez Canal in 1869 Aden became much more significant; with its excellent natural harbor and modern port facilities, it became one of the busiest ports in the world. More important, it commanded the nearby Bab al-Mandeb straits, a potential chokepoint in the southern approaches to the Suez Canal, Europe's gateway to the Far East.

This strategic location made Aden a worthy prize, and several countries attempted to dislodge the British by establishing control of its hinterland or allying with local shaikhs to put pressure on British positions. As a result, by the mid-1930s the area had been divided into two political jurisdictions. On the Red Sea coast an Imam, chosen by the tribes of the adjacent highlands, dominated the coastal tribes and those in the southern region close to Aden's immediate hinterland. Partly in reaction, the British had moved out from their colony in Aden and established two protectorates. The boundary between the Imamate and the West Aden Protectorate cut through many tribal areas, and the Imams of Yemen never accepted its validity or the fact of British rule.

The Soviets, recognizing an ally no matter how objectively reactionary, signed a treaty of friendship with Imam Yahya in 1928.[2] The tie was purely symbolic, for the USSR was not in the arms business yet and had no military capability to threaten the British in Aden. In any case Yahya was deeply religious, reactionary, and intensely suspicious of all foreigners. The Soviets could try to encourage him to do what he was going to do anyway, but it is doubtful that they had any impact.

By the mid-1950s, when Moscow renewed its interest, the situation in southwest Arabia had not changed very much. Yemen was still in a lamentable state of backwardness and poverty under Yahya's son, Ahmad, and still divided on religious lines between the tribes of the northern highlands and the coastal and southern regions. Ahmad was carrying on the struggle for Britain's expulsion from Aden and the Protectorates, but also felt threatened by a British plan to create a federation and some semblance of self-rule in the Protectorates, a scheme which might appeal to Yemenis in the southern regions (who had tribal and religious ties with Protectorate tribes), never happy with the Imam's rule.

Thus the Imam needed help, and Moscow recognized that its aims would be furthered by providing it; in late 1955 it signed another Treaty of Friendship. By this time the Soviets had embarked on a strategy of developing relations with the Third World, using their enhanced military, political, and economic resources. They and their allies extended economic aid to Yemen, and, more important, provided arms on easy terms. The arms were obsolete and the quantities small, but they were more than adequate to reequip Yemen's small military forces and allow the Imam to distribute his older weapons to maintain the loyalty of tribal allies. The arms encouraged Ahmad to intensify his struggle with the British; this was an ideal conflict from the Soviet point of view: small-scale (thus unlikely to drag them into a confrontation with Britain), long-running (thus likely to increase Yemen's dependence on the USSR for training, spare parts, ammunition and replacements), and not susceptible to a British victory (thus likely to weaken Britain's power and prestige throughout south Arabia, with possible consequences in the Persian Gulf).

However, the Soviets discovered that the influence generated by their military and economic aid was very limited. They were able to encourage Ahmad to do what he wanted to do in any case, but they were not able to dissuade him from moves contrary to their interests. Thus he established relations with the Chinese, who set up an economic aid program that was more visible and successful than the Soviets'; in 1961 he broke with Nasir, abandoned almost completely his fight with the British, and accepted small amounts of U.S. aid.

Moscow's quest for an influential position seemed to have been revitalized in September 1962 when a coup by the army (a group with close ties to the Soviets), led by Colonel Abdullah as-Sallal (known to be pro-Soviet) proclaimed the Yemen Arab Republic (YAR). The new regime's first pronouncements not only suggested that it would adopt a pro-Soviet foreign policy but also promised economic, social, and political reforms so sweeping that by their example they might shake the British in Aden and the pro-Western conservative rulers in the rest of the Arabian Peninsula. The YAR, it appeared, would further Soviet goals in the region.

First the new regime had to have help. The Imam had escaped, and with financial assistance and arms from Saudi Arabia had rallied many of the tribes; it appeared that the republican armed forces were not strong enough to ensure the survival of the republic. Moscow did not respond directly,[3] for the YAR needed trained troops, not more weapons, and the Soviets were not willing or able to make that effort. However, they were willing to support with funds and propaganda Jamal Abd al-Nasir's eagerness to undertake the defense of the YAR while spreading his influence on the peninsula. At the same time, the USSR facilitated Egyptian logistics by building a modern airport near the YAR capital city, Sanaa, and by expanding the main port of Hodaydah (which they had built); these two facilities, particularly the airport, were also intended to extend Soviet access to the Red Sea region in the future.

The Soviet strategy of leaving direct intervention to the Egyptians was risk free and relatively low cost, but it demonstrated the disadvantages of entrusting foreign policy goals to a third party. First, the Egyptians were sensitive about their position and reluctant to see direct Soviet involvement with the YAR; thus even the signing of a new 20-year Treaty of Friendship (an extremely important type of transaction between the USSR and Third World countries), during the well-publicized visit of as-Sallal to Moscow in March 1964, was not announced at the time.[4]

Second, the Egyptians were never able to control more than one-third of the country; Nasir's prestige declined, and the Soviets' with it. Third, as the Egyptians gradually assumed control of the Sanaa government, Yemenis' dislike of them increased and the Soviets' popularity inevitably declined. At the same time, as-Sallal became generally perceived as an Egyptian puppet and this, together with Egypt's inability to force a military conclusion to the civil war, gave impetus to the emergence of a 'third force' of Yemeni politicians eager to find a political solution by compromising with the royalists. Finally, by entrusting the military situation to Nasir, Moscow lost any influence it might have had over the outcome. Nasir rejected Soviet suggestions that he use some of their military aid to rebuild and strengthen the republican army, and the chance for a strong, radical YAR which could influence events on the Peninsula disappeared, given the *coup de grace* by the Egyptian defeat in Sinai at the hands of Israel in July 1967 which forced Nasir to withdraw his troops.

In their wake was installed a moderate regime in Sanaa which espoused not only republican principles, positive neutrality, and nonalignment, but also negotiations with the royalists to end the war. The war, however, continued, with the royalists having the upper hand. By mid-December they were besieging Sanaa and seemed certain to destroy the republic. Moscow demonstrated its commitment to the republic's survival with an emergency airlift of small arms and ammunition, and also combat aircraft with technicians and ground crew; moreover, such was the urgency of the situation that for the first time in a nonaligned state, Soviet pilots flew combat missions. This was a measure of some desperation, but a royalist victory would have meant the loss of a considerable investment and of a strategic position on the Red Sea coast. (It would also have left exposed the most recent and vulnerable addition to the 'progressive' Arab states, the People's Republic of South Yemen, proclaimed on November 30, 1967.) The emergency military aid undoubtedly helped to save these Soviet interests; further shipments of tanks, jet fighters, and light weapons in the spring of 1968 enabled the republican regime to stabilize the military situation.

In October Yemeni Prime Minister Hasan al-Amri travelled to Moscow and after meetings with Soviet Premier Aleksei Kosygin,

Defense Minister Andrei Grechko, and economic aid officials, came away satisfied. The communiqué registered Soviet willingness to support the republic, referring to discussions on "ways of further cooperation in the economic field" and further Soviet help in "strengthening the defense capability of the Yemen Arab Republic."[5] Following the visit, more arms arrived.

However the weapons were not enough to enable the weak army to extend the regime's control. Republican leaders, tired of the years of fighting and seeing no prospect of military victory, concentrated on a political solution. By July 1970 their stance had become sufficiently moderate, even conservative, for them to invite royalist participation in their regime. Saudi Arabia agreed to end its support of the royalists and extend diplomatic recognition to the republic.

By that time Sanaa was also engaged in expanding its sources of economic aid, having resumed diplomatic recognition with West Germany in return for aid, with the prospects bright for U.S. and British aid. The Soviets did not approve; but despite millions of dollars in economic aid, 50 military aircraft, large amounts of other military aid, and 200 advisers, their disapproval availed them nothing. It was reported that in February 1970 when royalist forces, making their last attack, took Sadah, Soviet advisers urged the government to react forcefully; it refused in order not to harm developing relations with Saudi Arabia. Moscow also tried to head off Yemen's resumption of diplomatic relations with Bonn by hinting that Soviet arms would be available only from East Germany; nevertheless, the YAR became the first Third World country to switch its diplomatic relations back from East to West Germany. All the USSR could do was to reduce its economic aid. However, it dared not carry this too far, lest it simply drive the North Yemenis closer to the West. Thus the aid projects already begun continued, but no new military or economic aid was promised.

In any case, by then a much more promising state, the People's Republic of South Yemen (PRSY), had emerged in Aden and the Protectorates, with a regime that professed Marxism-Leninism as its guiding principle. Ironically, in the infighting in South Arabia prior to independence, the Soviets had backed the wrong national liberation movement, and partly because of this relations between the USSR and the PRSY were somewhat hesitant at first (see below, pp. 15-19.) However, they warmed up as the young regime was threatened by émigré forces on its borders and as the Soviets saw that their advantage lay in helping it to survive.

What has been behind the intense interest of outsiders in the conditions in and policies of North and South Yemen? Recent motives seem not to differ very much from historical motives. They can be roughly categorized into economic, political, and military-strategic.

ECONOMIC

There is little if anything indigenous to the YAR and the PDRY to excite the interest of outside powers. They are two of the poorest countries in the world. Some parts of both have adequate rainfall and they can sustain agriculture, but it is small-scale and dependent on irrigation, and therefore expensive. Neither country has significant exports, neither possesses mineral wealth, and alone on the Arabian Peninsula neither possesses oil. Aden is situated on a fine natural harbor; during the British tenure modern port facilities and a refinery were constructed. However the departure of the British, the closure of the Suez Canal, the advent of supertankers, and the shortage of development capital in the PDRY have all contributed to the running down of these facilities. There seems to be little in the solely economic sphere to attract outside powers. Their economic weakness does seem to open the way for outside powers to use economic aid to gain influence. However, the scope of their economic problems and the proven unsuitability of economic aid as a means of generating lasting influence in the Third World serve to dampen interest in the long run.

POLITICAL

There is more of political interest in the area. In general, the Soviets have for decades believed that the Third World countries and national liberation movements are powerful potential allies in the antiimperialist struggle. In the Arabian Peninsula region, all societies have been undergoing unsettling modernization and change which, in conjunction with the Arab-Israeli conflict, have resulted in varying shades of anti-Western feeling. Moscow has hoped to capitalize on this situation to reduce Western presence and influence while expanding and consolidating its own; however, it has not had much success in persuading the oil-producing countries, whose resources are so vital to Western economies, to establish normal relations. Only in the Yemens have the Soviets succeeded in establishing the kind of relations which might be translated into influence. (This they have accomplished through the flexible application of an impressive variety of instruments: economic aid, propaganda and political support, naval visits, support for national liberation movements, exploitation of regional conflict, and most important, military presence and aid.)

Although the Yemens are on the periphery of the Arabian Peninsula, they are not peripheral to the political stability of its member states. The YAR provides a significant portion of Saudi Arabia's labor force;[6] a radical government in Sanaa could have a destabilizing effect on Riyadh, and at least (if Moscow had sufficient influence) might be used to give the Soviets some leverage over Saudi policy. Thus Moscow has consistently attempted to improve its state-to-state and military-to-military relations with the YAR. The PDRY, with its policy for most of the past decade of supporting national liberation movements, has been a destabilizing factor, particularly with regard to Oman, which borders on the Persian Gulf oil countries and on the Strait of Hormuz. The Soviets have seen in its radicalism a possible instrument for the achievement of Soviet goals, and have nurtured and helped to defend it.

For the Western industrialized countries the political importance of southwest Arabia lies primarily in its contiguity to the oil states of the Gulf, particularly to Saudi Arabia. Perceiving a precarious stability in these states, the West's objectives are to ensure that the instability of the YAR and the radicalism (and Soviet connections) of the PDRY do not spread, and if possible to promote the development of a stable, pro-Western government in Sanaa.

MILITARY-STRATEGIC

It is the strategic position of the PDRY which most excites the interest and concern of outside powers, now as in the past. It lies close to Persian Gulf oil and adjacent to vital Western sea lines of communication, both the Red Sea route to the Suez Canal (and Israel) and the oil route from the Gulf. It is also reasonably well placed to assist projection of power into the Horn of Africa, the Red Sea, and the Persian Gulf. The United States in particular sees the PDRY as a potential threat to Western positions; it is controlled by an inimical government, allied to Moscow with its growing military might, and plays host to significant contingents of Soviet and Cuban military advisers; it has itself provided support to rebel movements in neighboring countries, a fact which leaves its conservative neighbors (including the YAR) and the United States prone to anxiety.

Soviet military-strategic interest in southwest Arabia has grown considerably in the past decade, as its developing ability to project power gave freer rein to its will to intervene in distant climes and to be regarded as a global power. Moscow's claim that events in the Middle East are of vital concern to the security of the USSR has expanded to encompass not just the contiguous Northern Tier and the volatile central (Arab-Israeli) region, but also the periphery. The interests of the superpowers have thus overlapped as the importance of the Arabian Peninsula has grown, and both have rushed to expand their military presence. For Moscow, this necessitated the acquisition of secure access to naval and air facilities from which to conduct and/or threaten both defensive and offensive operations; to do this the Soviets have worked to develop as close ties as possible with their friends on the periphery, especially the PDRY. Generally, in both Yemens as elsewhere in the region, the Soviet aim has been to reduce and expel U.S. military presence, or if that has not been possible, to stop its growth and limit its freedom of action.

NOTES

1. For details on ancient and modern conditions in southwest Arabia, cf. M.W. Wenner, *Modern Yemen 1918 - 1966*, (London: Oxford University Press, 1967); J. Peterson, *Yemen: The Search For a Modern State* (Baltimore: Johns Hopkins University Press, 1982); R.W. Stookey, *Yemen: The Politics of the Yemen Arab Republic* (Boulder: Westview Press, 1978); R.W. Stookey, *South Yemen: A Marxist Republic in Arabia* (Boulder: Westview Press, 1982).

2. For a detailed examination of Soviet reactions to events in southwest Arabia 1917-1970, cf. the author's *The USSR and Arabia: The development of Soviet policies and attitudes toward the countries of the Arabian Peninsula* (London: Central Asian Research Centre in association with the Canadian Institute of International Affairs, 1971).

3. In that era, the USSR had not yet adopted a forward military policy, and did not have adequate lift capability. Moreover, in October 1962 it was embroiled in the Cuban missile crisis, and did not wish to involve itself in a distant civil war.

4. Remarkably, this treaty was not mentioned again until 1968, when the Soviet Ambassador to the YAR referred to it as having been signed in 1967. [Y. Roi, *From Encroachment to Involvement* (New York: Wiley, 1974), pp.

496-97.] I found only two other references to it in Soviet sources until it came up for renewal in 1984. This continuing inattention probably stems from the Soviet shift to South Yemen in the 1970s, and the concurrent concern of the YAR not to antagonize Saudi Arabia unduly.

5. *Middle East Record 1968*, p. 51.

6. In 1975 40 percent of the Saudi Arabian immigrant work force came from the YAR (and 8 percent from the PDRY). J.S. Birks and C.A. Sinclair, "Migration and Development: The Changing Perspective of the Poor Arab Countries," *Journal of International Affairs* 33 (Fall/Winter 1979):286. At the peak of the oil boom, over a million workers from the YAR were in Saudi Arabia.

PART II

MOSCOW AND THE PDRY: THE DEVELOPMENT OF A LOYAL ALLY

2
MOSCOW: HESITATION AND COMMITMENT TO THE PDRY (1967-73)

FROM INDEPENDENCE (NOVEMBER 1967) TO THE CORRECTIVE MOVEMENT (JUNE 1969)[1]

The withdrawal of the British from South Arabia created new political and strategic realities and opportunities in the region; from Aden, the British for 130 years had dominated the Indian Ocean, the Arabian shore of the Persian Gulf, and the approach to the Suez Canal. Even more important was the potential political impact of this indication of weakness in the dominant power in the oil-rich Gulf. In Moscow's eyes, this victory of the national-liberation movement might well spread into Oman (where a new rebel movement had already taken root in Dhofar) and then into the 'feudal shaikhdoms' of the lower Gulf, and finally, perhaps, into the prize of prizes on the Arabian Peninsula, Saudi Arabia. Moveover, because of the historical and cultural ties between southern and northern Yemen, it was possible that the more radical southerners could inject some revolutionary fervor into the flagging republican movement in the north. The radical force that had eluded Moscow in Sanaa was surely to be found in the new People's Republic of South Yemen, proclaimed on November 30, 1967 in Aden.

The Soviets, however, seemed tentative in their early relations with the PRSY. They did extend recognition to the new republic immediately, and welcomed the declarations by its president Qahtan as-Shaabi as to its aims: positive neutrality and nonalignment, a strong state sector in the economy, and agrarian reforms. In mid-December a small Soviet delegation arrived in Aden to set up a diplomatic mission and discuss aid possibilities. Six weeks later a PRSY delegation led by the Minister of Defense arrived in Moscow for a 14-day visit, attended by considerable publicity. President Nikolai Podgornyy indicated a significant degree of Soviet interest by receiving the delegation for "conversations on questions of mutual interest" in a "friendly atmosphere"; the following day they met with Soviet Defense Minister Andrei Grechko, with whom they had "a warm and friendly conversation on matters of mutual interest."[2] There was no communiqué. This was not too unusual for this type and level of visiting delegation; however, a communiqué would have given Moscow the opportunity to show off a new success for the national liberation movement, a new friend in the Arab World. The lack of a communiqué (and a later description of the talks as "frank") may have indicated Soviet uncertainty about the new regime, or concern not to arouse alarm in North Yemen. It may also have indicated the unhappiness of the South Yemeni delegation, which must have been hoping for the announcement of a major arms deal to show the new regime's enemies (both internal and external) that it had a powerful friend.

Although no agreements were announced, it became evident that Moscow had promised some arms during this visit; two weeks later all the British soldiers who had remained under contract to train the PRSY military were abruptly dismissed. In mid-March 1968, two ships arrived in Aden with Soviet arms, but were diverted to the YAR when the South Yemeni army attempted to destroy the NLF's leftists.[3] After this unrest had subsided, a Soviet military mission arrived in Aden to study the republic's military requirements; the outcome was a smaller gift of light weapons in July (probably an indication that Moscow wanted to wait and see if the army was actually under control). Despite the PRSY's manifest need for economic aid, the Soviets did not offer any; they were in no great hurry to get too deeply involved.

There were many reasons for such reluctance. The Soviets had backed the wrong horse in South Arabia, supporting the Front for the Liberation of South Yemen (FLOSY) until its final defeat. Surprisingly, they apparently had had no direct connections with the National Liberation Front (NLF) prior to its victory (probably because of Jamal Abd al-Nasir's hostility toward the NLF for rejecting his leadership);[4] this despite the NLF National Charter (1965) which, although not Marxist, was anticapitalist and prosocialist, and the praise of NLF leader Qahtan as-Shaabi for Soviet "support at international meetings and for the attention given to South Arabia in the [Soviet] press and radio."[5] Although the small South Arabian communist party, the Popular Democratic Union (PDU), had supported the NLF in the struggle, it was hostile to Nasirism and possibly therefore distanced from Moscow. More importantly the PDU and the Marxist elements in the NLF were suspect in the Kremlin because of the infiltration of Maoism into the country.[6]

A more prosaic reason for the tentative Soviet approach was simply the chaotic economic and political situation in the PRSY. The closure of the Suez Canal, with a consequent drop in the number of ships using Aden's port facilities, and the departure of the British military, had dealt a severe blow to Aden's economy. In addition, British subsidies had accounted for 60 percent of the defunct Federation's budget, and when the British government abruptly cancelled its promised compensation payments in 1968, the PRSY was in very dire straits. A broad Soviet commitment to the country could have meant a large annual subsidy just to keep it running, and substantial amounts of additional aid if any progress in economic development was to be made. Moreover, the longevity of the new regime was quickly put in doubt. After independence, the factional infighting which had characterized the NLF since 1965 had intensified.[7] This had strong personal and tribal underpinnings, but it appeared in public as an ideological battle between 'moderate' and 'leftist' factions. The 'moderate' faction was led by Qahtan as-Shaabi, whom the Soviets accepted as a 'bourgeois democrat,' whose government had proclaimed the PRSY's positive neutrality and quickly established relations with the USSR. He was in fact a radical, but of the 'Arab socialist' stripe, desiring social and agrarian reform, but somewhat pragmatic on the economic question. He and his faction were willing to delay radical reforms in order not to threaten the economy further, to work within the existing state and economic structures, and even, apparently, to solicit U.S. aid.[8] The 'leftist' faction had a number of leaders, the most prominent of which initially was Abd al-Fattah Ismail. It was based on the 'secondary leadership' of the NLF, those who had stayed in the country during the liberation struggle and led the fighting. Committed Marxists, they bitterly opposed as-Shaabi's more moderate policies and busily proselytized among the NLF rank and file.

The dispute came to a head at the Front's Fourth Congress at Zinjibar in early March 1968. The left, presenting a radical program, swept all before it. Decisions were taken to "begin immediately to form councils of workers [aimed apparently at removing some of as-Shaabi's power], to carry out radical agrarian reform in the interests of the poor peasants, to take effective measures to liquidate foreign capital and create a state sector, to purge the civil service and army, and to create a popular militia"; a special resolution was also passed on the necessity of developing friendship and cooperation with the USSR and the other socialist countries.[9] In a further resolution, the NLF pledged to "take up its historical responsibilities toward the Arab Gulf and all areas of the Arabian Peninsula for the elimination of the international imperialist and reactionary forces."[10] Abd al-Fattah Ismail put the seal on this, the most radical program of social, economic, and political transformation yet proclaimed in the Arab world, with a ringing declaration of class war. The leftists' program was Marxist with a South Yemeni face, and Moscow did not entirely approve. Moscow radio gave it very brief coverage a week later, mentioning its choice of the "non-capitalist path" and its support of the socialist camp; interestingly, the broadcast made particular mention that a resolution had dealt with the transformation of the NLF into a "pioneering socialist party" encompassing "all the people's progressive, vigilant, and active forces"[11] – something the Soviets had been anxious to see established in all friendly countries in the developing world, with little success. Other Soviet writers commented favorably on some aspects of the program, but were clearly concerned about its Maoist and 'ultra-leftist' facets.

It may be, of course, that the immediate Soviet ambivalence to the congress was simply due to events in Aden overtaking it. Army officers, reacting to leftist demands for a thorough-going purge of their ranks on political grounds, staged a 'mini-coup' on March 19, arresting many of the left leadership. As-Shaabi dissociated himself from this action and ordered them released, but used the confused situation to exclude the left from leading positions in the party and government. The resolutions of the Fourth Congress were not implemented, and the leftists retreated to their power bases.

Immediately a threat arose on the borders. At independence, most of the shaikhs and thousands of people supporting them or fearful of what the new order might bring had fled into the YAR and Saudi Arabia. Some of these had found support, particularly from

Riyadh where King Faisal had been alarmed by the appearance of a radical regime on his southern borders. They organized themselves (or were organized) in camps on the South Yemeni border, and armed with U.S. weapons began in early 1968 to conduct raids; these the South Yemeni forces had trouble containing. The raids, and the money and weapons flowing across the border, encouraged the traditional antigovernment instincts of some of the tribes. Thus in July 1968, the tribes of the Radfan district, the midwives of the anti-British struggle, took up arms against their putative soulmates in power in Aden. The tribal unrest was crushed, but only with great difficulty; Qahtan as-Shaabi was forced to turn again to the NLF militants to save his regime. This provided the leftists with an *entrée* back into the corridors of power and they decided to abandon their overt opposition, rejoin the government, and work to displace as-Shaabi by political means.[12]

In the meantime the pressure on the frontiers continued. Saudi Arabia was actively supporting the counterrevolutionary forces. The conservatives now in power in Sanaa would not or could not control the groups based in its territory. The Sultan of Muscat was hostile. Further afield, the British had reneged on their aid promises. The United States continued to have diplomatic relations, but refused to consider economic aid; moreover, Washington was aiding the counterrevolutionaries at least passively by not interfering with the Saudis' channelling of U.S. weapons to them. Thus, isolated by their conservative neighbors and by their own revolutionary pronouncements, the South Yemenis were pushed in the direction of the USSR — a direction to which they were predisposed in any case.

The unrest in South Yemen may have impressed on the Soviet Union that the NLF had not endeared itself to the population during its first nine months of power, and that some assistance in economic development and in security matters was becoming necessary. On the other hand it may have been growing Chinese interest that prompted Moscow to look to its own aid program. In any case, the summer and autumn of 1968 saw a vast increase in the number of delegations exchanged, and the negotiation of several aid agreements.

Soviet activity was intense in comparison to the previous period. In June, three ships of the new Indian Ocean squadron visited Aden for four days. The visit was part of a 'show the flag' cruise by the Soviet Navy, intent on establishing its presence in the Indian Ocean; it also served to demonstrate that Aden had a powerful friend.[13] A more extensive military aid agreement was signed in August, as a result of which PRSY missions visited Moscow in November and December; in late January 1969 ten MiG-17s, air-to-surface rockets, antiaircraft guns, portable radar equipment, ammunition, and spare parts arrived, accompanied by about 50 technicians and advisers.[14] In December, a large Soviet delegation visited Aden for three weeks of discussions about economic cooperation, including assistance in economic planning, in geological exploration, and in the development of a merchant marine and fishing industry. On January 2, another group of five Soviet ships began a six-day visit in Aden, and to top it all off, the day they left, a circus troupe arrived.

As a climax to all this activity, Qahtan as-Shaabi arrived in Moscow on January 28, 1969 for a ten-day visit, seeking economic and military aid. The visit was well publicized, with full pomp and ceremony on their arrival and departure, and regular interviews with as-Shaabi. He responded with fulsome praise for Soviet experience ("a genuine school for the South Yemeni people") and for Soviet support in South Yemen's struggle for liberation.[15] (He did not elaborate.) The Soviets in turn complimented the South Yemeni people on their courageous fight against the continuing machinations of imperialist and reactionary forces.

That the Soviet Union did not fully approve of as-Shaabi, however, was evident during the visit. The protocol was correct, but no more; President as-Shaabi was met by and had talks with Podgornyy and a number of officials. Leonid Brezhnev's absence was not a slight since as-Shaabi was not formally the leader of the NLF; Brezhnev's presence would have been an extraordinary sign of Soviet support. However, as-Shaabi, as Prime Minister and Minister of Defense of the PRSY, might justifiably have expected to see Kosygin or Marshal Grechko; neither appeared for any of the talks or social events. A hint of Soviet displeasure with the South Yemeni president appeared in Podgornyy's dinner speech welcoming as-Shaabi:

> We are convinced that the *unity of all patriotic forces of the republic*. . . is the main condition for frustrating the hostile schemes of imperialism and reaction."[16] (Emphasis added.)

Moscow disapproved of as-Shaabi's attempts to exclude the NLF's leftist faction from power. It was also unhappy at his unwillingness to break relations with the United States and West Germany or to establish relations with East Germany. (The Kremlin's unhappiness over the latter was made quite clear in the communiqué.[17]) Further evidence of trouble was the allusion in the communiqué to an "atmosphere of absolute frankness and mutual understanding," with "a wide exchange of opinions on questions of Soviet-South Yemeni relations"; these are terms which denote sharp differences over a wide range of subjects, and interestingly, they differed from a description by TASS earlier in the visit of the talks being held in a "friendly atmosphere," with a "fruitful exchange of opinions."[18]

The initiative for these changes in wording probably came from the South Yemeni side. The absence of a further military aid package when the PRSY was still being threatened by émigré forces must have been very disappointing. Further, the economic agreement (although significant when compared to past Soviet aid to Aden) was only a fraction of what the PRSY needed, and did not include enough budgetary aid to ease the crippling financial burden with which Aden had been struggling since independence. The agreement promised a 14 million dollar loan, to be repaid in trade or convertible currency, for irrigation projects to open land for cotton cultivation, for construction of short-wave radio transmitter in Aden and health and education facilities, and for harbor improvements in Aden. There was also an agreement to begin weekly flights between Moscow and Aden, and others in the culture, trade, and technical fields. The most important of these dealt with Soviet assistance in the creation of a modern fishing industry: the Soviets would provide a fleet, a cannery, and a training and research center in the PRSY and would take young South Yemenis to the Soviet Union to train them in modern fishing methods; it further provided that Soviet research vessels would make periodic visits and that scientists from both countries would use them to study the Gulf of Aden and adjacent waters.[19] As a result, the Soviets increased their use of Aden's port facilities (although on what conditions is not clear) and were given the right to develop the anchorages off Socotra Island which have been the Soviet Navy's main Indian Ocean 'facility' ever since.

Although the results of his visit were disappointing, as-Shaabi could take some comfort. There were, after all, the beginnings of an aid program. Moreover, in the communiqué the Soviets had promised to "give economic and cultural assistance to the People's Republic of South Yemen and to help it strengthen its defensive capabilities," and Podgornyy had declared the Soviet Union to be a "reliable friend" of the PRSY. More help would be forthcoming. In any case, as-Shaabi had nowhere else to turn; hemmed in by the 'reactionaries and imperialists' on his borders, and by the NLF leftists demanding even closer ties to the socialist countries, he made the best of it. After the disgruntled opening of the communiqué, the two parties announced the "coincidence or similarity [of views] on pressing issues of the international situation." The first step in the creation of a loyal ally had been taken.

Action on some of the aid agreements began immediately. In March 1969, Moscow awarded 50 scholarships for South Yemenis to train as pilots in the USSR. In May a Soviet military mission spent ten days in the PRSY and a fisheries delegation surveyed existing facilities in several coastal towns. The number of South Yemeni academic students in the USSR and Eastern Europe rose from 30 in 1967 to 220 in 1968 and 315 in 1969, slightly more than half of whom were in the USSR.[20]

However, none of this helped to improve the economic situation in the short run, as the economy continued to show a five percent negative annual growth rate. (The value of aid actually disbursed in 1969 from all sources was $1 million in grants and $5 million in development loans.[21]) As-Shaabi tried to halt the erosion of his popularity by purging the army of 'traditional and disloyal elements,' but this merely weakened his position more. In the meantime the NLF leftists had been working to undermine him in the party, and in June 1969 his position deteriorated completely, and he and his close associates were forced to resign.

FROM THE 'CORRECTIVE MOVEMENT' TO THE FIFTH CONGRESS OF THE NATIONAL FRONT (MARCH 1972)

The new leadership of the NLF High Command and the PRSY was vested in a five-man Presidential Council. This group, generally dominated by Salim Rubay Ali and Abd al-Fattah Ismail, was well to the left of as-Shaabi. However, the radicals were by no means united; Ismail was a North Yemeni who wished to create a Soviet-style Marxist state with close ties to the USSR, whereas Rubay Ali had strong tribal connections and was somewhat wary of dependence on the Soviet Union, in any case preferring some aspects of the Chinese model.[22] Factional infighting had not disappeared from the South Yemeni political scene.

The Soviets appeared to recognize the positive and negative aspects of the South Yemeni situation. Moscow radio welcomed briefly the new government's statement that it would "rely in its domestic policy on the masses." It was more enthusiastic about Aden's foreign policy declaration to "support national liberation movements" and also to "strengthen its relations with the socialist camp, in the first place with the Soviet Union."[23] The new regime, it was felt, represented a step toward the unity of the Arab world, under radical *aegis*; it was also clearly a step forward in the antiimperialist struggle, as witness its first foreign policy act, to recognize the German Democratic Republic. As regards its internal policy, Moscow noted with approval its clear adoption of the noncapitalist path of development and its intention to unify all progressive forces into a vanguard socialist party. However, they also noted Ismail's condemnation of

> . . . left wing extremists [who] play on the revolutionary sentiments of the masses and call for a more or less immediate establishment of socialism, jumping across the stages of development necessary in this country.[24]

This reference was to the existence of a strong Maoist faction; at a time when China was building a significant presence in the PRSY and aiding the rebellion in neighboring Oman, and when tension on the USSR-China border was high, it must have given Moscow pause when considering its relations with the new regime. A decision was taken to continue its aid program, but not openly to associate itself too closely with any faction in Aden, pending clarification of the internal picture. Thus, no high-level delegation was invited to the USSR after the Corrective Movement, and very little attention was paid to South Yemen in the Soviet media.

However, in August the Soviets offered a 7-million ruble loan for agricultural development projects,[25] and their military aid program continued on the lines already negotiated. A Soviet submarine visited Aden in August. Regular monthly supply flights began. Another group of South Yemenis arrived in the USSR for training as pilots. It was reported that in a PRSY military display marking the sixth anniversary of the beginning of the anti-British struggle for the first time all of the armaments were Soviet.[26] This must have been meant as a signal of Aden's intent to align itself with the Soviet Union, for Moscow has reequipped only onethird of the South Yemeni armed forces by then. More concrete evidence came in October as the PRSY broke relations with the

United States. Furthermore, the regime had begun to establish training camps for Palestinian guerrillas [particularly those of Naif Hawatmeh's Popular Front for the Liberation of Palestine (PFLP)] and for international terrorist groups.[27] In addition, the new regime was adopting internal policies which made its intentions clear; the most important of these was the November decree nationalizing foreign banks, insurance companies, and trading firms. These policies reinforced the hostility of South Yemen's neighbors; the nationalization decree swelled the ranks of the regime's enemies in Saudi Arabia, and in November and December the cross-border clashes sharpened.

Still Moscow did not increase its support, either material or verbal. The reasons for this reluctance were not articulated immediately,[28] but were rooted in the continuing political and economic instability. It was quite possible that the ideological instincts of the leftists would lead to political collapse or economic bankruptcy. Land reforms had hardly been implemented; the tribal system was still intact, and the tribes had in no way been incorporated into the new political order. Aden had lost one-third of its population and some believed that the new economic policies would destroy what was left of its modern economic sectors. The officer corps of the army had been thoroughly purged; this meant that it was probably under political control but that extensive training would be necessary before it became an effective force. Furthermore, its absorptive capacity was still very limited. In the international arena, the Soviets were pursuing détente. Washington had thus far shown little interest in the Indian Ocean (despite the Soviet squadron there), and Moscow may have feared that too much activity in the PRSY could arouse the United States. In the Middle East, Soviet leaders were watching with great concern the war of attrition between Egypt and Israel, which may have influenced them to avoid involvement in another potential quagmire. Finally, the South Yemeni leftists were not proving to be very tractable; despite the weakness of the country and its growing isolation from all but the socialist camp, they had refused to support the Soviet-sponsored United Nations Resolution on Palestine. Moreover, the October coup in Somalia which brought Siad Barre to power may have seemed to offer a greater return for the limited resources Moscow was willing to devote to the region.

Even so, relations were beginning to warm up. In October 1969 the first South Yemeni Ambassador to the USSR presented his credentials to Podgornyy, who declared that the Soviets would continue to supply all possible aid to the PRSY. In the same month South Yemen signed economic agreements with the GDR. In November Moscow proffered a 2 million ruble loan to promote trade. Then in December, the National Front (NF) leadership took a large step toward establishing a vanguard party when they invited the leaders of the Baathist People's Vanguard Party and the Communist Popular Democratic Union to join the Cabinet. Shortly thereafter the question of unifying the three parties began to be discussed again. The NF further improved its standing with the Kremlin by staging an extensive campaign to celebrate the 100th anniversary of the birth of Lenin in April 1970. For several months a national committee "representing all sectors of society" organized celebrations which were the most enthusiastic and extensive in the Arab world,[29] to the point of arousing the concern and anger of South Yemeni *ulema* and the local Muslim Brotherhood (who accused the leaders of communism and atheism); a Libyan newspaper pointed out irately that while these celebrations had been going on, the NF had completely ignored the birthday of Muhammad.

For the Soviets, however, the celebrations showed the progressive character of the regime and this was reflected in the three-week visit in April 1970 of a PRSY delegation led by Abd al-Fattah Ismail to Moscow for the Lenin Centenary celebrations. This was the first high-level South Yemeni delegation to be invited to Moscow since the June 22, 1969 regime change (and the first visit by Ismail), and it demonstrated that the Soviets had at last decided that the NF showed enough promise to be worth cultivating. The delegation met with Boris Ponomarev (the Head of the CPSU Central Committee's International Department, which had the responsibility for contacts with foreign Communist parties and other friendly groups) in an "atmosphere of friendship and mutual understanding"; a communiqué was issued (an unusual occurrence after meetings with him, probably intended to underline the step forward in relations). It declared that "the CPSU and the National Front... are united by common interests and aims...."[30] The South Yemeni side, recognizing the symbolic value of this assertion, acknowledged the necessity of bringing the PDU into a ruling coalition, and "highly appreciated the all-round assistance" of the Soviet Union to a number of embattled peoples. Interestingly, there was no statement of appreciation for Soviet support to the PRSY; this probably indicated that the South Yemenis wanted more material support as well. A further outcome of the meeting was reported in June, when Ismail announced that the CPSU had agreed to help build the NF's party cadre and to provide special educational courses[31] (party-to-party assistance which indicated much greater support, for it had previously been rendered only to those Third World states with which Moscow had very close relations). In August an NF delegation visited the CPSU's Higher Party School, a South Yemeni model of which the Soviets were building in Aden. (It opened in January 1971, staffed largely with Soviet lecturers.)

In military matters there were no startling developments following Ismail's political breakthrough. Military supplies continued to arrive; a small number of Soviet advisers worked with the army, which was still being brought under reliable political control. In August 1970, there were reports that a unit of Soviet naval infantry had conducted an amphibious landing exercise on Socotra. As the émigré forces stepped up their attacks, Defense Minister Ali Nasir Muhammad went to Moscow on an unofficial visit at the end of September; while there he met with the Soviet First Deputy Defense Minister and almost certainly asked for more military help.

In the meantime, however, President Salim Rubay Ali had embarked on a course of which the Soviets strongly disapproved. On August 1 he arrived in China for a two-week visit, during which he met both Zhou Enlai and Mao Zedong (higher-level meetings than had yet been accorded South Yemeni leaders in Moscow). During the visit the Chinese government granted South Yemen long-term interest-free loans totalling $43 million for various agricultural projects, a textile factory, and road-building (the Aden-Mukalla road, first land link between the western and eastern parts of South Yemen).[32] Agreement was also reached on the provision of Chinese weapons and training for the PRSY militia (which may have concerned the Soviets because it threatened to break their monopoly on arms supplies to Aden). Most galling to Moscow however were the indirect criticisms in the communiqué of the USSR's position on the peaceful solution to the Arab-Israeli question,[33] and the announcement that Zhou Enlai would visit the PRSY in the future. However, in October Abd al-Fattah Ismail provided reassurance as to his loyalty with a visit to the GDR for party-to-party talks. This paved the way for a 1971 economic cooperation agreement and an agreement to have East German experts organize South Yemen's police and security forces.

Internally, South Yemen was being moved in directions that the Soviets approved albeit sometimes at a speed and by methods that made them nervous. In the fall, a new agrarian reform law was decreed which limited private ownership of land, encouraged the formation of agricultural cooperatives, and created state and collective farms. These were objectives with which the Soviets sympathized, although with some trepidation; they understood only too well the probable impact of collectivization on the primitive agricultural sector of the PRSY. Moreover, the tactics by which the NF encouraged more rapid redistribution of land (*intifadhat* or peasant insurrections, seizing large landholdings even before the agrarian law went into effect) had Maoist overtones and was likely to disrupt agriculture even more.[34] A new Constitution, drawn up with the advice of East German experts, was promulgated at the end of 1970; it established a Soviet-style parliamentary system and proclaimed that the society and government should be developed on the basis of the "principles of scientific socialism." It also changed the country's name to the People's Democratic Republic of Yemen, thereby laying claim to legitimacy as the government of a united Yemen. In its other aspects the Constitution was less radical than might have been expected; for example, it included the *petit bourgeoisie* among the classes forming the basis of the national democratic regime; it also declared Islam to be the state religion (while subjecting it to the restriction that the freedom of religion must not contradict the "principles and spirit of the Constitution").

The Soviets indicated their approval of the South Yemeni situation and their growing interest in the country by sending a high level delegation to attend the independence anniversary celebration. (This brought the number of Soviet delegations in South Yemen at the time to four; two of the others were looking at cooperation in education and fishery development; the third and most important was working with the South Yemen planning authority, helping to draw up the country's first three-year development plan.) *Pravda* published a lengthy article praising the PDRY for its antiimperialist stands "on the very frontier of the mighty Anglo-American Persian Gulf oil 'empire'."[35]

However, this article indicated Soviet reservations by not mentioning the radical social and economic policies being pursued in South Yemen. Other works also indicated that the Soviets were well aware of the backwardness of the country and the strength of Islamic customs, and of the dangers of moving too quickly.[36] R.A. Ulianovski, the authoritative analyst of Third World ideological trends (and Deputy Head of the CPSU Central Committee's

Information Department), put the PDRY into proper (Soviet) perspective with two articles in early 1971.[37] Ignoring completely South Yemeni pretensions to scientific socialism, he wrote that the revolutionary democrats, while "gaining ground," were far from complete victory. He pointed out in general that the noncapitalist path was a "complex process" with stages that could not be skipped. He then went on to stress (although without referring specifically to the PDRY) the need to reduce food imports by promoting peasant agriculture, and the need to earn foreign currency. He indicated that private capital, both domestic and foreign, should be involved in development and only gradually brought under state control, and warned that the nationalization of private domestic trade (which had not yet been done in South Yemen, but was being planned) could "have an adverse effect on normal economic life, giving rise at times to discontent." Here was a clear statement of Moscow's concern that the radical policies of the South Yemeni leaders would weaken their domestic support, at a time when North Yemen seemed to be returning to the conservative Arab fold and the reactionaries were reportedly massing in Saudi Arabia. Moreover, the criticism is remarkably similar to an article on the PDRY in *New Times* the previous summer reproving unnamed leaders who wanted to leap over all stages of the revolution and nationalize and collectivize everything; such a policy, the author concluded, "can only ruin the economy utterly and undermine the faith of the people in socialist principles."[38] Apparently the Soviets were continuing their efforts to moderate the zeal of South Yemen's leaders, and they may have been relieved when Aden invited an International Monetary Fund (IMF) delegation for consultations about the PDRY's economy in late December.

Reports and events in early 1971 and Ismail's participation in the CPSU's 24th Congress indicated that, their reservations notwithstanding, the Soviets had made the commitment to help to preserve the regime and to compete with the Chinese for influence there. At the same time, perhaps because of the reservations, it seemed that Moscow was not yet ready to make a substantial investment in the PDRY. Thus, work continued on a number of small projects, mostly in the agricultural, fishing, and health sectors,[39] drawing on the original aid package of February 1969. Soviet trade with the PDRY was fluctuating but minor; the Soviets imported almost nothing from the PDRY, and its exports were in 1969 and 1970 less than half of China's, and less than five percent of the PDRY's total imports.[40]

In the sphere of national defense the émigré raids from Saudi Arabia and the YAR continued, apparently at an increased level; there seemed to be a fear in Aden that the Saudis would attempt to drive to the Arabian Sea coast and annex the Hadhramaut. Moscow took note of this situation, and began to assist in constructing an airfield in the Sixth Governorate (the easternmost section of the PDRY) in order to allow quicker resupply of government forces there. However, there were Soviet advisers on the ground, and Moscow therefore knew that the reports of fighting were exaggerated, that the émigré forces in Saudi Arabia and the YAR were hopelessly disunited and that in the only pitched battle fought so far, the PDRY forces had won handily and captured large quantities of (U.S.) weapons.[41]

Thus, Moscow felt under little pressure to accede to the South Yemeni requests for more arms made when Abd al-Fattah Ismail and Defense Minister Ali Nasir Muhammad visited Moscow at the end of March 1971 for the 24th Congress of the CPSU. That military matters were the only items of interest for both sides is clear from their schedule of meetings. Both South Yemenis met with Soviet Defense Minister Marshal Grechko for "friendly talks" upon arrival on March 29; Ismail was not reported to have seen any other high official, but Muhammad met "in a friendly atmosphere" with Chief of General Staff Matve Zakharov and again with Grechko and General Aleksei Epishev (Chief of the Main Political Directorate of the Soviet Army and Navy) on April 13. On April 14 he had a "friendly" visit with Admiral Sergei Gorshkov, Commander-in-Chief of the Soviet Navy and Deputy Minister of Defense. Then on April 28 he met again with Grechko in a friendly atmosphere to discuss questions of mutual interest.[42] Muhammad revealed that the discussions "reviewed in detail the dangers facing the revolution, and the plots by world imperialism and reaction."[43] He certainly asked for more material support. For their part, the Soviets' chief interest was their desire for greater access to South Yemen's military facilities, particularly for more extensive naval privileges in Aden. (This of course was not reported; however, it is known that the Soviets did try to get increased access in the early 1970s. Ali Nasir's meeting with Gorshkov, the impending U.S. naval exercise in the Arabian Sea involving an aircraft carrier, the Anglo-American agreement in December 1970 on the use of Diego Garcia Island in the Indian Ocean as a military base, and the promised withdrawal of Britain from the Persian Gulf at the end of 1971, all make it probable that the issue came up for discussion in April.) The PDRY's Defense Minister refused. Nevertheless, there is some indication that he took home a new military aid agreement;[44] if this were true, the Soviets for some reason did not implement it, for arms deliveries did not expand in 1971.

As for the CPSU's 24th Congress, Moscow gave no indication that it considered the PDRY to be more promising than any other Third World country. Brezhnev talked of "further activating the world-wide anti-imperialist struggle" but made no mention of the PDRY. Kosygin spoke of mutually advantageous economic relations as though serious that they should be the basis for Soviet trade and aid; the South Yemeni delegation, with nothing to sell, could not have found that reassuring. Moreover, Ismail was not invited to address the Congress, but was relegated to speak to "one of Moscow's party organizations"; he responded with a speech that stressed the PDRY's internal changes about which the Soviet were not too enthusiastic, which did not mention Soviet support for the PDRY, and which stressed that his country had a "more acute need than ever" for aid and support.[45]

By autumn the Soviets were ready to expand their military aid program. It is not possible to pinpoint the exact reason for this; a number of events during the summer no doubt contributed to it. At the end of May, Abd al-Fattah Ismail (who had remained in the USSR for medical treatment after the 24th Congress) had a very successful meeting with Mikhail Suslov, the ideological watchdog of the Politbureau. The meeting was described as being held in a "comradely" atmosphere (the first time that heavily symbolic term had been used with regard to the PDRY), in a "spirit of friendship and mutual understanding." They discussed ideological issues, including the national-liberation movement and noncapitalist development, and Suslov must have liked what he heard, for without a reciprocal declaration he stated that "the Soviet people value highly and support the struggle of the South Yemeni people"; both then expressed their desire to develop friendship and cooperation.[46] Abd al-Fattah had a powerful friend in court.

Another set of events which may have influenced Moscow to increase its support for the PDRY related to the changing strategic situation in the Red Sea and Indian Ocean. The USSR-Egypt Treaty of Friendship and Cooperation in May 1971, the failure of the

Communist coup in Sudan in July, the PFLP commando attack on the Israeli-chartered tanker Coral Sea from the PDRY in the same month, and subsequent reports (never verified and likely planted by Aden) that Israel was establishing some kind of presence on Ethiopian islands in the Red Sea, possibly encouraged the Soviets to think they could and should move to dominate the southern end of the Red Sea. At the same time the U.S. announcement that the U.S. Navy would begin to send more patrols into the Indian Ocean (because of the expanded Soviet naval presence there) undoubtedly raised the value of access to Aden for the Soviet Navy, both for ships and shore-based air support and reconnaissance.

In its internal activities during the summer the PDRY regime was moving in directions favored by Moscow. In June, after a government declaration that no further nationalization was intended, President Salim Rubay Ali urged South Yemenis (particularly, one presumes, those working abroad) to invest in economic development projects at home. At the beginning of August, Prime Minister Muhammad Ali Haythem, the last major holdover from the as-Shaabi era and reputedly a true moderate who favored policies that would encourage the Arab oil states to provide aid, was removed from his government and party posts and went into exile; a purge of his supporters in the government and army followed. His replacement, Ali Nasir Muhammad seemed to indicate that Aden was moving closer to the Soviets when in an interview he said that the PDRY "did not oppose" a political solution to the Arab-Israeli question provided that Palestinian rights were not prejudiced.[47] Shortly after that, a delegation returned from Rumania and the GDR with agreements on strengthening party-to-party relations, a sign that the NF was gaining acceptance. A final reason for the Soviets to supply new military aid was that the situation on South Yemen's borders seemed to be deteriorating, even though Aden was now able to apply some measure of air support. Clashes continued all along the border, and it appeared by autumn that Saudi Arabia had been able to unify the various forces under one command; were that true, not only the Hadhramaut was in danger, but also the regime in Aden.

This set the stage for Ali Nasir Muhammad's visit to Moscow September 29 to October 2, 1971 where he was welcomed with ceremony [including (for the first time for a South Yemeni dignitary) his picture on the front page of *Pravda*] and met with Kosygin and Grechko, and other officials. The visit was a success for the PDRY.

Aden received a new loan to be used for fishing industry development, irrigation and land reclamation projects, technical training, and mineral and oil prospecting.[48] More importantly, the Soviets apparently agreed to increase arms shipments; Kosygin made a point of saying at the welcoming dinner that the Soviet Union would do "everything necessary" for the successful implementation of the agreements on cooperation in different fields.[49] Although the communiqué only "affirmed their desire to continue to promote cooperation in the political, economic and cultural and other fields,"[50] arms shipments did expand rapidly in 1972.

That relations between the two countries were still touchy, however, was indicated by the language of the communiqué. The talks were said to have taken place in an "atmosphere of frankness, friendship and mutual understanding"; there was a "frank exchange of opinions" with regard to "questions of mutual relations and cooperation and also about the present international situation." These were code-words for broad disagreement, accentuated by the specific reference to disagreement in their views on bilateral and international relations. The bilateral disagreements probably centered around South Yemen's military and economic needs. Despite the new loan, the USSR had provided only a relatively small amount of economic aid, and lagged behind China in this field; Muhammad's disappointment with the level of aid was indicated by his little lecture on the Soviets' internationalist duty at his luncheon for Kosygin in Moscow,[51] and by his failure to mention military aid in his postvisit statement to the Aden media. The international disagreements seemed to be less serious. The PDRY did not support the Soviet position on a political solution in the Middle East. There was no mention of Bahrain and Qatar, whose recent independence was decried in Aden as an attempt by imperialism to legalize its status in the region, but whose governments the USSR had recognized. However, the South Yemeni side did support the Soviets on a variety of other international issues, and to emphasize that there was not total disagreement they "expressed great gratitude" for Soviet assistance in developing the PDRY's economy, strengthening its defense might, and training its national cadres. Kosygin in turn accepted an invitation to visit the PDRY at an unspecified date. Interestingly, both sides apparently ignored the issue of increasing U.S. naval activities in the Indian Ocean, although each was evidently concerned about it. Four months previously, Brezhnev had even suggested discussions on great-power demilitarization of the Indian Ocean.[52] However, by October the Kremlin had apparently decided that it wanted to keep Soviet ships in those waters, and that its interests lay in not aggravating the littoral countries' fears of a great-power naval arms race in the region.

Nevertheless, in the next six months the Indian Ocean played a role in the improvement of relations between the two countries, as Aden's potential strategic value became more evident and as South Yemen's security crisis grew. The Indo-Pakistan war in early December 1971 raised the level of Soviet involvement in South Asia and concurrently the level of U.S. interest; a U.S. navy carrier task force made a prolonged visit to the Indian Ocean, and Washington announced that henceforth the Navy would carry out more frequent patrols in the area. In the same month Britain completed its withdrawal from the Persian Gulf and the United States quickly negotiated a treaty with Bahrain to allow continued use of its naval facilities by the small U.S. MIDEASTFOR.

These events produced both a potential opportunity and problem for Moscow. The newly independent Gulf states seemed both weak and ripe for radical change, but the Soviets had no presence in the Gulf. Moreover, if the United States was going to try to fill the vacuum presumed to exist after the British left, Moscow believed it must have the ability to counter that move. Therefore, its relations must be improved with the PDRY, where the Soviets had a presence, and where the government was supporting a rebellion in Dhofar which might contribute to the process of change in the Gulf. At the same time, Aden was looking for better relations with Moscow for the same reasons, and also because the threat from Saudi Arabia and the YAR seemed to be building. In October a large battle was fought in the Bayhan area, which the PDRY army seems to have won, supported by tanks and planes; according to one report Soviet advisers had been instrumental in planning the South Yemeni victory.[53] Sporadic fighting continued, and Aden was undoubtedly grateful for the delivery of more supplies and a number of MiG-17s in early 1972. The dispute over their different policies toward the new Gulf states was not important enough to affect relations in any lasting way. It obviously rankled Aden,[54] but there was nowhere else to turn; both Moscow and Beijing, as well as most of the Arab states, had recognized the new states.

The economic aid programs and exchange of delegations with the USSR and Eastern Europe continued. China's aid persisted at a significant level; however, Moscow may have been less concerned about the Chinese ability to gain predominant influence in South Yemen as it saw China's revolutionary fervor moderate and its rapprochement with the United States develop. President Salim Rubay Ali, generally considered China's man in the PDRY, gained favor in Moscow with his fulsome praise for Soviet aid while on board Soviet ships visiting Aden in October 1971.[55]

Thus by early 1972, the stage was set for much closer relations between the two countries.

FROM THE NATIONAL FRONT'S FIFTH CONGRESS (MARCH 1972) TO THE OCTOBER WAR 1973

In the late 1970s, Soviet writers were unanimous in their analysis of the Fifth Congress: it was a watershed in the lives of the PDRY's people, having adopted a program that looked to the ideas of scientific socialism and the experience of the socialist countries, and that set the country firmly on the path to becoming a 'state of socialist orientation.'[56] At the time, however, Soviet reaction was much more subdued. The Soviet Union did not send a delegation, and the CPSU Central Committee's telegram of greetings stated only that the NF was "performing the tasks of the national democratic revolution."[57] Reflecting the still somewhat uncertain relations between the two countries, there was no indication that the CPSU considered itself to be in a close party-to-party relationship with the NF. However, the Central Committee did indicate its interest in better relations by its flattering reference to the "vanguard position" which the NF was said to occupy in the Arab national liberation movement and the struggle against imperialism. In addition, Soviet analysts praised the NF's resolution to unify all the progressive forces in the PDRY and its continued support for national liberation movements in the Arabian Peninsula and elsewhere.

For its part, the National Front seemed to be indicating unhappiness with the Soviets. Aden radio in its coverage of the Congress quoted from various telegrams, but said only that one had been received from the CPSU. In its report on the congress resolutions, the radio reported that one had "supported the development of the best relations with the states of the socialist camp"; no specific mention was made of relations with the Soviet Union.[58] The playing down of the Soviet connection may have been the result of maneuvering inside the NF which led to Salim Rubay Ali's elevation (temporarily) to a dominating position in both government and party. (A report published in 1974 of an interview with Ismail and Ali at the congress makes it very clear that it was only Ismail who talked of strengthening relations with the CPSU and the Soviet Union; a later book implied that the NF's relations with China had been disturbingly close at the time.[59])

As usual, the Soviets did not allow such annoyances to interfere in practical policies and did not respond openly. China was moderating its foreign policy and withdrawing from the Dhofar cause; it was possible that Rubay Ali would see he could not rely on Beijing to help him maintain his ascendancy, and would switch to a more reliable patron. Moreover, the external threat to South Yemen intensified in the spring with attacks in the west, in the Hadhramaut and from Oman; it appeared briefly in mid-March 1972 that a full-scale war would break out with the YAR. Only the USSR and its allies could (or would) provide the military assistance to deal with this level of threat. More important to Moscow, however, was the apparent rapid improvement in its position in the Middle East with the signature of the USSR-Iraq Treaty of Friendship and Cooperation on April 10. With global détente developing, it must have seemed an opportune moment to shift the 'correlation of forces' a bit more by tightening relations with the PDRY. To accomplish this, Kosygin met Ismail during his visit to Baghdad; also on the agenda was the improvement of relations between the PDRY and Iraq. Ismail's talks with the Iraqis were a definite success for all three parties, as the PDRY and Iraq strengthened their relations and echoed each other in supporting Gulf revolutionaries and attacking imperialist intrigues. Closer relations lessened both countries' isolation, caused Saudi Arabia some concern, and promoted the 'progressive' cause in the Persian Gulf.

Throughout the spring and early summer of 1972 the pace of Soviet-South Yemeni contacts quickened. Official delegations were exchanged, such as that led by PDRY Interior Minister Muhammad Salih Muti to discuss, among other things, increased contacts between the new NF youth movement and the Komsomol. Religious delegations from each country visited the other in early May.

The Soviets continued their wide variety of aid projects, and expanded their activities (without increasing their aid) in the fisheries sector, which with agriculture remained the chief forms of their economic aid program. However, the chief beneficiary of increased Soviet interest was the military aid program. Arms deliveries increased dramatically, totalling approximately $20 million in 1972 (a fourfold increase over 1971).[60] The Soviets were even reported to have paid the PDRY army for three months when the government ran short of cash.[61] Moscow's interest in South Yemen was further increased in July by the sudden weakening of two of its positions in the region. In early July the YAR announced its resumption of diplomatic relations with the United States, a move which the Soviets (and the South Yemenis) saw as being aimed at Aden and Moscow at a time when tension on the border was high. Then in mid-July Anwar Sadat expelled Soviet advisers from Egypt. This threatened the whole edifice of Soviet policy in the Middle East, but the Soviets could do nothing except reinforce their standing in fall-back positions in Syria, Iraq, and the PDRY. It was reported that several hundred of the expelled advisers were sent directly to Aden.[62]

At the time (early August), the political situation in the PDRY was extremely difficult to interpret, even by South Yemeni standards. President Rubay Ali seemed to be in control. Abd al-Fattah Ismail had been sent on a tour of various Communist countries. While he was out of the country, Rubay Ali embarked on "his own version of the Cultural Revolution,"[63] (the '7 Glorious Days') bringing thousands of peasants and workers into Aden to demonstrate against the bureaucratization of the party and government, and in favor of salary cuts for bureaucrats. This revolutionary upsurge upset Ismail who was reported on his return to have accused Rubay Ali of pursuing as-Shaabi's policies by seeking personal prominance and the restoration of one-man leadership.[64]

If these Maoist-tinged policies of Rubay Ali disturbed the Soviets, they were no doubt reassured by his remarks to the new Soviet Ambassador, calling the USSR a "strategic ally."[65] Moscow must also have been pleased at the rapid development at this time of PDRY-Cuban relations; diplomatic relations had been upgraded in May, and a Cuban Communist Party delegation visited in mid-August and signed an economic cooperation agreement. The new relationship was sealed with Abd al-Fattah Ismail's visit to Havana in late October for discussions with Fidel Castro.

The war which broke out on the PDRY/YAR border in late September 1972 (see Chapter 6) seemed to cause the Soviets to shift in favor of Rubay Ali. It has been speculated that the Ismail faction provoked the fighting, because of its interest in uniting the Yemens under the NF's leadership, and also because of a wish to bolster Ismail's popularity in the upsurge of patriotic feeling when war broke out.[66] Moscow was unhappy with the war, for it feared irreparable damage to its already cool relations with the YAR if it had to declare openly its support for the PDRY. (It was clear, however, that its sympathy and interests lay in Aden.) Although PDRY Prime Minister Ali Nasir Muhammad stated that "the Soviet Union will not stand with folded arms in the event of an invasion of South Yemen,"[67] the claim was never repeated by a Soviet spokesman or analyst. The only open indication of Soviet thinking was an Aden radio broadcast on October 3, which said that "the Soviet Ambassador explained to Salim Rubay Ali the stand of the friendly Soviet Union on the aggression against Democratic Yemen";[68] this implied political support, but the word "explained" indicated that the Soviet stand was far from being enthusiastic support for whatever military or political aims the South Yemenis might have. Abd al-Fattah Ismail certainly realized this, and lashed out at the Soviet Union for "inadequate" aid; "the socialist camp's assistance for us," he told the Beirut weekly *Al-Hurriyah*, "has not sufficed to enable us to fight the dangers of the imperialist-reactionary conspiracy."[69] This criticism could not have endeared him to Moscow. Salim Rubay Ali, on the other hand, had cabled his thanks to Brezhnev, Kosygin, and Podgornyy for the "Soviet support in the struggle against imperialism and reaction."[70]

The South Yemeni President's relationship with Moscow was buttressed during his visit November 21-25. One of the purposes of his trip was to explain the Yemen unity agreement which he was about to sign, and to solicit Soviet support for it. Another was to seek closer military ties to neutralize the 'imperialist-reactionary conspiracy' on his country's borders, but also to allow South Yemen to step up its support for the Dhofari rebel movement in Oman; in addition, he sought more economic aid and Moscow's recognition (and approval) of his predominant status in the Aden regime. The visit was a great success. Rubay Ali was met at the airport with appropriate ceremony by Kosygin, Gromyko, and Ponomarev, and was accorded the "warmest" welcome in Moscow.[71] His picture was printed in *Pravda*, which stated that he "invariably comes out for close friendship and cooperation with the Soviet Union and the other socialist countries."[72] In his dinner speech, Rubay Ali gave the USSR fulsome praise for its support of the PDRY and of other struggling peoples, and announced South Yemen's desire for even closer relations. Perhaps seeking to elevate himself and his country into the magic circle, he addressed his Soviet hosts as "Comrade." Kosygin did not reciprocate, and even alluded to the need for "realistic" policies, in accordance with South Yemen's "objective conditions and potential." However, he did say in conclusion that the Soviets highly valued the PDRY's policy of strengthening relations with the Soviet Union.[73]

The communiqué was long, and covered many topics. The meetings between Kosygin and Rubay Ali were said to have been held in an atmosphere of "friendship and complete mutual understanding";[74] i.e., although some differences did exist, each side understood the other's position, and the differences would not be allowed to interfere with the development of closer relations. In internal PDRY matters, Rubay Ali stressed the continuation of policies of which Moscow approved, such as expanding the state sector, and paid lip service to the unification of patriotic forces, although not of the more favored "progressive" forces; he was known to be lukewarm toward that project. The Soviet side let that pass, and was said to "highly appraise" Aden's progressive reforms. The South Yemeni side expressed its gratitude to the Soviet Union for its assistance in strengthening the PDRY's defense capability and in invigorating the economy and training national cadres. However, some reticence could be discerned in the South Yemenis' description of the Soviet aid program, as it merely "noted the successful development of cooperation."

In regional matters the Soviets shared Aden's views about the threat of imperialism and reaction (the United States and Saudi Arabia) to its existence. They welcomed the PDRY's efforts to normalize relations with the YAR, but the communiqué pointedly did not mention the unity agreement; Moscow probably had reservations about it. For the first time in an official communiqué, the Soviets came out strongly in support of the national liberation movement in the Arabian Peninsula. The South Yemenis thanked the Soviet Union for its (unspecified) efforts to preserve peace in the region, and for its military aid. In international affairs, the views of the two sides were said to be in "coincidence or proximity" on all major issues. The South Yemeni's gave Soviet policies in the Middle East strong support, thus refuting Sadat's complaints about those policies:

> The PDRY party-government delegation *highly appraised* the Soviet Government's *consistent and constructive* foreign policy in the Near East and... expressed *profound gratitude* to the Soviet Union for its *constant support* for the Arab peoples' just struggle for freedom and independence.... (Emphasis added.)

(However, it should be noted that a political solution to the Middle East question was not mentioned; presumably the South Yemenis still opposed it).

For this support (and because the Soviets had obviously decided on greater involvement with the PDRY) Rubay Ali and South Yemen received significant rewards. The many references in the communiqué and in Soviet publicity to the "party-government delegation" emphasized his position in the party leadership, as well as his better-known government post. This, he hoped, would strengthen him in his struggle with Abd al-Fattah Ismail, the NF's General Secretary. The Soviets signed new economic, technical, trade, and cultural agreements, which were reported to involve a loan of approximately $20 million.[75] Agreements were reached on the expansion of contacts at various levels of government and public organizations and, more significantly, on the party level. Perhaps to underline this, Rubay Ali invited Kosygin (again), Podgornyy (again), and Brezhnev to visit; the invitations were accepted with gratitude (again). Finally, the Soviets promised to increase their military aid program.

The visit was thus mutually satisfying. Each side received much of the support it had hoped for, and each enhanced its position. The PDRY, by inviting closer ties to the Soviets, had increased its security and furthered its revolutionary aims in the region; the Soviet Union, by agreeing, expected to ensure the preservation of an increasingly useful friend, to improve its strategic position in the south end of the Red Sea in order to partially offset its setback in Egypt, and to improve the revolutionary potential of the Arabian Peninsula.

To be sure, there were some disappointments. Rubay Ali was not received by Brezhnev; the Soviets were not ready to invest that level of prestige in him. None of the Soviet leaders set a date for a visit. Rubay Ali failed in an apparent attempt to establish an "inseparable link" between the struggle of the South Yemenis and the liberation movements of the Gulf on the one hand, and the struggle of Palestinians for liberation of the Israeli-occupied territories on the other;[76] to have established this link would have given South Yemen added prestige in the Arab world, and a better guarantee of Soviet assistance. There were as well other differences remaining between the two sides, as evidenced by references in two brief reports of the visit to an "exchange of views."[77]

Nevertheless, the two countries lost no time demonstrating their closer ties. Early in December a CPSU delegation made a brief visit to conclude a protocol on party cooperation for the coming year. The delegation held talks with Abd al-Fattah Ismail, Salim Rubay Ali, and Ali Nasir Muhammad, and the joint communiqué laid heavier emphasis than usual on South Yemen security and on the liberation movement. At the end of the year, Ali Nasir Muhammad travelled to Moscow to attend the festivities celebrating the 50th anniversary of the founding of the USSR. While there he met with Kosygin and Podgornyy, and was accorded the honor of addressing the joint session of the CPSU Central Committee and the Supreme Soviet. In his speech he likened the PDRY to Cuba — distant, surrounded by enemies, depending on help from the socialist countries. He made clear his country's commitment: "you are our allies and we take a common stand with you toward all questions of principle."[78]

OBSERVATIONS

At the end of 1972 the PDRY and the USSR were poised to enter a new stage in their relationship, one which would see South Yemen actively (although not consistently) helping Moscow to work toward some of its foreign policy goals, and in turn moving toward a favored status in Soviet sympathies as a 'state of socialist orientation,' closely tied to and heavily dependent on the socialist camp. However, it should be remembered that the PDRY was already heavily dependent on the socialist countries. Aside from small amounts from Kuwait and international agencies, all economic development aid came from Communist sources, with the USSR, Eastern Europe, and China each disbursing approximately equal amounts (although China had promised more than either of the others). In addition, it appears that the Soviets and/or the Eastern Europeans also provided undisclosed amounts of financial aid to ease the PRDY's budgetary deficit (which in 1972-73 was 9.6 million dinars in a budget of 21.6 million dinars[79]). These sums, not large in absolute terms, and not enough to allow economic growth, were vital to the PDRYs survival.

In their economic and technical assistance the Communist countries avoided showpiece projects and concentrated on agriculture and irrigation, fisheries development, road construction, resource exploration, a few light industrial plants, and medical assistance. The Soviets also did some port improvement (mainly for the fishing fleet, apparently, for the Soviet Navy did not change its pattern of visits or its use of Aden despite increasing its deployments in the region) and repaired the runway at Khormaksar airport to keep it up to international standards. Advisers from all the donor countries worked on South Yemeni projects and were engaged in on-the-job training. Several hundred South Yemenis were studying in Communist countries, with about 50 new scholarships added each year. The Soviet Union donated textbooks and lecturers for party training programs and particularly for the Higher School of Scientific Socialism, where thousands of South Yemenis took short and long courses in Marxism-Leninism and organizational methods.

In the short run, however, it was the Soviet Union's military aid which had ensured the new republic's survival. Although again not large in absolute terms (about $30 million[80]), it was enough in a poorly armed region to counter the constant low-level border raids by émigré groups and the occasional pitched battle. Soviet military advisers (about 200 by the end of 1972[81]) had helped to reorganize and retain the armed forces and to create a small air force. Assistance from East Germany in organizing and running police and security services, and from China in organizing and arming a popular militia, contributed greatly to the regime's control.

The regime by the end of 1972 did seem to be in control, and this was undoubtedly a factor in Moscow's decision to establish closer ties. The army had been purged and repurged and was now under tight NF rein. Together with the army, the security service and militia extended that control to all parts of the country. Tribalism was rife, and threatened many of the regime's reforms, but not its control. The political power of the clergy had been broken, but Islam continued to be taught in the schools (albeit by secular teachers) and religious observance was tolerated.[82] The economy was still in disastrous shape, but the groups that might have led the disaffection on this issue had fled abroad. (It was estimated that of a population of 1.6 million at independence, almost one-quarter had fled the country by 1973.[83]) On a positive note the regime had worked hard to create a number of subordinate organizations involving peasants, women, trade unions, and the young to help spread its message and control; the young, particularly, were said to be "loyal, enthusiastic and radically politicized."[84] The only political groups outside the NF had been coopted and were being absorbed. There were still disputes over who should run the country, but these were now confined to the NF leadership, in which all major factions seemed to support closer ties with the Soviet Union.

In the spring and summer of 1973 the Soviets seemed to be acknowledging that they had more options than just Rubay Ali. In January *Pravda* published an interview with Abd al-Fattah Ismail in which he lavishly praised the Soviet Union and the ideas of scientific socialism.[85] In early March, Ali Nasir Muhammad arrived to follow up on the general military aid agreement signed during Rubay Ali's visit. The visit was a success; although no details were revealed other than a statement about developing "all-round cooperation,"[86] it was probably at this meeting that the USSR agreed to provide a dozen top-of-the-line MiG-21s (although they did not arrive until 1975 because of the necessity of resupplying Egypt after the October 1973 War). Furthermore, actual arms shipments doubled over the 1972 level, reaching $40 million.[87] Muhammad had a "warm and friendly" meeting with Marshal Grechko, and then was received by Leonid Brezhnev, the first South Yemeni to be accorded this honor. The fact that the meeting took place with the third-ranking member of the ruling PDRY triumvirate rather than with the top-ranking member four months previously, and its description as a "warm, comradely" meeting,[88] indicates that the Soviets had finally decided to pursue their interests in the country vigorously. The publicity accompanying the visit seemed to reflect the new policy by promoting the PDRY to a somewhat higher stage of development; it was noted that the PDRY constitution had proclaimed scientific socialism as the theoretical foundation of the political system, and the PDRY was called "one of the countries where the struggle for national liberation has been transformed into a struggle for deep social and economic changes which accord with the basic interests of the masses."[89]

The restoration of Abd al-Fattah Ismail to Soviet favor was completed in the summer of 1973. There were no particular reasons evident for this, although Rubay Ali's upgrading of Aden's relations with Beijing may have been a factor. In any case, in August Ismail visited Moscow for talks on strengthening party-to-party ties (another sign of Soviet willingness to develop closer relations), and while there was received by Brezhnev in a "warm and comradely atmosphere."[90] During the talks, both parties called for further development of "all-round relations and collaboration," and Ismail expressed "profound gratitude" for Soviet support of South Yemen and the Arab struggle. There was, however, an "exchange of views" on several issues. Moreover, the PRDY's application for observer status in the Council of Mutual Economic Assistance (CMEA) was turned down. No formal communiqué was issued, an indication that Ismail's objections were quite strong. However, the fact that the talks were reported in both countries showed that they did not want to make too much of their differences.

Whatever the ups and downs of political relations, the Soviet and Soviet-allied aid programs continued to develop, led by military aid. Besides new supplies of weapons, more Soviet advisers were reported to arrive. Moreover, the first contingent of Cuban military advisers (variously reported to be 500 or 150 strong) arrived, with "significant military equipment"; they were reported to be taking over from China the training of the militia, helping to train the regular army, training Dhofari guerrilla forces, Palestinians, and international terrorist groups in their South Yemen camps, and piloting PDRY Air Force planes.[91] It appeared that the *quid pro quo* was being revealed in the summer, as Beirut diplomatic sources reported that a Soviet naval team had inspected the PDRY coastline near Mukallah (in the east) for potential facilities; the same report and others stated that the Soviet Navy enjoyed special privileges in the port of Aden.[92] (It should be noted, however, that other sources, including the Director of the CIA, have cast doubt on this.[93])

Other Soviet aid programs continued at roughly the same level as the previous year, as South Yemen drew on previous credits. The Soviets negotiated a fish canning project in keeping with the kind of economic development projects they were involved in elsewhere in the Third World; in return for helping to set up and run the plant, they would receive part of its product in payment.[94] Soviet planners were also sent to evaluate the three-year economic plan and to develop a five-year plan. Various delegations were exchanged, including one led by PDRY Minister of Culture and Information (and Communist leader) Abdullah Abd ar-Razzaq BaDhib; this was his first visit and demonstrated that the NF leaders felt confident in the effectiveness of their absorption of the South Yemen Communists, and in their ideological relationship to Moscow.

NOTES

1. This section draws from the author's *The USSR and Arabia* (London: Central Asian Research Centre, 1971), pp. 111-15.
2. U.S., Foreign Broadcast Information Service, *Daily Report: USSR* (hereinafter cited as FBIS/USSR), February 8, 1968, p. aa31.
3. *Middle East Record* 4(1968); 846.
4. F. Halliday, "Soviet Relations with South Yemen," paper delivered to the International Symposium on Contemporary Yemen, Exeter University, July 15-18, 1983.
5. *Mizan Supplement A* 8 (January-February 1966): 4.
6. J. Kostiner, "Arab Radical Politics: *Al-Qawmiyyun al-Arab* and the Marxists in the Turmoil of South Yemen, 1963-1967," *Middle Eastern Studies* 17 (October 1981): 466-67.
7. Cf. F. Halliday, *Arabia Without Sultans* (New York: Penguin Books, 1979), Ch. 8; F. Halliday, "Yemen's Unfinished Revolution: Socialism in the South," *MERIP Reports*, no. 81 (October 1979): R. W. Stookey, *South Yemen: A Marxist Republic in Arabia* (Boulder: Westview Press, 1982).
8. U.S., Congress, House, Committee on International Relations, Special Subcommittee on Investigations, *Diego Garcia 1975: The Debate over the Base and the Island's Former Inhabitants* (Washington, D.C.: Government Printing Office, 1975), p. 86; M. Wenner, "South Yemen since Independence," paper presented to the International Symposium on Contemporary Yemen, Exeter University, July 15-18, 1983.
9. I.A. Aleksandrov, *Narodnaia Demokraticheskaia Respublika Iemen* (Moscow: Iz. Nauka, 1976), p. 229.
10. G. Lenczowski, *The Middle East in World Affairs* (Ithaca, N.Y.: Cornell University Press, 1980) (4th ed.), p. 649.
11. *FBIS/USSR*, March 13, 1968, p. aa22.
12. F. Halliday, *Arabia Without Sultans*, p. 237. The new tactic was adopted after Abd al-Fattah Ismail returned in August from convalescence in Bulgaria. There is no evidence that he received advice on the new line, but it seems reasonable to speculate that he did, given the Soviets' acceptance of as-Shaabi and their wariness at the time of "adventurers" who tried to jump historical stages.

13. Arguably, this visit could be taken as a sign of Soviet approval for as-Shaabi. However, Moscow was almost certainly concerned only with its naval ramifications; i.e., the Soviets had decided to establish a permanent naval presence in the Indian Ocean and were looking for a base or at least access to port facilities. Aden was an obvious choice, and if as-Shaabi was willing to give access to the Soviet Navy, the Soviets were willing to appear to give their approval to him.

14. E. Einbeck, "Moscow's Military Aid to the Third World," *Aussenpolitik* (English ed.) 22 (1971): 468; *Izvestiia*, December 19, 1968; *New York Times*, March 3, 1969.

15. *FBIS/USSR*, February 10, 1969, p. A32; *FBIS/USSR*, January 30, 1969, p. A8.

16. Ibid., p. A7.

17. The communiqué may be found in *FBIS/USSR*, February 10, 1969, pp. A34-37.

18. *FBIS/USSR*, February 3, 1969, p. A8.

19. I. A. Aleksandrov, op. cit., p. 198; U.S. Department of State, Bureau of Intelligence and Research, *Educational and Cultural Exchanges between Communist Countries and the non-Communist World 1969* (Washington: Department of State, 1969), p. 63; *Mizan Supplement A*, 11 (January-February 1969): 9.

20. U.S., Department of State, op. cit., p. 63; interestingly, Soviet figures are much lower. A table in I. A. Aleksandrov, op. cit., p. 301 shows 14 PRSY students in the USSR in 1968-69 and 20 in 1969-70.

21. P. Wiles (ed.), *The New Communist Third World* (New York: St. Martin's Press, 1982), p. 182.

22. R. L. Bidwell, *The Two Yemens* (Boulder: Westview Press, 1983), pp. 230-1, 239, 248.

23. *FBIS/USSR*, June 30, 1969, pp. A43-A44.

24. A. Vasilev, "Nadezhdy Iuzhnogo Iemena," *Pravda*, September 14, 1969, p. 4.

25. *Arab Report and Record*, August 16-31, 1969, p. 334. Later it was reported that another 5 million rubles had been added to the loan. *Arab Report and Record*, February 1-14, 1970, p. 96.

26. *Egyptian Gazette*, October 14, 1969.

27. C. Sterling, *The Terror Network: The Secret War of International Terrorism* (New York: Holt, Rinehart & Winston, 1981), p. 90.

28. Later, after Ismail had departed the scene, analysts displayed Soviet discomfiture over these measures. Cf. V. Ozoling and R. N. Andreasyan, "Some problems arising in the process of the noncapitalist development of the PDRY," a paper presented to the International Symposium on Contemporary Yemen, Exeter University, July 1983, p. 9, in which the authors state that "the revolutionary authorities ventured to take radical measures without sufficient socio-economic foundations, seeking to do away with backwardness at one stroke."

29. I. A. Aleksandrov, op. cit., p. 100. The Lenin celebrations in the Third World were considered by the CPSU Central Committee as a top priority

vehicle for Soviet propaganda. V. Sakharov, *High Treason* (New York: Ballantyne Books, 1980), pp. 242-43.

30. *FBIS/USSR*, April 28, 1970, p. A13.
31. U.S., Foreign Broadcast Information Service, *Daily Report: Middle East & North Africa* (hereinafter cited as *FBIS/MENA*), June 5, 1970, p. B2.
32. A. Sylvester, "South Yemen - the Revolution Tightens its Grip," *New Middle East*, no. 28 (January 1971), p. 34; M. Abir, *Oil, Power and Politics: Conflict in Arabia, the Red Sea and the Gulf* (London: Cass, 1974), p. 131. These loans brought total Chinese aid to South Yemen to $55 million, as against $14 million from the USSR.
33. A. Yodfat, *Between Revolutionary Slogans and Pragmatism: The People's Republic of China and the Middle East* (Brussels: Centre d'Etude du Sud-Est Asiatique et de l'Extreme Orient, 1979), pp. 50-1.
34. For a description of the *intifadhat*, cf. F. Halliday, *Arabia Without Sultans*, pp. 248-49.
35. *Current Digest of the Soviet Press*, (hereinafter cited as *CDSP*) 22 (January 26, 1971):31.
36. Cf. L. A. Basin and O. Gerasimov, *Narodnaia Demokraticheskaia Respublika Iemen* (Moscow: Iz. Mysl, 1971): R. Sharipova and R. Aliev, "Islam v segodniashnem Iemene," *Nauka i Religiia*, no. 9 (September), 1975, pp. 54-55.
37. Prof. R. A. Ulianovski, "Leninism, Soviet Experience and the Newly-Free Countries," *New Times*, nos. 1 and 2 (January 1 and 13), 1971, pp. 18-21 and 20-24.
38. A. Vasilev, "Visiting South Yemen," *New Times*, no. 30 (July 29), 1970, p. 29.
39. For a list of Soviet aid activities, cf. *FBIS/MENA*, February 19, 1971, p. B2.
40. P. G. Alkhimov and V. L. Gusarov, *Ekonomika Narodnoi Demokraticheskoi Respubliki Iemen*, (Moscow: Iz. Nauka, 1976), pp. 145, 148.
41. *FBIS/USSR*, March 17, 1971, pp. B7-8.
42. *FBIS/USSR*, March 30, 1971, p. 15; *FBIS/USSR*, April 14, 1971, p. B4; *FBIS/USSR*, April 15, 1971, p. B2; *FBIS/USSR*, April 28, 1971, p. B6.
43. *FBIS/MENA*, May 19, 1971, p. B1.
44. On May 18, Ali Nasir stated that the Soviets were "fully prepared to give the PDRY additional aid in all areas." (*FBIS/MENA*, May 19, 1971, p. B1). On June 26 a report stated that he "revealed that military agreements had been concluded to provide the armed forces with arms to strengthen their ability. . . ." (*FBIS/MENA*, June 28, 1971, p. B1). No dates were given, however.
45. *FBIS/USSR*, April 16, 1971, p. I37.
46. *FBIS/USSR*, June 1, 1971, p. B6.
47. *FBIS/MENA*, September 8, 1971, p. B3.
48. *FBIS/MENA*, October 14, 1971, p. B3.
49. *FBIS/USSR*, October 1, 1971, p. B1.
50. The communiqué may be found in *FBIS/USSR*, October 12, 1971, p. B18.

51. "Under these conditions [imperialist plots], dear comrades, it is the duty of the friendly states led by the Soviet Union to render us support and assistance." *FBIS/USSR*, October 7, 1971, p. B5.
52. *Pravda*, June 12, 1971.
53. *An-Nahar Arab Report* 2 (December 13, 1971); 1-2.
54. Cf. Ali Nasir Muhammad's interview in *FBIS/MENA*, October 28, 1971, p. B5.
55. *FBIS/MENA*, October 4, 1971, p. B1.
56. Cf. O. Gerasimov, *Iemenskaia revoliutsiia 1962-1975 gg.: problemy i suzhdeniia* (Moscow: Iz. Nauka, 1979), pp. 197-203; A. Guskov, "Kursom progressivnykh preobrazovanii," *Aziia i Afrika Segodnia*, no. 3 (March), 1976, pp. 26-27; V. Naumkin, "Demokraticheskomu Iemenu - 10 let," *Agitator*, no. 19 (October), 1977, pp. 44-45.
57. *FBIS/USSR*, March 3, 1972, p. B12.
58. *FBIS/MENA*, March 7, 1972, pp. B1-2.
59. A.M. Vasilev, *Puteshestvie v 'Araviia Feliks'* (Moscow: Iz. Molodaia Gvardiia, 1974), p. 76; O. Gerasimov, op. cit., p. 207.
60. U.S., Arms Control and Disarmament Agency, *World Military Expenditures and Arms Transfers 1970-1979* (Washington, D.C.: ACDA, 1982), p. 124.
61. *FBIS/MENA*, March 7, 1972, p. B2.
62. *FBIS/MENA*, November 3, 1972, p. B1.
63. F. Halliday, "Soviet Relations with South Yemen," p. 13.
64. *FBIS/MENA*, September 5, 1972, p. B1.
65. J. Pennar, *The USSR and the Arabs - The Ideological Dimension* (New York: Crane, Russak, 1973), p. 117.
66. M. Abir, op. cit., pp. 111, 118 fn. 100.
67. A. Haselkorn, *The Evolution of Soviet Security Strategy 1965-1975* (New York: Crane, Russak, 1978), p. 78.
68. *USSR and Third World* 2 (September 11 - October 22, 1972): 534.
69. *FBIS/MENA*, November 15, 1972, p. B1.
70. *Arab Report and Record*, November 1 - 15, 1972, p. 542.
71. *FBIS/USSR*, November 27, 1972, p. B5.
72. *FBIS/USSR*, November 21, 1972, p. B2.
73. *FBIS/USSR*, November 24, 1972, pp. B1-5.
74. The communiqué is reprinted in *FBIS/USSR*, November 29, 1972, pp. B7-11.
75. M. Abir, op. cit., p. 100.
76. Rubay Ali put this point forward in his dinner speech. *FBIS/USSR*, November 24, 1972, p. B5. The South Yemenis attempted to give it momentum at a conference of Gulf liberation movements in Aden two weeks later, but were not able to convince any of the major "progressives."
77. *FBIS/USSR*, November 22, 1972, p. B4; *FBIS/USSR*, November 24, 1972, p. B6.
78. *FBIS/USSR*, December 29, 1972, p. AA5. Muhammad was one of only six non-communists to address this session.
79. I. A. Aleksandrov, op. cit., p. 175.
80. U.S., Arms Control & Disarmament Agency, op. cit., p. 124.

81. U.S., Department of State, Bureau of Intelligence and Research, *Communist Governments and Developing Nations: Aid and Trade in 1973* (Washington: D.C.: Department of State, 1974), p. 13.

82. F. Halliday, *Arabia Without Sultans*, p. 242.

83. R. L. Bidwell, op. cit., p. 228.

84. J. B. Bell, *South Arabia: Violence and Revolt* (London: The Institute for the Study of Conflict, 1973), p. 12.

85. *FBIS/USSR*, February 2, 1973, p. B3.

86. *FBIS/USSR*, March 8, 1973, p. B14.

87. U.S., Arms Control and Disarmament Agency, op. cit., p. 124.

88. *FBIS/USSR*, March 8, 1973, p. B13.

89. Ibid., p. B14.

90. *CDSP* 25 (September 5, 1973): 15.

91. *FBIS/MENA*, March 13, 1973, p. B5; D. L. Price, "Moscow and the Persian Gulf," *Problems of Communism* 28 (March-April 1979): 9; C. Sterling, op. cit., p. 253. Ms. Sterling's book implies that the PDRY became the most important training ground for international terrorists in the 1970s.

92. *USSR and Third World* 3 (July 16 - September 2, 1973): 424; N. Novik, "On the Shores of Bab al-Mandab: Soviet Diplomacy and Regional Dominances," *Crossroads*, no. 2 (Winter 1979), p. 69.

93. U.S., Congress, Senate, Committee on Armed Services, Subcommittee on Military Construction, *Military Construction Authorization FY75* (Washington, D.C.: Government Printing Office, 1974), pp. 147, 163.

94. *Ezhegodnik BSE 1973*, p. 298. This was the first deal of this type negotiated with South Yemen.

3
THE PDRY: *ZIGZAGY* IN ITS RELATIONS WITH THE USSR (1973-78)

FROM THE OCTOBER WAR TO THE NF'S UNIFICATION CONGRESS (OCTOBER 1975)

The October War ushered in new conditions in the relationship between the PDRY and the Soviet Union. The Soviets embarked on an activist, interventionist phase of foreign policy toward the Third World, or at least those parts of it where the 'correlation of forces' favored the USSR. In support of this policy, they demonstrated an impressive new capability to project power. However, after the war, as Sadat turned to Washington, the Soviets were forced to focus their attention on their other Arab friends. South Yemen, perhaps for the first time, became truly important to Soviet basic interests. With the reopening of the Suez Canal in the foreseeable future, a strong presence at the south end of the Red Sea was desirable. Moreover, with the Peninsula oil states (especially Saudia Arabia) having finally launched their oil weapon against the United States and Western Europe, and with Washington's decision to send more frequent naval patrols into the Arabian Sea, it made good sense to maintain a position close by and adjacent to major oil shipping routes.

The South Yemenis recognized this increase of interest and, for the most part, welcomed it. At the same time, the October War gave them increased flexibility. Their strong stand against Israel and their cooperation with Egypt in blockading the Bab al-Mandeb to ships bound for Israel won the approval of the Arab mainstream. The conservative oil states joined the mainstream during the war, and they too became better disposed toward Aden; in turn, their anti-U.S. oil policy made them more acceptable in Aden's eyes. The prodigious increase in their oil revenues also made the peninsula oil states (in particular Saudi Arabia) the potential source of amounts of economic aid wildly beyond what the Soviets and their allies would or could provide. There was, of course, a catch; the Saudis still suspected leftist radicals of harboring worse intentions toward them than did the United States, and if South Yemen wanted aid, it would have to moderate its policies. Salim Rubay Ali appeared receptive, Abd al-Fattah Ismail not. The old power struggle intensified, not to be resolved until mid-1978.

Renewed Soviet interest in South Yemen surfaced soon after the October War ended, and resulted in a feverish round of messages, visits, and agreements which lasted throughout 1974. It began with a warmer than usual Soviet message on the PDRY's national day, that the Soviet Union "greatly apprecites the PDRY's friendship and cooperation with the Soviet Union and other socialist countries."[1] Then at year's end a Soviet delegation arrived to discuss modernization of Aden's airport, a sure sign of strategic interest. In February there were two visits of Soviet ships. (Naval visits continued throughout 1974, 1975, and 1976 at a rate almost three times higher than in any previous year,[2] consistent with the much greater interest being shown by both superpowers in the region's waterways. Early in 1974 Moscow launched a determined propaganda campaign to convince Indian Ocean littoral states that they were threatened not by the Soviet Union, which wanted only that the Indian Ocean be declared a 'zone of peace,' but by Western navies and particularly by Washington's decision to expand Diego Garcia into a "powerful nuclear naval base".[3])

Contacts continued in March 1974, with the arrival of a middle-level CPSU delegation to discuss inter-party relations and other issues. Once again there was less than complete agreement on international issues, and while the Soviet side promised to continue to support the national liberation movement on the Arabian Peninsula, the PDRY stopped short of that. The South Yemen side thanked the Soviets for their "all-round support" and endorsed the deepening of party relations.[4] It was a satisfactory visit but not overly warm, and this is perhaps best explained by a trend apparent in Aden, identified with Rubay Ali, to begin to improve relations with non-socialist countries. Of more concern to the Soviets were the signals Rubay Ali was sending to the United States. In March 1974 he responded to representations from Paul Findley (Republican Congressman from Illinois) on behalf of a constituent imprisoned in Aden on a spying charge in January 1973 by inviting Findley to come to Aden and releasing the man into his custody; at that time he made it clear to Congressman Findley that he would welcome relations with the United States.[5]

Moscow may well have not objected to the first approach. The second approach they certainly did not like; however they responded not by being critical, but by stepping up their aid program somewhat and by returning to focussing their approval on the party and its leader Abd al-Fattah Ismail. Thus, on the anniversary of the June 22 "Corrective Movement," *Pravda* stressed the threat from the reactionaries and imperialists to the PDRY, and referred to the NF as a "vanguard organization of the people" (one step below a communist party in the Soviet hierarchy of labelling parties).

However, the signing of a Soviet-Somali Fifteen-Year Treaty of Friendship and Cooperation on July 11, 1974, must have caused the South Yemeni leaders to wonder whether the Soviets simply wanted to keep the PDRY 'on hold' while they pursued their real regional interests elsewhere. Aden immediately sent a delegation of military government and party officials led by Abd al-Fattah Ismail to Moscow. The South Yemenis must have counted the visit a success. After meeting with Podgornyy, Suslov, Gromyko, and Grechko (Brezhnev was on a visit to Poland) the South Yemeni side was promised assistance in strengthening its defense capability, and an agreement on economic and technical cooperation was signed. No details were reported about the defense agreement which may have been simply to continue the high level of arms shipments (in response to tension on the YAR border after the military coup in June). It was also reported that the Soviet Union had cancelled $50 million in South Yemeni debts during the visit,[6] no small concession considering the state of South Yemen's economy.

The communiqué[7] referred to a "friendly, cordial atmosphere," but also to a "detailed exchange of views on bilateral relations and their further development," an indication that problems still existed. Another indication was that the South Yemenis "expressed satisfaction with" (not "highly valued" or some such phrase) the cooperation between the two countries. It dealt with international issues on which both sides could agree, but did not mention reconvening the Geneva Conference, something the Soviets wanted very badly at the time. It is interesting to note that the comminiqué did not mention the national liberation struggle in the peninsula, although Ismail had referred to it in his dinner speech.[8] There had been no indication that the Soviet Union had foresworn these movements; thus it may have been that Ismail was speaking out of turn, fighting a rear-guard action against the more pragmatic, less revolutionary foreign policy in the region which the Rubay Ali faction was beginning to implement. (South Yemeni media attacks on Saudi Arabia all but stopped in early summer.)

The internal dispute over the foreign policy line (actually, of course over power) within the NF raged on until the middle of 1978, and was largely responsible for the tortuous twists and turns of the PDRY's policy statements. On one side was the more pragmatic faction, led by Salim Rubay Ali, Chairman of the Presidential Council and Deputy Secretary-General of the NF. This faction, although dedicated Marxists all, recognized that only the oil states could provide the amount of economic aid that South Yemen badly needed. Getting it would entail downplaying revolutionary activities and rhetoric, and loosening the PDRY-USSR connection; by no means did they contemplate breaking the connection, which provided them with almost all their arms and ultimately protected South Yemen against the machinations of powerful enemies (and of aspiring patrons like Saudi Arabia). The other faction, led by Abd al-Fattah Ismail, Secretary-General of the NF and member of the Presidential Council, who was supported most of the time by Ali Nasir Muhammad, Prime Minister and the last member of the Presidential Council, favored retaining close ideological and other ties to the Soviets, although they did not wish to be, or to appear to be, under Soviet control.

Rubay Ali's quest was made easier by regional events as they developed after mid-1974. First, the highly emotional issue of Aden's support for the Dhofari guerrillas was becoming irrelevant as they were gradually pushed out of Dhofar in 1975. Second, the thaw between the PDRY and the conservative Arab states, which had begun as a result of the October War, led to agreements by Saudi Arabia and the United Arab Emirates (UAE) at the Rabat Conference in October 1974 to join Kuwait in giving economic aid to the PDRY (although indirectly). Third, the possibility of a further thaw was enhanced by the assassination in March 1975 of Saudi Arabia's King Faisal, a bitter opponent of communism and leftist radicalism in any form.

It is not clear to what extent the Soviets disapproved of Rubay Ali's policy. It held potential advantage for them, if it could be used to improve the USSR's relations with Saudi Arabia. They were not averse to Riyadh's funding South Yemen's economic development, as long as this did not weaken their positions in South Yemen. The danger was, of course, that the PDRY's leader would go too far toward Riyadh; since the Saudis appeared to have bolstered their dominance over North Yemen through the al-Hamdi coup, this must have seemed a real threat.

However, there was little the Soviets could do except look to the Ismail faction in the regime (not an insignificant group) to prevent this from happening. A heavy-handed approach, such as cutting off aid, could backfire as it had done in Egypt. In September Ali Nasir Muhammad went to Moscow. Kosygin stressed Moscow's "invariable" support for the PDRY and "the identity of the positions of both sides," but an exchange of opinions was said to have occurred specifically on the topic of the southern Arabian Peninsula.[9] (Confusingly, Kosygin also promised support for "the normalization of the situation in the south of the Arabian Peninsula." An examination of the South Yemeni and Soviet positions regarding the region (see below, pp. 132, 167-68) shows that at the time both held moderate positions regarding the Dhofar war; the normalization statement probably refers to that situation. However, the Soviets were engaged in a propaganda campaign against Riyadh, largely as a result of the al-Hamdi coup; if Ali Nasir held to the policy set by Rubay Ali, the sides would clash.)

In the first nine months of 1975 there were few exchanges of delegations between the two countries; reflecting the interest of both Ismail and Moscow in closer ties, the groups from the PDRY tended to be connected with party work. The Soviets sent a delegation led by Semen Skachkov, the head of the State Committee for Foreign Economic Relations, to discuss economic cooperation. Although his talks were said to have been "cordial," the Aden radio reports indicated that he was on the defensive. On his arrival he "expressed the hope that the talks would take place in a friendly atmosphere"; on his departure he declared that "the success of the talks indicates that in future matters will be carried out more successfully."[10]

In April, an article by Abd al-Fattah Ismail was published in *World Marxist Review*, a clear sign of Moscow's favor. At about the same time, Moscow began to use Radio Peace and Progress to comment on the situation in the Arabian Peninsula. An 'unofficial' Soviet station which had begun broadcasting in Arabic only the year before, Radio Peace and Progress reflected the more radical urges in Soviet policy, generally taking a much harder line on international issues although often attributing its comments to foreign sources. In this case, it was used to remind its listeners of the threat posed to South Yemen by the imperialists and reactionaries, the very groups with which Salim Rubay Ali was flirting.

In the meantime, Rubay Ali continued to pursue his goal of more flexibility. It must be emphasized, however, that he was not trying to cut Soviet-South Yemeni ties. He visited the GDR in August 1974; he sent his Foreign Minister Muhammad Salih Muti to talk to Gromyko in Cairo on the eve of Muti's first trip to the Gulf states. Muti also visited Cuba in August 1975. In addition, ties were strengthened with Iraq. Less commendably in Moscow's eyes, Rubay Ali also renewed his ties to China during a visit in November 1974.

However, it was the South Yemeni overtures to the conservative Arab states and the West which drew the most attention. In September 1974, Rubay Ali visited Cairo for talks with Sadat. In an interview he insisted that it was not Aden's policy to export revolution; further, in repeating South Yemeni denials of President Gerald Ford's claim that the Soviets had a naval base in Aden, his tone was conciliatory. Moreover, he declared that the Red Sea was an "Arab Sea,"[11] a claim the Saudis and Egyptians were also asserting, and one the Soviets became very nervous about, once the Suez Canal reopened. Rubay Ali was also reported to have promised to cease supporting the Dhofar war and to have discussed ways of establishing "collective Arab control of the southern end of the Red Sea."[12] His new foreign policy line was emphasized in a possibly even more startling way a few days later when it was announced that the PDRY and West Germany had agreed to restore normal diplomatic relations.[13] At about the same time the two remaining U.S. citizens in South Yemen prisons were released. On November 30, he announced that Aden, which had good relations with Kuwait, wanted friendly ties with Bahrain, Qatar, and the UAE, and hoped for good-neighborly relations with Saudi Arabia. The Gulf states responded; Muti visited them in February and March 1975 and had "good and useful talks."[14] In an apparent signal of good faith to the conservative Arab states, Muti was sent to Jiddah in July to participate in the Islamic Conference Foreign Ministers' meeting. In addition, during 1975 the PDRY indicated that U.S. participation in economic development projects would be welcome.[15] Finally, U.S. activities, such as the MIDLINK naval maneuvers in the Indian Ocean in November 1974 and the decision by Congress in July 1975 to expand the facilities on Diego Garcia, were not received with the same amount or degree of vituperation as had been normal, although the Soviet media campaigned bitterly against them.

The Rubay Ali faction was on top, but by no means paramount. The Ismail faction was not without weapons. Between May and July 1975 the South Yemeni public was treated to a spy trial which received unprecedented publicity. As a result of the trial a State Security Law was passed which forbade South Yemenis from talking to foreigners except on official business; it was aimed specifically at contacts with other Arabs,[16] and was probably meant in part to embarrass Rubay Ali as he sought to expand contacts with those very Arabs. Moscow may also have taken heart from the Sixth Congress of the National Front which took place in March 1975. The Congress reelected Ismail as its General Secretary and passed resolutions that were regarded in the Soviet Union as "affirming the progressive orientation" of the country, and "continuing the construction of socialism." The Congress "highly assessed" Soviet aid and stressed the need to develop cooperation with socialist countries and with the world communist and national liberation movements.[17] Ismail, in a press conference, seemed to support better relations with the Persian Gulf states, but also backed the Dhofar guerrilla movement (PFLO), and was distinctly cool toward Saudi Arabia. The Congress apparently followed his lead and did not endorse further moves toward Riyadh. This congress was followed in short order by congresses of the Communist Popular Democratic Union (PDU) and the Baathist People's Vanguard Party (PVP). Their sole purpose, it seems, was to endorse the idea of union into a single party of progressive forces as soon as possible, an idea which Ismail and the Soviets, but not Rubay Ali, had been urging since 1968.

FROM THE UNIFICATION CONGRESS TO MID-1976

This was accomplished at the Unification Congress October 11-14, 1975, which linked the three parties in the United Political Organization-National Front (UPONF), in which as the name suggests, the NF was the dominant force. The UPONF was to be a transitional party, charged with creating a vanguard party of the workers which would be guided "in theory and in practice... by the principles of scientific socialism."[18] This was considered a defeat for Salim Rubay Ali, who was known to be opposed to a heavily bureaucratized vanguard party which would control the activities of the government. In addition, the Congress passed resolutions on foreign policy which were highly supportive of national liberation movements (including the Dhofari movement), the socialist camp, and the various causes that the Soviet Union supported; furthermore the UPONF Program declared that the socialist countries were South Yemen's "strategic allies."[19] (Significantly, however, the resolutions did not attack 'Arab reactionaries' and instructed the leadership to "continue following the policy of peaceful coexistence with countries with different social systems."[20])

The Soviets greeted the Congress with enthusiasm. In their messages to the PDRY leaders, the Soviet leaders addressed them as "dear comrades," praised their internal policies, and expressed "confidence that the decisions of the Unification Congress will be a new stimulus to the further consolidation of the close friendly relations among our parties, peoples and states."[21] Since the downfall in the 1960s of Nkrumah, Ben Bella, and Sukarno, Moscow had been urging favored Third World noncommunist leaders to institutionalize their power and policies in vanguard parties which included local Communists at all levels, including the policy-making level. So far, none had, but in the PDRY the process seemed well under way.

Thus the Soviets continued their attentions to Aden. (They did not expand their activities; at the time there seemed little need, and Somalia was still their favored client in the region.) In mid-November 1975, an economic delegation signed a protocol, which led to the infusion of $24 million in new Soviet aid in 1976,[22] mainly in agricultural projects, oil prospecting, education, and fisheries.

Such aid was insignificant when compared to the money the Saudis had to offer, however. This fact, together with domestic political factors, the continuing depressed state of the economy, and the effective end of the Dhofar rebellion, enabled Rubay Ali to achieve sufficient support to carry on with his rapprochement with Saudi Arabia. On March 10, 1976, this came to fruition with the announcement that the two countries had extended diplomatic recognition and would exchange Ambassadors. The Saudis were reported to have promised $100 million in development and badly needed budgetary aid, with $40 million of this having been paid before relations were established.[23]

The Soviet reaction to this announcement was correct but cool. Moscow radio characterized the normalization of relations as a "positive" initiative, which should "help to consolidate stability in the Arabian Peninsula"; the broadcast then went on to imply that Saudi Arabia was still pursuing hostile policies toward the PDRY.[24] Although the Soviets were probably glad to see a new source of funding appear, they could not have been anything but concerned at the size of the aid package (compared with actual South Yemeni drawings of Soviet aid of $6.6 million in 1976) and at the probability that it could be repeated year after year if the Saudis so desired. The joint statement about the normalization must have worried Moscow about the effect of Saudi money; it referred to "the spirit of Islamic and Arab fraternity," to "religious, historical and cultural ties" between South Yemenis and the other peoples of the Arabian Peninsula, and to their "common destiny." It also mentioned "preventing foreign interference" in the region,[25] by which Aden no doubt meant the United States, but Riyadh definitely meant the Soviet Union. (That Moscow's concerns were justified about the power of Saudi money and the anti-Soviet uses to which it would be put was demonstrated by Sadat's abrogation of the Soviet-Egyptian Treaty on March 14, and his cancellation of the Soviet Navy's privileges in Egyptian ports three weeks later.)

Nevertheless, there was little Moscow could do except be patient and try to limit the damage which could be done to its position in South Yemen. This it did by continuing its military and economic aid programs. Perhaps more importantly in the long run, the Soviets did what they could to increase the prestige of Abd al-Fattah Ismail, and quietly encouraged the development of the UPONF and of CPSU-UPONF contacts. Ismail had addressed the 25th Congress of the CPSU at the beginning of March 1976; his speech had expressed extreme gratefulness at Soviet assistance and been given prominence in the Soviet media.[26] He had been received by Mikhail Suslov and Boris Ponomarev in "warm, friendly discussions" during which the two sides condemned "reaction." Leonid Brezhnev had spoken "with profound satisfaction of the growing cooperation between the USSR and the PDRY,"[27] and the latter had been included in the new category of (presumably) reliable Third World allies, countries of 'socialist orientation.' (However, it could not have escaped Soviet attention that the announcement of normalization of relations between South Yemen and Saudi Arabia was timed to follow closely the return of Abd al-Fattah Ismail from his prestigious visit to the Soviet Union.)

There followed a parade of delegations to and from the socialist countries, as well as Somalia and Ethiopia (with whose radical government both Moscow and Aden were beginning to develop relations). In June two Soviet Navy ships paid a formal visit to Aden, and received unprecedented attention in both countries. Ali Nasir Muhammad went on board and stressed that the PDRY was the loyal and sincere friend of the Soviet Union; the Soviets for the first time publicized a naval visit to the PDRY.[28]

During the same period, however, South Yemeni delegations were busy consolidating the new relations with Arab 'reactionaries.' This task fell largely to the Foreign Minister Muhammad Salih Muti, who in short order visited and met the rulers of the UAE, Qatar, and Bahrain; in early May he met Saudi Arabia's Crown Prince Fahd in a "cordial and brotherly spirit," and in late July (while Ismail was in Moscow) King Khalid and Oil Minister Shaikh Yamani, and Fahd again. As a result of these visits, it was reported, the Saudis had promised to build an oil pipeline network from the Persian Gulf to a huge modern oil terminal it would build on the South Yemeni coast (to bypass the Straits of Hormuz).[29]

In June Ismail departed for a lengthy stay in the Soviet Union. While this was primarily for health reasons, he did manage a number of official functions. He met Andrei Kirilenko and Ponomarev for "warm, comradely" discussions in which he expressed "profound gratitude to the CPSU and the Soviet people."[30] He discussed economic matters with the chairman of the State Committee for External Economic Relations (possibly to try to convince Moscow to loosen the purse strings in order to offset Saudi aid). On August 2 he received an honorary doctorate from Moscow State University for his "contribution to the theory of the contemporary national liberation movement and the transformation of the bourgeois democratic revolution into socialist revolution." In his acceptance speech, Ismail emphasized the invariable wish of South Yemenis to broaden the friendship and cooperation between the two peoples. (A noticeable contrast in tone was evident in Rubay Ali's speech two weeks earlier on the anniversary of the Corrective Movement, when he laid great stress on fraternal relations with Arab countries, and praised the support received from peninsula and Gulf brothers, adding his thanks to the socialist countries almost as an afterthought; he did not mention broadening the relations.[31])

MOSCOW AND ADEN IN MID-1976

By mid-1976 the Red Sea region had taken on new significance and new complexity for the Soviets. The Suez Canal had reopened, given them easier access to the Indian Ocean; but Sadat was hostile and Egypt, Saudi Arabia, and the Sudan were beginning a campaign to establish the Red Sea as an "Arab Lake" by drawing the YAR, PDRY, and Somalia into some kind of security arrangement, aimed, it appeared, at Israel, the USSR and later Ethiopia. It became imperative that Moscow guard its interests by cementing its ties with Somalia and the PDRY. At the same time, new opportunities were opening up in Ethiopia.

Furthermore, as the lift of military personnel and equipment to Angola in mid-1975 had shown, Moscow had developed the capability to indulge its wish to involve itself more effectively and forcefully in parts of the Third World. The southern Red Sea region was a natural focus; parts of it were undergoing rapid change, and the United States was nowhere ensconced. Moreover, the Soviet military already had access to airfields and naval facilities which made the region an excellent staging post. Complicating the task of extending Soviet positions, but also making it more essential in the eyes of the Kremlin and the Soviet military, was Washington's decision in the fall of 1975 to expand Diego Garcia into a full-fledged base, and the widespread reports that the United States had concluded an agreement with the Sultan of Oman for the use of the British airbase on Masirah Island.[32] While expanding its political campaign against foreign bases in the Indian Ocean region by giving qualified support for the first time to the U.N. General Assembly's proposal on making it a zone of peace,[33] Moscow also looked to the security of its access to facilities there.

In this developing situation, the PDRY assumed a more important position in Soviet eyes (although one which was secondary to Somalia's for another year). In 1976 and 1977 the Saudis tried to use aid and promises of aid to wean Aden away from the Soviet Union. Were this tactic successful, it would ruin Moscow's Red Sea strategy; moreover, it might even open Aden to the U.S. Navy, undermining Moscow's Indian Ocean strategy. That the Soviets were concerned about the prospects of Saudi success (in undermining Soviet positions in Syria as well as in the PDRY and the Red Sea region) was evident in the latter half of 1976, as the Soviet media thundered about Saudi reactionaries, Saudi ties to the United States which was the mainstay of Israel and imperialism, and Saudi attempts to split the Arab progressive forces.[34]

By this time, Soviet positions and investment in the PDRY were substantial, particularly in the military and security spheres. The USSR and its allies were the sole suppliers of weapons and training for South Yemen's armed forces, militia, and security service. Communist-bloc advisers were to be found in all of these institutions, although their numbers were not great. (In 1977, the CIA estimated, there were 350 Soviet and 350 Cuban military advisers in the country, and 875 South Yemeni military personnel training in communist countries.[35]) East German security experts were still involed in the security service. The terms of Soviet military aid, the cancellation of some of South Yemen's arms-related debt, and apparently some budgetary aid had enabled the PDRY to more than double the size of its armed forces (to 21,000), to equip them with weapons which were as good as or better than those in other countries of the region, and to carry the burden of allocating 40-50 percent of government spending to defense and security.[36] By 1976, it was estimated, the Soviets had supplied $185 million in arms to the PDRY.[37]

In economic assistance the Soviet and allied aid was much less impressive although by no means negligible. It was sensibly directed at agriculture, fishing, and a few light industries; the Soviets had become quite involved in the South Yemeni fishing industry, providing boats, training, and storage and canning facilities. (In the latter they appear to have been overenthusiastic; a 1978 study showed that capacity was 430,000 tons/annum while the annual catch was 20,000 tons.[38]) The CIA estimated that by 1977 there were about 1,000 Soviet, East European, and Cuban economic advisers in the country;[39] in addition, frequent delegations and short-term visitors were sent to study or work on various projects. Several hundred South Yemeni students were studying in the Soviet Union,[40] and Soviet teachers were at the University of Aden and the Higher School of Scientific Socialism, as well as at lower school levels. The CIA and Department of State estimated the value of Soviet aid by 1977 as only $39 million, and East European aid $21 million.[41] This seems too low; the Economic Counsellor of the Soviet Embassy in Aden claimed in 1972 that the Soviets were giving $29 million annually; later sources were more conservative, evaluating total Soviet nonmilitary aid (committed, though much of it not disbursed) at approximately $100 million.[42] Whatever the true sum, by 1977 the Soviet aid program was receiving less than enthusiastic acclaim, because of its relatively small size and its sometimes poor quality. There were also complaints at the time that the Soviets were undervaluing the fish delivered to them as repayment for their aid, and were using their privileged position in the PDRY's fishing industry to overfish South Yemen's waters.[43] This made Saudi and other Arab aid commitments (many of them grants or if not, on generous terms, and none of them tied to Communist-bloc workmanship) more attractive.

Finally, the Soviets provided ample political aid, both international and internal. The former took the shape of continual reassurances of Soviet support for the regime against external and internal enemies; while undoubtedly very important in the early years, it was probably taken for granted by 1977. In internal political affairs, the Soviets rendered important assistance, both by providing a model for the South Yemenis, and experts to assist the PDRY regime in developing the party and related organizations by which to control the country.

The results for Moscow of these various aid programs were not inconsiderable, but neither were they overwhelming. The Soviet Navy had access to the port facilities at Aden and used them. There is some question, however, whether the Soviets had totally free access. They did not in any case routinely use Aden for refuelling and replenishment; these were normally done at their anchorages near Socotra and elsewhere. More important was their access to

Khormaksar airport near Aden, which they used not only for military supply flights, but also for long-range reconnaissance flights over the Red Sea and Indian Ocean; in addition, there were reports in mid-1976 of a new airbase being built near Aden for Soviet use only.[44] All in all, however, Moscow was more interested at that time in developing the facilities at Berbera (Somalia), which were more extensive (including a missile-handling facility and a communications facility). The economic aid program was a drain on the Soviet economy, yielding only goodwill (and not always that, because it was now expected and did not always function properly), access to fishing grounds (not to be discounted, although the Indian Ocean catch was a small part of their total), and some fish. The results of their political aid program looked more promising. The PDRY consistently supported Soviet positions on most international issues. A vanguard party was being developed; relations between it and the CPSU were growing closer. Moscow's thinkers had come to believe that such a party would be a guarantor of long-term relations between the Soviet Union and a Third World country. It seemed possible that the PDRY would prove that belief true.

There were problems, however—the same problems as bedeviled Moscow in other parts of the Third World. The economy was very weak despite (or because of) being more closely aligned to the socialist model than most Third World countries. There were no mineral resources, little good land, and few reliable sources of water; agriculture was susceptible to drought and floods which no land reclamation projects could tame. The country was as far from feeding itself as ever. The problem of developing human resources seemed more likely to be brought under control than elsewhere in the Third World, with well-organized education and literacy programs, but as elsewhere, there was little one could do with an education. The result: emigration of skilled and semiskilled workers. The regime attempted to halt this flow in 1974, but by 1977 had relaxed its restrictions because the remittances were too important a source of foreign currency.[45]

The economic conditions created pressures on Aden to moderate its ideological stance, renounce its patron in Moscow, and bask under a shower of oil money. No one in the regime was willing to pay the full price, but a familiar figure haunted Moscow: the charismatic leader with enough popularity, strength, and will to be able to (or to think he or she is able to) manipulate the country's foreign policy and the country's patrons and would-be patrons in ways he or she thinks will increase its prosperity and independence.

FROM MID-1976 TO THE ASSASSINATION OF YAR PRESIDENT AL-HAMDI (OCTOBER 1977)

The Soviets had responded to Salim Rubay Ali in the way they had responded to other such figures. They had dealt with him when it was necessary for the preservation of their positions, while quietly encouraging, if possible, his rival. By autumn 1976, their concern over the developing situation in the Red Sea led them once again to court Rubay Ali (while by no means forsaking Ismail) to try to limit the damage the Saudis could do.

At the same time the political situation in Aden remained fluid, as the two factions maneuvered to try to gain ascendancy. Salim Rubay Ali was not always able to implement his foreign policy; nor indeed, was he always consistent in the pursuit of that policy. This situation produced various contortions and balancing acts in South Yemeni-Soviet relations and South Yemeni-Saudi relations over the next 12 months. Thus in the fall of 1976 a UPONF delegation visited various European Communist Parties and the Soviet Union, and Ismail made a speech expressing strong support for the Dhofari guerrilla movement as did Foreign Minister Muti at the United Nations; the three South Yemeni leaders sent a telegram to the Kremlin expressing profound gratitude and the desire to strengthen ties, and played host to Admiral Gorshkov. On the other hand, Rubay Ali sent a warm message to King Khalid, and in his National Day speech praised support for the PDRY from "fraternal states headed by Saudi Arabia, the Gulf states and Egypt";[46] South Yemeni and Saudi Arabian ambassadors were exchanged, and South Yemen accepted Saudi mediation and released an Iranian pilot shot down over the PDRY.

Having thus received the message that the PDRY's foreign policy orientation had not yet been decided, both the Saudis and the Soviets pressed their suit in 1977. Riyadh agreed to sell crude oil to the Aden refinery at a discount, and then, with the Gulf States, agreed to become partners in a unique joint ownership plan which would see a modern oil complex built around the refinery. These were agreements of vast potential importance for the PDRY; like all nonoil countries it was suffering badly from the oil price increases.

Moreover, the refinery was its largest industry even though it was operating at only 20 percent of capacity; it had been starved for oil both because of Aden's political isolation and because the refinery was outdated. The agreement with Saudi Arabia and the other Gulf states promised to correct both of these conditions. The Saudis combined these promises with attempts to convince the PDRY to begin to normalize relations with Oman. As the fighting in the Ogaden region of Ethiopia slowly intensified, and the Ethiopian regime became much more radical following Mengistu Haile Mariam's coup in February, Riyadh's attempts to draw the PDRY (and Somalia) into its preparations for a Red Sea security pact seemed to be bearing fruit; both participated in the Taizz Conference in March (see Chapter 6).

For its part, Moscow stepped up its aid efforts and political activities, mostly apparently with an eye to the situation developing on the Horn of Africa. The Soviets began shipping 10,000 barrels per day of crude oil to the Aden refinery for the use of the Soviet Navy in the Indian Ocean; it seems that the Soviets anticipated increased naval activity in the Indian Ocean and/or the possibility of losing access to storage facilities in Somalia. Moscow also contracted to use some of its promised aid for lengthening the runways and for other airport improvements at Aden.[47] In addition, arms shipments were reported to have picked up in early 1977; these consisted mostly of small and medium weapons, but also included a sizable consignment of tanks.[48] General economic aid increased, and after a visit to Aden in March the Deputy Chairman of the State Committee on Foreign Economic Relations, V. Mordvinov, declared that the volume of Soviet technical aid to the PDRY would increase fourfold between 1976 and 1980.

That the Soviets did not do more (such as signing an agreement for a major new aid package, or delivering high-profile, high-prestige weapons like planes) suggests that they were fairly confident by early 1977 that South Yemen would not defect. They had several opportunities to test the waters, besides using their large embassy staff. Gorshkov had visited in December; Ali Abd ar-Razzaq BaDhib talked with Ponomarev while attending the World Peace Forum in Moscow in February. Soviet First Deputy Defense Minister General Sergei Sokolov visited Aden in mid-February; it was probably at this meeting that arrangements were made to send 30 Soviet tanks from South Yemen to Ethiopia for use in the Ogaden against the Somalia invaders,[49] a move that was bound to anger the Saudis. Further indications of the PDRY's fidelity were received during Castro's first visit to Aden in March. His main purpose was to convince the Ethiopian, Somalian, and South Yemeni leaders to agree on the federation proposal then being promoted by Moscow in a desperate attempt to avoid a full-scale war between its old and new friends on the Horn. Castro's mission failed, but apparently the South Yemenis were willing to go along with it.

South Yemen's participation ten days later in the Taizz Conference with the leaders of Sudan, the YAR, and Somalia must have given Moscow pause, however. Convened with the backing of Saudi Arabia and Egypt, the conference was probably meant to begin to create an anti-Soviet security pact around the Red Sea. However, Rubay Ali was not willing to go that far (nor, probably was the YAR's al-Hamdi) and the joint statement mentioned only keeping the Red Sea as a "zone of peace,"[50] a phrase with a multitude of interpretations, but one also which the Soviets have made their own.

On the question of PDRY-Oman relations, Rubay Ali moved toward accommodation, a position not favored at the time by Moscow; it was reported that a South Yemeni envoy would visit Muscat. However, the Ismail faction managed to nullify the initiative; that brought Saudi Foreign Minister Prince Saud to Aden for talks with Salim Rubay Ali. The latter must have soothed his concern over the Oman situation and the provision of South Yemeni tanks for Ethiopia, for on his departure he spoke of strengthening relations and increasing cooperation in the field of development.

On May 10, 1977, Muhammad Salih Muti arrived in Moscow. The attention accorded him indicated the concern with which Moscow was regarding the Red Sea. In two days he: discussed economic relations with Skachkov; discussed the further development of party-to-party relations with Ponomarev; talked to Gromyko; and, most importantly, discussed Red Sea matters with Brezhnev. This was an unusual honor for a Foreign Minister, as was the publication in *Pravda* of a photograph of the meeting. The meetings were not entirely successful—the phrase "exchange of views" cropped up in all the talks and in the communiqué, and the report of his discussion with Brezhnev used only the word "friendly," rather than a more enthusiastic catch-phrase.[51] Moscow would have liked the PDRY to join in its castigation of what it called Saudi Arabia's attempt "to knock together a closed military and political grouping in the Red Sea"[52] (i.e., one that excluded the Soviet Union), and in its call for the consolidation of all progressive forces to oppose this attempt. The South Yemenis were not willing to be this direct, but did acquiesce in a communiqué which expressed concern at the "attempts being made by imperialist *and reactionary* forces to create fresh hotbeds of international tension" in the Red Sea region.[53] (Emphasis added.) The South Yemen side also acknowledged the "great importance" of Soviet assistance and expressed support for the Middle East peace initiative which Brezhnev had launched in March. In return Brezhnev promised that the USSR would continue to assist the PDRY (a promise that the South Yemenis may have been anxious to get, considering the huge new demands on the Soviets from their new African friends) and invited Salim Rubay Ali to visit, a certain indication that he was not considered beyond the pale. Thus, while the Soviets could not be completely satisfied with this meeting, it did serve to underline the ties between the two countries and to restore to a certain extent their contacts with the Rubay Ali faction in Aden.[54] In addition, the two sides joined for the first time in a call for the liquidation of foreign (i.e., U.S.) bases in the Indian Ocean region. Moscow had stepped up its political campaign in the wake of Carter's unexpected declaration in favor of complete demilitarization of that ocean (quickly amended to "mutual military restraint").

Throughout the late spring and early summer of 1977, few contacts were reported between Moscow and Aden. PDRY contacts with the Gulf countries were more frequent, with Muti visiting the UAE and Saudi Arabia to promote bilateral relations, particularly economic aid, and Muhammad visiting Kuwait and Iraq. However, the indications were that South Yemen's foreign policy continued to be closer to Soviet than to Saudi wishes. In May Mengistu cited the PDRY as Ethiopia's only friend in the area, and in June Iraq's Vice-President found no encouragement for his plea for support of Aden's former friends in Eritrea. Aden radio continued to broadcast reports of PFLO activities, and both Abd al-Fattah Ismail and Ali Nasir Muhammad spoke of "material and political" support for them in June; this, an indication that Rubay Ali (who appeared to be willing to abandon quietly the Dhofari cause) was still not completely in charge of South Yemen's foreign policy, effectively sabotaged any movement toward Oman.

Nevertheless, in mid-June the Saudi Arabian Development Fund signed a long-term loan agreement worth $20 million to finance an electric power project in South Yemen. On July 18 at long last came the announcement that Salim Rubay Ali was to visit Riyadh on July 31, a visit which would presumably set the seal on the new relationship with Saudi Arabia. Alarmed, especially in view of Ethiopia's defeats in the Ogaden and Moscow's deteriorating relations with Somalia, the Soviets invited Ali Nasir Muhammad for a brief unofficial visit July 28-29. Muhammad met Skachkov briefly for talks on the further development of Soviet aid, but his main discussions were with Soviet Defense Minister Marshal Ustinov. The meeting was undoubtedly timed to diminish the warmth of Rubay Ali's reception in Saudi Arabia and to undercut the impact of that 'historic' visit; it demonstrated that the Ismail faction was still strong, and perhaps gaining ground. The discussion, "warm and friendly," probably centered on the situation in the Horn and the contingency that the Soviets might need Aden's facilities should they decide to intervene; the report of the meeting (admittedly brief) gave no hint of any South Yemeni objection.

Salim Rubay Ali's talks with King Khalid and Crown Prince Fahd during his three-day visit to Taif appeared to go well. It was announced following the meeting that Khalid would visit Aden later in the year. The communiqué[55] referred to a "spirit of love, fraternity, and true cooperation" and to a "spirit of Arab and Islamic fraternity"; however, since it also referred to the "historical neighborliness" of the two countries, these phrases could have been more for the sake of form than accuracy. The South Yemeni side seemed to give more than it received; a paragraph in the communique emphasized the importance of dialog in settling Arab differences, a reference to PDRY–Oman relations. Another paragraph referred to the need to preserve the Red Sea as a zone of peace and to "keep it free of any international conflict or ambitions"; this was a much more ambiguous phrase than the South Yemenis usually used, and the Saudis certainly intended it to refer to Soviet ambitions; at the same time, however, the 'Arabism' of the Red Sea was not mentioned. There was no mention of the subject nearest to Rubay Ali's heart– more Saudi economic aid.

This omission undoubtedly contributed to the deepening conflict within the regime in Aden. Despite the early reports in 1976 of massive aid, and the actual commitment of about $50 million in project aid and some unspecified budgetary aid,[56] the Saudis had remained cautious about promising large sums for long-term development before the PDRY's orientation was settled. Thus nothing had come of the joint Arab plan for modernizing and expanding the Aden refinery. The deal signed in May to refine 1 million tons of Saudi oil annually was slow in starting up (and was in fact cancelled by late October[57]). This is not to say that Arab aid, much of it from the peninsula oil states, was insubstantial; far from it.[58] However, it never lived up to expectations, and many in the regime were unhappy with the actual and likely political and ideological costs. Furthermore, some of the Saudi grant aid went directly into a separate fund which Salim Rubay Ali used to promote specific projects under the direction of his own appointees (in order to bypass the bureaucracy). Some of the projects and some of the appointees turned out to be very unsuitable.

A deepening of the factional conflict was discernible almost from the time Rubay Ali returned from Saudi Arabia. On August 7, 1977, Salih Muslih Qasim, the PDRY Interior Minister (and member of the Ismail faction) visited Addis Ababa; a week later Muti went to Somalia. These visits were reported by some as attempts at mediation; it seems more likely, given South Yemen's gradual tilt toward Ethiopia, that Qasim's visit was to affirm PDRY support. (This was reported in *al-Ahram*, which also said that there were 180 South Yemeni "military experts" assisting Ethiopian forces.[59] Other sources reported that the PDRY had supplied more tanks, and that South Yemenis were training Ethiopian pilots on MiGs supplied by the PDRY.[60])

Then in early September at the Arab League Foreign Ministers' Conference, reports surfaced that the PDRY had joined Sudan, the YAR, and Somalia in deciding to hold a conference of Arab Red Sea states to discuss Red Sea security and a permanent Red Sea security force; more spectacularly, rumors spread that Salim Rubay Ali would meet Jimmy Carter to discuss U.S.-PDRY relations.[61] These were not denied in Aden. Shortly thereafter a South Yemeni economic delegation visited Moscow for a scheduled meeting of the Soviet-PDRY joint economic committee. Its leaders had an unexpected meeting with Ponomarev and his deputy Karen Brutents, who were undoubtedly concerned to get more information about these reports. They did not, however, receive much satisfaction—the report of the meeting referred to an "exchange of views" on the development of relations.[62]

The South Yemeni President's appearance at the United Nations at the end of September seemed to confirm the rumors. Despite Rubay Ali's having just concluded a successful visit to Cuba, and despite his declaration of total support for the Dhofaris in his speech to the General Assembly (after which the Omani Under-Secretary for Foreign Affairs and the PDRY Ambassador to the U.N. traded shrill accusations), U.S. Secretary of State Vance had a successful meeting with him in private. Congressman Paul Findley, who met both Rubay Ali and Muti privately, has said that Muti believed that Washington would quickly send a mission to Aden to discuss normalization of relations.[63] Rubay Ali also had a "warm and friendly" talk with Andrei Gromyko, in which an "exchange of views" on the Horn was reported, but also a "mutual desire to continue to deepen and strengthen friendship and cooperation."[64] From Moscow's point of view, however, this sentiment must have been far outweighed by the prospect of U.S. involvement in the PDRY.

In the meantime, in Aden the Ismail faction had not been idle. While Rubay Ali was abroad, a meeting of representatives of UPONF and the Popular Front for the Liberation of Palestine advocated a "progressive Arab front" to oppose "imperialist, Zionist *and reactionary* designs" in the Red Sea region (emphasis added), and praised the struggle of the PFLO.[65] In early October the visit of an Ethiopian delegation brought the two countries closer, and on October 11 they signed an economic cooperation agreement. Ismail's speech on the anniversary of the Radfan uprising hinted that a power shift was taking place. Despite difficulties, he said, the UPONF had reached the "objective conditions which are accelerating its shift to a vanguard party"; the vanguard party would be formed in the second half of 1978.

Ismail's confidence, despite the strong opposition of Salim Rubay Ali to this move, indicated that the latter's star was descending. In retrospect (although it was not at all clear at the time) the removal on October 24 of the Defense Ministry from the hands of Prime Minister Ali Nasir Muhammad and the appointment of Ali Antar, one of the Ismail faction, was also a sign that the balance was shifting against Rubay Ali. Although Muhammad was by no means opposed to close ties to the Soviet Union, he was not a hard-liner like Ali Antar, and more important, he was not a military man. By that time Moscow had already taken the decision in principle to intervene in the Horn on Ethiopia's side and Soviet military planners certainly realized they could lose their facilities in Somalia and in any case would need those of Aden. Internally the new result was to add another pro-Ismail voice to the top levels of government.

FROM OCTOBER 1977 TO THE FIRST CONGRESS
OF THE YEMENI SOCIALIST PARTY (OCTOBER 1978)

By this time, however, the Saudi-Soviet competition over South Yemen was virtually finished, the *coup de grace* being Aden's participation in the Soviet arms air lift to Ethiopia which began in November. The October 11 assassination of YAR President al-Hamdi on the eve of his first (and the first ever by a YAR President) visit to the PDRY, provided the penultimate blow. Mystery surrounds the reasons for, and the perpetrators of, the assassination; it appears to have been the result, at least in part, of a realization in Riyadh that South Yemen was going to remain aligned with the USSR no matter what the promises of Saudi aid, and its consequent fear that Yemeni rapprochement could lead to Yemeni unity on terms inimical to Saudi interests. The Saudis were already dragging their feet over the implementation of their aid. In South Yemen, the murder of al-Hamdi and the widespread belief that Saudi Arabia was behind it[66] cut the ground from under Rubay Ali's feet, particularly when added to the disappointment at Saudi aid. The President himself was apparently infuriated by the assassination, and made no attempt to control the damage done to Saudi-PDRY relations. By mid-November, the Saudi and South Yemeni Ambassadors had been withdrawn and the policy of rapprochement with Saudi Arabia abandoned.

In all of this, Ismail's position in the regime was strengthened, and both he and the Soviets hastened to reaffirm their ties. In October, *World Marxist Review* carried an article by him asserting that only scientific socialism provided the correct decisions in internal and foreign policy. Special attention was paid in South Yemen throughout the autumn to the approaching 60th anniversary of the October Revolution, with a party-government commission set up to supervise the celebrations; as with the Lenin anniversary in 1970, the PDRY was the only Arab country to show great enthusiasm. Abd al-Fattah Ismail led a high level delegation to Moscow for the event, speaking before he departed of the "strong militant bonds and links of principled solidarity" between the two countries.[67] During his speech to a combined meeting of the CPSU Central Committee and the USSR Supreme Soviet, he criticized (clearly but not by name) Saudi Arabia, its aid package, Eritrean guerrilla movements and Somalia, and affirmed South Yemen's support for the national liberation movement in Oman.[68] In a meeting with (Politburo member) Kirilenko, Ponomarev, and Brutents, Ismail expressed gratitude for Soviet "all-round support," and both sides confirmed their desire for "a further comprehensive development and deepening of relations" and their "unity of views on questions relating to the international situation."

The day after Ismail returned from the Soviet Union, Somalia's leader Siad Barre dramatically changed the picture in the Horn, the Red Sea, and the Indian Ocean by unilaterally abrogating Somalia's Treaty of Friendship and Cooperation with the USSR and ordering all Soviet and allied advisers out of the country. Moscow's position, carefully prepared to back up its naval presence in the Indian Ocean, was in ruins. Because of the inadequacy of Ethiopian facilities, the Soviets needed Aden's port and airport; in the short run, they needed a logistics base for their operations in Ethiopia and a transshipment point for Soviet equipment and Cuban personnel heading there; in the long run, they had to replace their lost facilities at Berbera, particularly the airfield for long-range maritime reconnaissance. Aden had become necessary to Moscow's activist foreign policy.

Soviet supply procedures were put into effect quickly and smoothly. There were no hasty trips between Moscow and Aden, indicating that the plans that had been prepared worked well, and that there was no significant opposition to them in Aden. Military equipment flooded into the country, most of it bound for Ethiopia, but a considerable amount was destined to stay. This was partly to refurbish South Yemeni stocks depleted by the earlier supply operation to Ethiopia, and partly to reward the PDRY for its cooperation with more modern equipment; these stocks accounted for much of the $120 million in arms delivered by the Soviets in 1977 (3 times the 1976 levels[69]). Along with the arms came Soviet and Cuban advisers; by early 1978 their numbers were estimated at 550 Soviets and 1,000 Cubans.[70]

This process threatened to make South Yemen once again the pariah of the Arab world, most of which was still verbally supporting Somalia (somewhat reluctantly) and Eritrea against Ethiopia with its Soviet backers. The Saudi leaders in particular were infuriated and immediately cut off any aid packages still functioning; furthermore they apparently succeeded in putting pressure on other Gulf Arab states to stop supplying crude oil to the Aden refinery and to cut back other types of economic aid. The PDRY's isolation was mitigated by

Anwar Sadat's trip to Jerusalem and Aden's immediate condemnation of it, but militant rhetoric began to flow between the Riyadh and Aden, and armed clashes on the frontier were reported late in 1977.

In these circumstances the renewed polarization of the peninsula was completed and South Yemen sought closer ties to the Soviets for protection, while the Soviets sought guaranteed access to Aden's facilities. At the end of November the two sides were reported to be discussing a draft agreement which would give the PDRY direct financial aid and modern weapons in return for naval access to port facilities improved by the Soviets, full use of the airport, and the right to establish communications bases in South Yemen to replace those the Soviets lost in Somalia.[71] Such an agreement was not signed at this time (rumor had it being signed in late spring 1978), but this did not appear to make any difference to the extensive Soviet use of the facilities during the Ethiopian air lift. The Soviet Navy's use of the port increased, commensurate with the surge of ships during the lift operation, and the drydock which the Soviets had stationed in Berbera was moved to Aden.

While all this military activity was going on, the two sides were also engaged in many nonmilitary contacts. At the end of November, Brezhnev and Kosygin sent a very warm "Dear Comrades" telegram on the tenth anniversary of the PDRY's independence.[72] In December a group of Soviet planning experts arrived in Aden to assist in formulating South Yemen's second Five Year Plan, and a Komsomol delegation and a group from the Soviet Afro-Asian Solidarity Committee visited.

South Yemeni participation in events in the Horn ended any hope of a diversified and flexible foreign policy for the PDRY; nevertheless, Rubay Ali apparently did not resist it, angered as he was with Saudi Arabia. He began to adopt a more militant stance, using the occasion of his tenth anniversary speech to express strong support for the PFLO and to state that relations with the socialist countries would expand. At the same time he did not completely abandon his former policy; in January he told Congressmen Findley (in Aden for a brief visit at his invitation) that he "hoped to discuss the establishment of full diplomatic ties with the U.S. soon"; he also asked him to carry his warmest greetings to President Carter.[73]

Rubay Ali's militancy in November had availed him little in any case. At its late December meeting the Central Committee approved a completely militant foreign policy line without even a face-saving nod to normal relations with Saudi Arabia; it also confirmed that the vanguard party would be established in the second half of 1978. Furthermore, he lost favor with the army's leadership over his refusal to dismiss several officers convicted of corruption while serving in the Arab peacekeeping force in Lebanon.

In early 1978 relations between the PDRY and the Soviet Union continued to grow warmer. In January the South Yemeni troops were withdrawn from Lebanon and sent to Ethiopia; reports spoke of 1,000-2,000 South Yemenis training Ethiopian troops and engaging in combat alongside Ethiopians and Cubans.[74] At home the growing antagonism with Saudi Arabia also led to closer ties with Moscow. In January and February there were several reports of clashes between remobilized émigré groups and Saudi forces on the one hand, and South Yemeni forces reinforced by Cuban officers on the other; in one of these actions, four Saudi planes were reported to have been shot down by PDRY MiGs[75] (one reason, perhaps, why the clashes did not develop into anything more serious).

In these circumstances, Prime Minister Ali Nasir Muhammad led a delegation which included the Defense Minister and Chief of General Staff to Moscow in February 1978. The delegation was greeted at the airport by Kosygin with much fanfare and publicity; Muhammad's picture was printed on page 1 of *Pravda* twice. He was received by Brezhnev, and had talks with Kosygin and Defense Minister Ustinov. The communiqué[76] registered widespread agreement on a large number of issues, including the situation in the Horn of Africa and the Middle East; the South Yemenis "stressed the need to strengthen relations between the Arab countries and the Soviet Union and other socialist countries," an endorsement the Soviets were particularly eager to get after Sadat's trip to Jerusalem. The sides again called for an end to foreign military bases in the Indian Ocean region, as the Soviets expanded their campaign now that they had lost Berbera.

Agreement was not total, however; the communiqué spoke of an exchange of opinions, and the Brezhnev-Muhammad discussions were said to have been conducted in an "atmosphere of friendship, frankness and mutual understanding." Perhaps because of the differences of opinion, the South Yemenis did not allow inclusion of Muhammad's call during a luncheon speech for the USSR to be included in any peace process in the Middle East.[77] Another interesting omission was the failure to attack 'reaction' in the Arabian Peninsula and the Horn or to express support for the PFLO either directly or under the rubric of the national liberation movement, although Ali Nasir had proclaimed strong support for it in East Germany, and had attacked "reactionary quarters" in his luncheon speech. It is likely that Moscow, heavily committed in the Horn, with South Yemen back on the team, was anxious that Aden not exacerbate the already tense situation on its borders.

The South Yemenis came away from the visit with a major new aid package (estimated at $90 million[78]) for development projects in the new Five-Year Plan, which went some way toward replacing the lost Arab aid; however, they apparently did not receive more budgetary aid. Nor, it would appear, were the Soviets completely satisfied. Kosygin in his luncheon speech made glowing reference to the memory of Jamal Abd al-Nasir (no doubt surprising the South Yemenis, who did not revere his memory in the least); the significance of this may have been that Nasir had granted to the Soviets extensive access to Egyptian military facilities; long-term access to Aden's facilities may still have been a problem. All in all, however, the trip could be deemed a success, and Kosygin again accepted an invitation to visit Aden. Certainly Muhammad billed it as a success on his return to Aden; probably for internal political reasons he ignored the "frankness," and referred to unanimity and complete harmony, and stressed the aid package.

Throughout the rest of the first half of 1978 Soviet-South Yemen ties continued to develop. In mid-March a CPSU delegation arrived to sign a new plan for party cooperation which provided for increased Soviet assistance in training UPONF cadres, particularly to the Higher School of Scientific Socialism. The agreement was presumably to assist in the development of the vanguard party, which Abd al-Fattah Ismail's faction was working very hard to promote. The visit was returned by a UPONF delegation in mid-May.

In military matters too, relations seemed to grow much closer. Reports began to appear in March of a major arms deal, perhaps negotiated during Muhammad's visit; the Soviets would supply 50 MiG-21s, surface-to-air missiles and T-62 main battle tanks, more advanced than any possessed by the YAR.[79] Then in May Admiral Gorshkov visited for talks with Ismail and Ali Antar about "friendly bilateral relations and ways of expanding them." Reports claimed that a secret 15-year military cooperation agreement was negotiated at this time, with provisions for: (1) a new naval base for the PDRY which would offer the Soviet fleet facilities for repairs, storage, communications, and monitoring (such as they had had in Berbera); (2) a new air force base near Aden which would offer facilities for the Soviets; (3) a major radar network covering the PDRY-Saudi Arabia and the PDRY-Oman border; and (4) Soviet assistance to South Yemen in the event of foreign aggression.[80] (It should be noted that (2) and (3) have been built, but (1) has not. If (4) was in fact agreed upon, it remains a deep secret.) There may have been some difficulty in these negotiations, for Ali Antar flew to Moscow with Gorshkov on May 22; another possibility is that the Soviets were unhappy with Aden's decision to withdraw its forces from Ethiopia in early June. A further possibility has nothing to do with a dispute; it was at about this time that the internal power struggle reached into the military with the arrest of 150 of Rubay Ali's supporters in the Army officer corps (for opposing the formation of a vanguard party),[81] and the Defense Minister may have been sent to brief the Soviet leadership.

The ebb and flow of the power struggle was also reflected in the regime's foreign policy moves that spring. At the end of March Ali Nasir Muhammad visited Kuwait to try to persuade the Kuwaitis to fulfill their aid commitments of the previous year, and to the UAE to look for new aid. He apparently received some small commitments, but was also urged to mend fences with Saudi Arabia. This was probably the reason for Interior Minister Salih Muslih Qasim's visit to Riyadh a week later. Nevertheless, Aden did not moderate any of the policies to which the Saudis objected. South Yemeni forces remained in Ethiopia, assisting the government's drive against the Eritrean rebels.[82]

On the other hand, the Soviets must have been annoyed when Muhammad visited Beijing, although he was very careful to keep his distance from Chinese references to Soviet "hegemonism." (This trip had been scheduled earlier, but had been postponed; one report claimed this was because of Soviet objections, but it is more likely that Aden was showing its displeasure over reports that China was considering diplomatic relations with Oman.) Muhammad came away with an economic and technical cooperation agreement which continued to draw on existing credits and which did not increase China's presence (by now insignificant) in South Yemen.

At the beginning of June, as Ali Antar visited the Soviet Union and Eastern Europe, the Kuwait press reported that Muti had asked Kuwait to help the PDRY to normalize relations with Saudi Arabia, in order to help Aden loosen its ties with the Soviet Union and Cuba.[83] This did not jibe with other South Yemeni activities. Within the country Cuban involvement with the militia was suddenly publicized.[84] East European delegations arrived in April for economic talks. Muti himself travelled to Cuba in June, and a South Yemeni trade delegation signed new agreements in Moscow. In mid-June Soviet Ambassador-at-Large L. Mendelovich visited Aden as part of a tour to generate support for Soviet disarmament and Indian Ocean proposals; he received enthusiastic support from Aden. (Interestingly, he did not speak with Rubay Ali.)

All of this must be set within the context of the internal power struggle which in the spring of 1978 was rapidly approaching its climax, and which was for the most part fuelled by internal political issues, personal ambitions, and tribal disputes.[85] Throughout the spring, Salim Rubay Ali, weakened by the failure of his move toward greater flexibility in foreign affairs and by his administrative practices and some bizarre economic policies,[86] gradually lost control over the government and military. His popularity, though still higher than Ismail's, was probably also affected by a succession of poor harvests caused by droughts or flooding since 1975.[87] In the meantime, Abd al-Fattah Ismail was working assiduously to strengthen his power base in UPONF by its reorganization into the new vanguard party.

In retrospect, Ismail seems to have won out by the beginning of May. His May Day speech announced the launching of formal activities to establish the new party, and two weeks later Rubay Ali himself was obliged to declare that "the formation of a vanguard party of a new type is one of the most important objectives" of UPONF and the people.[88] At the end of May there were the arrests of Army officers supporting him, and his replacement as Chairman of the important Armed Forces Organization Committee by a member of Ismail's faction. In June, restraints on the PFLO's activities seemed to be lifted. On June 21, Ismail was able to announce that the vanguard party would be formally established in October. By then Arab sources were openly speculating that Rubay Ali had been defeated and that his days as President were numbered.[89]

This certainly turned out to be true, although in a way which few would have foreseen, with Rubay Ali's execution on June 26, ostensibly for his part in the assassination of YAR President al-Ghashmi two days earlier. No one has yet produced a completely plausible explanation of these events, and it is unlikely that anyone ever will.[90] The least unlikely scenario is that the Ismail faction planted the bomb in order to 'frame' Rubay Ali, to finish him off together with the rapprochement he may have been planning with the pro-Saudi YAR President and the possibility of better relations with the United States. A State Department mission was due to arrive in Aden on June 27 to begin a dialog aimed at eventually improving relations.)

As a result of the assassination, fighting broke out in Aden, as Rubay Ali sought to prevent the Ismail faction from succeeding in their bid to blame him for the bomb and to overthrow him. The fight was an uneven one; Rubay Ali could count on only a few army units and his supporters, most of whom were some distance away in the Third Governorate; Ismail on the other hand could count on the militia, most of the army, and, most important, the air force. The fighting was over quickly, and Rubay Ali was executed.

The role of the Soviets and their allies in these events is not clear. The East Germans with the South Yemeni security service seem likely to have had some involvement in the assassination in Sanaa and the Soviets to have been aware of it. The Soviets appear not to have participated in the fighting in Aden; despite widespread reports that Cubans had flown the planes that bombarded the Presidential Palace, South Yemeni forces appear to have been capable of conducting the fighting themselves. There is no question that the Soviets supported Ismail to the extent they were needed. They flew in several hundred Cuban troops from Ethiopia to help out if necessary, and Soviet ships moved about in the Gulf of Aden as if to discourage any outside intervention.[91] This latter activity was just one of a series meant to warn off countries (the United States and Saudi Arabia) considered to be threatening South Yemen in its time of instability and to reinforce the mutual support between the Soviets and the now undisputed leaders of the PDRY. (A new Presidential Council was formed, with a distinctly pro-Soviet hue: Abd al-Fattah Ismail, Ali Nasir Muhammad (the Chairman), Ali Antar, Ali Abd ar-Razzaq BaDhib, and Muhammad Salih Muti.[92])

The most obvious Soviet efforts were political, consisting in the main of a blizzard of propaganda throughout July on the theme of the Saudi Arabian and U.S. threat to South Yemen.[93] In this brief campaign the Soviet media outdid even its South Yemeni counterparts. Moscow may by the intensity of the campaign have been trying to convince Riyadh and Washington of its commitment to the new regime in Aden in the hope that this would deter them from hostile actions which would in turn have forced the Soviets to respond. At the same time, it should be noted that the Soviets produced various vague expressions implying more active support. On July 4, *Pravda* published a statement by Ali Antar that "if South Yemen is obliged to fight, then it will not fight alone. The PDRY can count on aid from its allies — both within the Arab world and outside it." Two days later Moscow radio broadcast the statement to the Arab world that "the progressive forces will not leave it [the PDRY] alone to face the danger"; the armed forces' newspaper *Krasnaya Zvezda* made similar statements.[94]

For a few months it appeared that there was a real threat to the new regime. The new YAR government issued a stream of bellicose statements, there were reports of North Yemeni and Saudi forces massing on the borders, and some of the South Yemeni émigré groups and their radio were reactivated. On Saudi and North Yemeni urging, the Arab League announced a freeze on economic and diplomatic relations with the PDRY. Inside the PDRY, fighting between government forces and Rubay Ali supporters continued throughout the summer and sporadically in the autumn; widespread purges were carried on in the armed forces, party, and government.[95]

To help the new regime cope with these various problems the Soviets provided various types of assistance in addition to the general propaganda mentioned above. There were reports of Soviet ships being stationed in Aden and near Perim Island "for guard duty."[96] In mid-August (by which time the threat of hostilities was much reduced, although tension still existed on the PDRY-YAR border) a group of Soviet ships paid a well-publicized visit to Aden; its commander was received by Ali Nasir Muhammad and held a press conference (unprecedented in Aden) in which he praised the South Yemen's foreign policy and offered more Soviet assistance in developing the PDRY Navy.[97] Other sources claimed that the Soviet ships brought 500 Cuban soldiers who were promptly despatched to the border with the YAR.[98]

The Soviets also continued their high level of arms deliveries, and may have promised $50 million in economic aid to help offset the Arab League's sanctions against the PDRY;[99] aid disbursements were not, however, accelerated. This was clearly not enough to meet South Yemen's needs, and in early July Aden apparently asked to become a member of CMEA, doubtless hoping this would result in much higher aid levels (as it had for Cuba and Vietnam); Moscow only agreed to study South Yemen's needs.

As in the early 1970s however, Aden was in no position to bargain, and any unhappiness at the economic aid level did not find public expression. The members of the new leadership unanimously proclaimed their gratitude for Soviet assistance and their support for the Soviets, though in terms no more effusive than in the past. Abd al-Fattah Ismail claimed that one of Rubay Ali's greatest sins had been to sow doubts about relations with the USSR, and declared himself proud to be systematically developing close relations with the Soviets, who were extending "great assistance" to the PDRY.[100] Ali Nasir Muhammad praised the Soviet Union for its assistance to help South Yemen defend its revolution, and also declared that the PDRY would not participate in the proposed Red Sea security agreement.[101]

Nevertheless, Aden did not abandon itself to radicalism. For several weeks in July (until Washington rejected the idea) Muti insisted that the PDRY was still prepared to start a dialog with the U.S.[102] Aden officials (especially Muhammad and Muti), insisting that al-Ghashmi's assassination was Rubay Ali's work, called for dialog and peaceful relations with the YAR and even Saudi Arabia.[103] Regarding the latter, however, they were not consistent; this may have been the result of the ebb and flow of tension on the borders or perhaps of differences between them and Ismail — a new power struggle was already taking shape.

Signs of relative moderation were not a setback for the Soviets, for they were publicly commending (and reinforcing) Aden's 'restraint' and its desire for "friendship and good neighborliness with all Arab countries."[104] The last thing the Soviets wanted was a general outbreak of war in the southern Arabian Peninsula, now that they seemed within reach of their goal of having military facilities in a country which would be a dependable ally. With the demise of Rubay Ali, the Soviets gained easier access to South Yemeni facilities which they needed to replace those of Berbera; in particular the new airbase coutside Aden, with electronic observation and communications facilities, essential to Soviet staging, ocean surveillance, and power projection activities, was under Soviet control in all but name. The same was not true of Aden's port facilities, where the South Yemenis were more anxious to preserve appearances (since it was much more visible); Muhammad on a number of occasions insisted that the PDRY had not given bases to the Soviets, and this was said in the context of the port. The big drydock from Berbera which had been towed out of Aden in April 1978 to the Dahlac Islands off the coast of Ethiopia was not returned,[105] although it surely could have been put to better use in Aden, and the Soviets wanted it there. A year later Western intelligence sources were still reporting that the Soviet Navy was using Aden only for crew changes, minor repairs, and some refuelling and replenishment. The Soviets probably wanted more access, and Ismail was believed to want to grant it, but could not convince his colleagues; this was evidently an area of some sensitivity for the South Yemenis, and the Soviets could not insist. In any case, political events in the PDRY were moving in the direction of closer, perhaps even permanent, ties to the socialist camp with the establishment of the Yemeni Socialist Party in October 1978.

NOTES

1. *FBIS/USSR*, November 2, 1973, p. F6-7.
2. B. Dismukes and J. M. McConnell, *Soviet Naval Diplomacy* (New York: Pergamon Press, 1979), p. 68.
3. *FBIS/USSR*, February 28, 1974, pp. A11-12; V. Pavlovsky and Iu. Tomilin, "The Indian Ocean: Confrontation or Security?" *New Times*, no. 10 (March), 1974, pp. 4-5; Portniagin, A. D., "Kritika planov Pentagona v zone Indiiskogo okeana," *SShA: Ekonomika, politika, ideologiia*, no.3 (March), 1975, pp. 74-6.
4. *FBIS/USSR*, April 10, 1974, pp. F6-7.
5. Cf. U.S., Congress, House, *Congressional Record*, 93rd Cong., 2nd sess., 1974, pp. 16334, 16340.
6. "Aid - with Strategic Strings," *Soviet Analyst* 3 (October 3, 1974): 3. The Soviets did not publicize this decision, undoubtedly to avoid pressure from other debtors.
7. *Pravda*, July 26, 1974.
8. *FBIS/USSR*, July 19, 1974, p. F5.
9. *FBIS/USSR*, September 30, 1974, p. F6.
10. *FBIS/MENA*, June 17, 1975, p. C4; *FBIS/MENA*, June 25, 1975, p. C4.
11. *FBIS/MENA*, September 17, 1974, pp. C1-2.
12. *FBIS/MENA*, September 18, 1974, p. C2.

13. *FBIS/MENA*, September 18, 1974, p. C1.
14. *FBIS/MENA*, February 19, 1975, p. C8.
15. U.S., Congress, House, Committee on International Relations, Special Subcommittee on Investigations, *Diego Garcia 1975*, pp. 91-92.
16. F. Halliday, "Yemen's Unfinished Revolution: Socialism in the South," *MERIP Reports*, no. 81 (October 1979): 10.
17. *FBIS/USSR*, March 27, 1975, pp. F4-5.
18. A. Guskov, "Kursom progressivnykh preobrazovanii," *Aziia i Afrika Segodnia* no. 3 (March), 1976, p. 27.
19. O. Bogushevich, "Demokraticheskii Iemen: edinstvo revoliutsionnykh sil," in Akademiia Nauk SSSR, Institut Mirovoi Ekonomiki i Mezhdunarodnikh Otnoshennii, *Mezhdunarodnyi Ezhegodnik: Politika i Ekonomika 1976* (Moscow: Iz. Politicheskoi Literatury, 1976), p. 236.
20. *FBIS/MENA*, October 16, 1975, pp. C3-8; *FBIS/MENA*, October 17, 1975, p. C3.
21. *FBIS/MENA*, October 16, 1975, p. C8; *FBIS/USSR*, October 20, 1975, p. F3.
22. U.S., Congress, House, Committee on International Relations, *The Soviet Union and the Third World: A Watershed in Great Power Politics?* (Washington, D.C.: GPO, 1977), p. 125.
23. *Arab Report and Record*, March 16-31, 1976, p. 195.
24. *FBIS/USSR*, March 12, 1976, pp. F1-2.
25. *FBIS/MENA*, March 11, 1976, p. C2.
26. *Pravda*, March 3, 1976; *New Times*, no. 10 (March), 1976, p. 5; Ismail was the sixth foreign delegate to be quoted and the second from the Middle East.
27. V. Naumkin, "Southern Yemen: the road to progress," *International Affairs* (Moscow), no. 1 (January), 1978, p. 69.
28. *FBIS/USSR*, June 18, 1976, p. F5; *FBIS/USSR*, June 19, 1976, p. F12; *FBIS/USSR*, June 23, 1976, p. F5; *FBIS/MENA*, June 22, 1976, p. C6.
29. "South Yemen softens its Marxist line," *The Arab Economist* 9 (March 1977): 22; *FBIS/MENA*, April 24, 1976, p. C2.
30. *Pravda*, July 31, 1976.
31. *FBIS/MENA*, June 22, 1976, pp. C5-6.
32. The expansion of Diego Garcia was justified, ironically, by increased Soviet naval activity in the Indian Ocean and by Soviet facilities in Somalia (which would have been called a 'base' by Soviet propagandists had a Western power had them). Cf. B. W. Watson, *Red Navy at Sea: Soviet Naval Operations on the High Seas 1956-1980* (Boulder: Westview Press, 1982), Chapter 10, pp. 152-54, 216-21. Regarding the Masirah Island facilities, an agreement was not in fact signed for several years, and U.S. access has never been as great as Moscow and Aden claim; however, the intensity of Soviet and South Yemeni propaganda about it indicates the level of their concern.
33. The Soviets warned that nothing must interfere with freedom of navigation and pointed out that if the Indian Ocean were to be designated as a zone of peace while imperialist military bases remained, the USSR would be put in an "inequitable" position. (*FBIS/USSR*, December 2, 1975, pp. A10-11.)

Moscow was annoyed by the persistence of the littoral countries in including the Soviet Union in their call for an end to great-power naval competition and base-building in the Indian Ocean.

34. For example, cf. Yu. Tsaplin, "Teamed Up," *New Times*, no. 48 (November), 1976, p. 23; *FBIS/USSR*, July 26, 1976, pp. F5-6; *Ezhegodnik BSE 1976*, pp. 284-85; V. Aleksandrov, "Dynamic Progress," *New Times*, no. 42 (October), 1976, p. 15.

35. U.S., CIA, *Communist Aid to the Less Developed Countries of the Free World 1977*, (McLean, VA: CIA, 1978), pp. 3-4.

36. International Institute for Strategic Studies, *The Military Balance, 1973-4* (London: IISS, 1973); Ibid. 1976-7 (London: IISS, 1976); V. N. Burmistrov, "NDRI: pervoe desiatiletie nezavisimogo razvitiia," in E. A. Lebedev (ed.), *Istoriia i ekonomika Arabskikh stran: sbornik statei* (Moscow: Iz. Nauka, 1977), p. 24.

37. U.S., Arms Control & Disarmament Agency, *World Military Expenditures and Arms Transfers 1971-1980* (Washington, D.C.: ACDA, 1983), p. 114.

38. S. A. Chaudhry, *The People's Democratic Republic of Yemen: Review of Economic and Social Development* (Washington, D.C.: The World Bank, 1979), p. 33.

39. U.S., CIA, op. cit., p. 9.

40. The impact of education abroad should probably not be valued too highly. South Yemeni sources have said that virtually none of the students trained abroad until 1975 stayed in South Yemen, and that many of the military trainees returned from the Soviet Union "drunk and useless."

41. U.S., Department of State, Bureau of Intelligence and Research, *Communist Governments and Developing Nations: Aid and Trade in 1973* (Washington, D.C.: Department of State, 1974); U.S., CIA, *Communist Aid to the Less Developed Countries of the Free World 1976* (McLean, VA: CIA, 1977).

42. M. Abir, *Oil, Power and Politics: Conflict in Arabia, the Red Sea and the Gulf* (London: Cass, 1974), p. 125; S. A. Chaudhry, op. cit., p. 25. This figure should be compared with $125 million from Arab sources, $60 million from China, and $38 million from the IDA. F. Halliday, "Soviet Relations with South Yemen," paper delivered to the International Symposium on Contemporary Yemen, Exeter University, June, 1983, p. 16.

43. F. Grimaldi, "Rubay Ali steers a new course for South Yemen," *The Middle East*, no. 36 (October 1977): 21; F. Halliday, "Yemen's Unfinished Revolution: Socialism in the South," *MERIP Reports*, no. 81 (October 1979): 19.

44. *FBIS/MENA*, August 20, 1976, p. C3.

45. By 1977, annual remittances totalled $180 million, up from $33 million in 1973. R. W. Stookey, *South Yemen: A Marxist Republic in Arabia* (Boulder: Westview Press, 1982), p. 89.

46. *FBIS/MENA*, November 18, 1976, p. C5; *FBIS/MENA*, December 1, 1976, p. C4.

47. U.S., CIA, op. cit., p. 28.

48. The Economist, *Foreign Report*, March 9, 1977; *The Military Balance 1976-77*, p. 39.

49. M. Ottaway, *Soviet and American Influence in the Horn of Africa*, (New York: Praeger, 1982), p. 108.
50. *FBIS/MENA*, March 24, 1977, p. C6-7.
51. *Pravda*, May 12, 1977; *FBIS/USSR*, May 12, 1977, p. F1; *FBIS/USSR*, May 16, 1977, pp. F1-3; *Pravda*, May 13, 1977.
52. *FBIS/USSR*, May 16, 1977, pp. F4-5; V. Kudryavtsev, "Teni nad Krasnym Morem," *Izvestiia*, April 16, 1977.
53. *FBIS/USSR*, May 16, 1977, p. F2.
54. That Moscow still favored Ismail was made evident in a major *Pravda* article on May 22 by veteran political correspondent A. Vasilev, who wrote about many aspects of South Yemen, but quoted only Abd al-Fattah; he also claimed that Saudi Arabia was still intent on subverting or overthrowing the PDRY's regime.
55. *FBIS/MENA*, August 3, 1977, pp. C3-4.
56. F. Halliday, "Yemen: Aden under pressure," *The Middle East*, no. 41 (March 1978): 23; C. Legum and H. Shaked (eds.) *Middle East Contemporary Survey 1977-78* (hereinafter cited as *MECS*) (New York: Holmes & Meier, 1979), pp. 561-62.
57. F. Halliday, "Soviet Relations with South Yemen," p. 13; it was reported in *MECS 1977-78*, p. 665 that the Saudis never did ship any oil to the refinery.
58. The World Bank study in 1979 estimated that Arab countries had committed approximately $200 million and had disbursed over $100 million in grants since 1975. Unfortunately, the study does not break the figures down by country of origin. S. A. Chaudhry, op. cit. Another source estimates that although by 1978 OPEC countries had promised $280 million to the PDRY, only $65 million had been disbursed. D. Deese and J. S. Nye (eds.), *Energy and Security* (Cambridge, Mass: Ballinger, 1981), pp. 37, 188.
59. *MECS 1976-77*, p. 560.
60. *Arab Report and Record*, August 1-15, 1977, p. 659; *Arabia and the Gulf* 1 (November 28, 1977): 11.
61. *FBIS/MENA*, September 7, 1977, p. A6; *Arabia and the Gulf* 1 (September 19, 1977): 16.
62. *FBIS/USSR*, September 15, 1977, p. F2.
63. Rep. Paul Findley to the author, May 26, 1983.
64. *FBIS/USSR*, September 30, 1977, p. A1.
65. *Arab Report and Record*, September 16-30, 1977, p. 803.
66. Aden News Agency carried Moscow radio's report from Beirut that the North Yemeni National Democratic Front had claimed that the United States and Saudi Arabia had "directed the murderers." *FBIS/USSR*, October 27, 1977, p. F2; *FBIS/MENA*, October 31, 1977, p. C1. However, claims that this Aden report caused the break between Saudi Arabia and the PDRY ignore the already poor state of relations between them.
67. *FBIS/MENA*, October 31, 1977, p. C1.
68. *FBIS/USSR*, November 4, 1977, p. P11.
69. U.S., Arms Control & Disarmament Agency, op. cit., p. 114.
70. U.S., CIA, *Communist Aid Activities in Non-Communist Less Developed Countries 1978* (McLean, VA: CIA, 1979), p. 4.

71. *MECS 1977-78*, p. 665.
72. *FBIS/USSR*, November 30, 1977, p. F10.
73. N. Sakr, "Yemen: the hard choice ahead," *The Middle East*, no. 41 (March 1978): 22.
74. Cf. *MECS 1977-78*, p. 238.
75. *MECS 1977-78*, p. 662; The Economist, *Foreign Report*, February 1, 1978; *FBIS/MENA*, February 27, 1977, p. C1.
76. *FBIS/USSR*, February 6, 1978, pp. F3-6.
77. *FBIS/USSR*, February 3, 1978, p. F6.
78. U.S., CIA, *Communist Aid Activities in non-Communist Less Developed Countries 1978* (McLean, VA: CIA, 1979), p. 35; this was at least a ten-fold increase over 1977. Cf. *Ezhegodnik BSE 1978*, p. 263.
79. *An-Nahar Arab Report & MEMO*, March 6, 1978; *Washington Post*, March 20, 1978. The communiqué of Muhammad's visit did not even hint at an arms agreement.
80. *FBIS/MENA*, July 10, 1978, p. C4.
81. *FBIS/MENA*, May 26, 1978, p. C2.
82. *New York Times*, June 27, 1978. South Yemeni Forces were withdrawn in June; however, this could not be considered a victory for Rubay Ali; he was in eclipse by then. It was partly due to pressure from other pro-Soviet Arab governments (particularly Iraq) who were supporting Eritrea despite Soviet support for Ethiopia; it was, no doubt, also due to the dislike of that war in South Yemen and to Ismail's wish to improve his popularity in South Yemen.
83. *Arab Report and Record*, June 1-15, 1978, p. 420.
84. *FBIS/MENA*, April 18, 1978, p. C8; *FBIS/MENA*, May 25, 1978, p. C3.
85. For an excellent discussion of the forces behind the power struggle, cf. F. Halliday, "Yemen's Unfinished Revolution," pp. 3-20.
86. *Washington Post*, August 15, 1978.
87. F. Halliday, "Yemen's Unfinished Revolution," p. 7; *Ezhegodnik BSE 1976*, p. 284; S. A. Chaudhry, op. cit., p. 46.
88. *FBIS/USSR*, May 18, 1978, p. F4.
89. Cf. *Arabia and the Gulf* 2 (June 5, 1978): 3; *FBIS/MENA*, June 20, 1978, p. C7.
90. For a detailed exposition of the two least unlikely scenarios, cf. N. Novik, "On the Shores of Bab al-Mandab: Soviet Diplomacy and Regional Dominances," *Crossroads*, no. 2 (Winter 1979), pp. 83-94, and F. Halliday, "Yemen's Unfinished Revolution," pp. 18-19.
91. *FBIS/MENA*, June 28, 1978, p. C1. A. Yodfat to the author, July 1983.
92. It was suggested at the time that Muhammad was made President in order to divert public opprobrium for Rubay Ali's execution away from the unpopular Ismail. BaDhib was, of course, a veteran communist.
93. *FBIS/USSR*, July 6, 1978, p. F7; *FBIS/USSR*, July 7, 1978, pp. F6-7; for a summary of the propaganda campaign, cf. *USSR and the Third World* 8 (July-December 1978): 97.

94. *FBIS/USSR*, July 7, 1978, p. F6; *FBIS/USSR*, July 13, 1978, pp. F3-4.
95. *MECS 1977-78*, p. 661; *MECS 1978-79*, pp. 660-61, 717, 719.
96. *FBIS/MENA*, August 22, 1978, p. C3.
97. *FBIS/MENA*, August 22, 1978, p. C3. The visit was said to be "in keeping with an understanding"; this may refer to the secret defense agreement which was said to have been signed in May 1978; is so, it is instructive that the crisis was over before the visit occurred. The unconfirmed July visit would have been more in keeping with the spirit of this agreement; if it did indeed occur, it was unpublicized, and Moscow must have meant it to be a serious but controlled 'hands off' signal.
98. *FBIS/MENA*, August 21, 1978, p. C3.
99. Table 5:15 in P. Wiles (ed.) *The New Communist Third World* (New York: St. Martin's Press, 1982), p. 196 suggests that total Soviet aid to the PDRY in 1978 was $138 million. Of that, $90 million was committed during Ali Nasir Muhammad's visit in February.
100. *FBIS/MENA*, June 29, 1978, p. C10; *FBIS/MENA*, July 25, 1978, p. C3.
101. *FBIS/USSR*, July 17, 1978, p. F3; *FBIS/MENA*, August 8, 1978, p. C2.
102. *FBIS/MENA*, July 10, 1978, p. C2; *New York Times*, August 6, 1978.
103. *FBIS/MENA*, June 30, 1978, p. C7; *FBIS/MENA*, July 10, 1978, p. C4.
104. *Pravda*, July 8, 1978.
105. R. Remnek to the author, March 29, 1983; R. Remnek, letter to the editor, *Problems of Communism* 28 (November-December 1979): 109. The Dahlacs are very inhospitable, lacking even fresh water; they are, however, private. The Soviets may have valued this feature for working on their ships, particularly submarines. They may also have contemplated moving the drydock to an Ethiopian port once the Eritrean war ended. However, it is also possible that the South Yemenis and Soviets disagreed on its use in Aden; the drydock would have been a valuable factor in the modernization of the port facilities so badly needed, and it is hard to see Aden wanting to be rid of it unless the Soviets refused to allow it to be used for civilian ships.

4

THE PDRY: A STATE OF SOCIALIST ORIENTATION (1978–84)

FROM OCTOBER 1978 TO THE SIGNING OF THE USSR-PDRY TREATY (OCTOBER 1979)

The formation of the Yemeni Socialist Party (YSP) at its First Congress October 11 - 14, 1978 and the reorganization of the government structure in December institutionalized Abd al-Fattah Ismail's triumph. He was named general secretary of the party, and later chosen by the newly elected Supreme People's Council as the Chairman of its Presidium. Since both of these institutions, party and government, were organized on the Soviet model, Ismail thus occupied the two most powerful positions in the country.

There was no doubt as to the policy orientation of the new party. The party program declared that the YSP would "be guided by the theory of scientific socialism and the historical experience of socialist construction, above all that of the Soviet Union."[1] Ismail's statements at the Congress contained fulsome praise for the USSR, Aden's premier ally, its reliable friend. At the same time, he stressed the need to strengthen relations in all spheres with the socialist countries, relations which, he said, were "principled and strategic."[2]

The Soviets never went as far as to call their relationship a "strategic" one, and they were leery of the ideological claims of the YSP. However, they were obviously pleased with the direction Aden was taking; in Soviet ideological writing on the Third World, the PDRY was confirmed as one of the 'countries of socialist orientation,' a relatively new category of countries which the Soviets hoped would become their long-sought Third World allies.[3] The YSP was enshrined in the Constitution as the "leader and guide of the society and state," and the Soviets had been assiduously developing close ties with it. As has been noted, delegations of party workers in all sectors had been frequently exchanged between the PDRY and the Soviet Union and other socialist countries. Foreign communist party officials had helped to organize and build the YSP and its predecessor; after the upheaval in the summer of 1978, Cuban and Bulgarian delegations were brought in to help rebuild it. Soviet and other socialist country nationals were providing ideological and organizational training in the Higher School of Scientific Socialism and its affiliates. The PDRY was advancing along the trail Cuba had blazed;[4] Moscow must have been pleased, the more so since the cost had been relatively low (as compared, for example, to Soviet costs in Cuba or even in Ethiopia during the short Soviet-Ethiopian relationship).

That the cost was still low, even after the Arab League aid boycott, was partly due to Aden's continuing poor bargaining position, but also to events in another part of the Middle East. The Camp David accords unified the Arabs as nothing previously had done and pushed outrage at the PDRY well into the background. At the Baghdad Conference, which was convened in early November to formulate a common Arab response to Camp David, a reconciliation was announced between the Saudis and South Yemenis, and the Arab League boycott quietly abandoned. The full participation of Saudi Arabia in the conference also opened up the prospect at last of antiimperialist Arab unity, and a thaw in Soviet-Saudi relations. The Soviets pursued this possibility industriously; by early 1979 their media courtship seemed to be getting some results.

However, any chance of it being consummated was destroyed by burgeoning tension along South Yemen's borders, particularly that with the YAR. (See Chapter 7 for details.) Ismail, accusing the "reactionary Arab states" of stepping up hostile activities against the PDRY, called for help in mid-November. Relations with the Soviet Union, he said, were closer than those represented by "paper treaties" because they were based on proletarian internationalism; the Soviet Union would rush to the defense of the PDRY if the latter's regime were threatened.[5] There seemed to be a number of messages in this statement: first, a warning to the Saudis; second, a clear understanding by Ismail that the safety of his regime lay in its ideological and political positions, not in "paper treaties" (an interesting conclusion, particularly in light of the Soviet-Ethiopian treaty, about to be signed); third, a message to the Soviet Union that there was a 'strategic' link between the two countries, and that the Soviets would be expected to live up to their duty. The Soviets appeared to have taken these messages seriously. Two days later, the Soviet Ambassador to the PDRY "emphasized the readiness of the Soviet people to extend assistance to Democratic Yemen in any field and at any time."[6] Ideological support, and Soviet support for Ismail personally, was underlined by the publication of an article by him in *World Marxist Review*. At the end of January 1979, the two countries signed an economic and technical cooperation agreement with $36 million in new aid for agriculture, mineral prospecting, education, and port improvements in Aden. Moscow also stepped up its arms shipments, stationed surface-to-air missiles near the border and near Aden, and began to increase the number of its ships in the area. In January the Soviets promised to deliver more MiG-21s, 15 MiG-23s, and SU-22 fighter-bombers.[7]

There was, however, a contradictory trend in both South Yemeni and Soviet policy. Muhammad on several occasions expressed and the desire for tranquility in the region and stressed that the Soviets did not have bases in South Yemen. The Soviets continued their attempts at rapprochement with Riyadh, and possibly tried to restrain the South Yemenis. It seemed by mid-December that the moderate line was having some effect, as Aden radio reported that Muhammad had received a hand-written message from "his brother" Crown Prince Fahd regarding bilateral relations between the "brotherly" countries.[8] In the first two months of 1979 Abd al-Fattah Ismail joined in. After visiting radical friends in Libya and Syria, he paid a visit to Kuwait and Iraq (which was moving rapidly closer to Saudi Arabia in the wake of the Iranian revolution). While by no means ready to join the conservative camp, Ismail was preparing to visit Riyadh, apparently to begin a reconciliation with the Saudis. Foreign Minister Muti was in Riyadh to prepare for the visit when war broke out on the PDRY-YAR border on February 24. (The causes and details of this conflict will be examined in Chapter 7.)

The war appeared to have positive results for the Soviet Union. It demonstrated the military weakness of Saudi Arabia; combined with Saudi mistrust of the United States' willingness to support its friends, this seemed to make Riyadh willing to respond to earlier Soviet overtures. The conflict also demonstrated North Yemen's weakness, and when it ended in an agreement to unify the two Yemens, South Yemeni dominance seemed possible. On the negative side, however, the United States decided to station a carrier task force permanently in the Indian Ocean; it appeared to have begun establishing a military presence in North Yemen, and there were reports that it had concluded a military access agreement with Muscat. In this situation, if the unity agreement fell through (as was likely), and if Saudi Arabia turned back to the United States, South Yemen would be more isolated than before. Moreover, Saudi Arabia's unhappiness over the war probably contributed to its lack of enthusiasm about the Arab sanctions against Egypt proposed at the second Baghdad Conference, after Egypt had signed a peace treaty with Israel.

In this situation, the Soviets moved to bolster South Yemen's armed forces even more, with 150 T-54 and T-55 tanks and MiG-21s and SU-22s; as well, they promised to supply 50 T-62 tanks, 50 general purpose helicopters, and two patrol boats fitted with ship-to-ship missiles.[9] In addition, it was reported that the numbers of Soviet and Cuban military personnel had increased significantly and that Soviet and Cuban pilots were flying South Yemeni planes.[10] In all, the Soviet Union provided $250 million worth of military aid in 1979, almost double the 1978 level.[11]

This significant upgrading of the PDRYs military was more than a demonstration of support for a regional client. It was part of Moscow's attempt to take advantage of the upheaval in Iran to improve its position in the Gulf region and at the same time to prevent the United States from recouping its losses by establishing 'bases' in other countries, particularly Saudi Arabia and Oman. Thus Moscow continued its 'carrot and stick' approach to Saudi Arabia, implicitly threatening it by building up South Yemen's armed forces while also implicitly offering to rein in Aden and explicitly continuing its public overtures for normal relations. For Oman, Moscow had only threats. The same considerations of relative position were evident in the visit to Aden May 26-June 2 of the Soviet carrier *Minsk*, accompanied by five of the newest ships in the Soviet Navy. This was a political visit, part of a long tour by these 'prestige' ships to West Africa and the Indian Ocean. Their stay in Aden and its adjacent waters was longer than in any other port, an indication of the close relations between the two countries and of the tensions in the region. With high-ranking PDRY officials on board, the ships and planes put on an impressive display of their firepower and amphibious landing capabilities, calculated to impress their allies in South Yemen as well as less friendly countries in the region. In case Washington had missed the message of Soviet naval capabilities, the Soviets raised the intensity of their propaganda about the growth of U.S. naval presence in the Indian Ocean a notch, warning that it constituted a threat to the security of the USSR.[12]

During 1979 it became clear that both the Soviet and the South Yemeni leaders (especially Ismail) were making a major effort to cement political ties with each other and with other 'progressive forces' in the region. In early April, Muti went to Ethiopia, Somalia, and Djibouti, and a month later Ismail visited Ethiopia; observers speculated that they were attempting to resurrect the Horn federation idea. Aden also obliged the Soviets by participating in the Soviet campaign for Islamic legitimacy in the wake of Khomeini's fundamentalist revolution. Of necessity, part of this campaign was devoted to showing that Soviet Muslims had complete freedom of worship; another part was the announcement of a conference of Islamic clergy in Tashkent in 1980. The imam of the Mosque of Aden participated in the planning for this conference, and while in the USSR testified to freedom of worship there. (This publicity represented a concession by Aden. Although the PDRY is an Islamic country and has not closed down its mosques, and the leaders appear in them on religious holidays,[13] it is rare for a clerical leader to be sent abroad or to be quoted on religious matters.)

The month of June 1979 saw a flurry of visits, including a Soviet delegation led by General Epishev, Director of the Main Political Directorate of the Soviet Army and Navy. No hint emerged as to the content of his talks; possibly they dealt with PDRY support for the PFLO military activity which flared up at about that time, or with access privileges for Soviet nuclear submarines, one of which entered Aden's harbor in August; possibly he was sent to sound out the military on the power struggle which was heating up again in Aden. It is also possible that he went to examine the reorganization of the PDRY Army's party apparatus, in which the Political Directorate (which has close ties to its Soviet counterpart) took on an enhanced role.

This flurry culminated with Ali Nasir Muhammad's arrival in Moscow to attend a session of CMEA, in which the PDRY had been granted observer status, the first Arab country to achieve this. Symbolically, this was a very important event, for it seemed to signal the onset of an organic tie between the socialist camp and the PDRY and with it a much higher level of economic assistance. However, in the near term at least, this did not happen; foreign aid actually declined in 1979. Muhammad was given a friendly reception by Kosygin, Ustinov, and Ponomarev. Although differences of opinion still existed, both sides "expressed the desire to promote in every possible way the further development of friendly relations" between the two countries and their ruling parties.[14]

In view of the increasing Soviet military investment in and closer symbolic ties with the PDRY, the outbreak of the power struggle during the summer must have been of some concern; although there was little question about the commitment of any of the contenders (Abd al-Fattah Ismail versus Ali Nasir Muhammad and Ali Antar) to the socialist camp, the latter two were thought to be somewhat more pragmatic. The struggle was primarily between North and South Yemenis in the regime; Ismail, a North Yemeni by birth, apparently was determined to achieve unity with North Yemen under YSP domination by whatever means necessary, while the other two, southerners, preferred negotiations.[15] There was also a strong current of personality conflict and personal dislike of Ismail; his dogmatic, heavily ideological style helped to make him unpopular and his frequently expressed unyielding commitment to scientific socialism and the Soviet Union may have cost him popularity at a time when the economy was not working well and Soviet aid was perceived as neither very generous nor very efficient. If that was indeed the case, Moscow did not help their favored comrade by awarding him the Order of Friendship among Peoples (the first time this had been given to an Arab leader).

A meeting in June between the South Yemeni and Omani Foreign Ministers to discuss the possibility of settling their differences, even though unsuccessful, was a sign that the more moderate faction in Aden had grown stronger. A further sign came in mid-July as regulations governing the private sector in the PDRY were relaxed somewhat. The power struggle came out into the open in early August with a session of the YSP Central Committee which praised Ismail, but gave Muhammad control over a newly created Committee on State Security.[16] Ismail's power had declined considerably.

It was into this situation that Kosygin flew on September 16, 1979 for a two-day visit. Remarkably, it was the first visit made to the PDRY by a top Soviet leader, despite the closeness of the relationship for the past decade. Furthermore it was not a gala state visit; it seemed more an afterthought, tagged on to his more important six-day visit to Ethiopia. Despite this rather patronizing approach to the relationship, the Soviets doubtless hoped that the visit would further cement ties, and that Kosygin could bring to an end a conflict between Iraq and the PDRY.[17] His mediation was successful, although he was not able to restore warmth to Iraq-PDRY relations. In his goal of further cementing ties with Aden, Kosygin was less successful. The communiqué[18] indicated that his meeting with Ismail had gone better ("warm, friendly conversation") than the one with Muhammad ("complete mutual understanding," code words for agreement to disagree on some issues). One area of disagreement was in the economic aid field; no new assistance was forthcoming. The communiqué made it clear that the Soviets were expecting even closer political relations, but the South Yemeni side did not appear enthusiastic. The two sides expressed "complete coincidence of views" on a wide range of international issues (including the now-standard call for the elimination of existing foreign military bases in the Indian Ocean); however, the glaring omission of any references to south Arabia made it obvious that there were serious differences between them on the very issues most important to the PDRY. This was not very surprising; not only was the South Yemeni regime badly split on the questions of relations with their neighbors, but the Soviets were also pursuing divergent policies. They wanted South Yemen to develop good relations with the YAR and Saudi Arabia (opposed by Ismail) to make it easier for Moscow to develop relations with these countries; at the same time they were interested in a hard-line response to Oman (opposed by Muhammad), primarily in the interest of undermining the Sultan and preventing the United States from acquiring a base on his territory. Thus it was no wonder that the two sides could not find enough common ground to include south Arabia in the communiqué.

FROM OCTOBER 1979 TO ISMAIL'S OUSTER (APRIL 1980)

In light of events in October, Kosygin may have had a third goal: to carry a draft Treaty of Friendship to Aden and to press for its signature. If this was the case (and it stands to reason that the Soviets would not expect a lesser figure to be able to overcome the resistance within the regime), the South Yemenis did not accede for a few weeks. The warmth of Soviet greetings on the October 14th anniversary,[19] the attendance of three high-ranking Soviet officials at a reception at the PDRY Embassy in Moscow on that occasion, and the despatch of a CPSU delegation (although curiously not a high-level one) to the celebrations suggest that Aden had agreed to the Treaty by then.

The Treaty was the result of a coincidence of interests and concerns at the time. The Soviets had probably been ready to sign one for at least a year, to consolidate their position both in the PDRY in case of a leadership change, and in the region. It was particularly important to them now as they faced the deteriorating situation in Afghanistan. Abd al-Fattah Ismail would probably have been glad to sign one at any time since June 1978; he was especially keen in the fall of 1979 as his grip on the regime weakened.

One of the factors which convinced the other faction was a compromise to which Ismail apparently agreed: a greater reliance on peaceful methods for unifying the two Yemens, and an attempt to improve relations with Saudi Arabia. At the beginning of September he and Saudi Prince Abdullah had met in Libya; neither side even admitted the meeting. Nevertheless, at the end of the month, Ismail told an interviewer that relations with Riyadh were based on "mutual respect and non-interference in internal affairs"; furthermore, he stressed his "desire to establish good and normal relations with the Kingdom."[20] However, the most important factor in the decision to sign a treaty was the unease among all factions in Aden over regional developments. The U.S. Navy now deployed a carrier task force regularly in the Arabian Sea; Washington was talking about creating a rapid deployment force, and Oman was rumored to be putting Masirah Island at its disposal. Oman itself was promoting a plan for the defense of the Strait of Hormuz which would involve the U.S. Navy and the Gulf oil states. Although these measures were directed at Iran, Aden's leaders in their isolation could see them as being aimed at themselves, a view that the Soviets were not loath to reinforce. An additional factor was probably the resumption of Soviet arms shipments to North Yemen at this time; there may have been a feeling in Aden that it was necessary to sign the Treaty in order to preserve the 'special relationship' with the Soviets, and to influence the Soviets not to provide enough weapons to allow the YAR to threaten the PDRY.

Thus on October 24 Ismail visited Moscow with a high-level delegation. The visit was a resounding success, with extensive publicity including Ismail's picture and biography on the front page of *Pravda*. He was met at the airport by Brezhnev (the first foreign dignitary in months to be accorded this honor), and the two held two sessions of talks (in startling contrast to the visit just a week before of Syrian President Assad, who did not meet Brezhnev at all). In this dinner speech Brezhnev referred to the PDRY as "particularly close" to the Soviet Union, an "ally in the struggle against imperialism."[21]

The communiqué[22] revealed that there continued to be some differences, in their views on the situation in southern Arabia and, interestingly, over "questions of cooperation" between the CPSU and the YSP. The Soviets approved of the development of peaceful relations between the Yemens, which may not have been much to the liking of Ismail. For the most part, however, the communiqué expressed a large measure of agreement. The South Yemenis stated their "profound gratitude" for Soviet assistance. Cooperation in all fields was said to be "assuming an increasingly stable and long-term nature." Ties between the parties and between mass public organizations in the two countries were to be strengthened. The PDRYs economic development plan was to be coordinated with those of other CMEA countries. Various agreements were signed.

The most important document signed during the visit was of course the 20-year Treaty of Friendship and Cooperation.[23] Similar to most of those signed by Moscow with non-Communist Third World countries,[24] it committed the two sides to long-term all-round cooperation (Articles 1, 3, 4), and to cooperation to "insure the conditions for preserving and further developing their people's socioeconomic gains" (Article 2, which some analysts believe could be used as a pretext for Soviet intervention to halt an unwelcome regime change). It includes the usual clauses related to defense matters:

> The high contracting parties will continue to develop cooperation in the military sphere on the basis of the relevant agreements concluded between them in the interests of strengthening their defense capability (Article 5).

> The high contracting parties will consult with one another on important international questions directly affecting the two countries' interests.[25]

> In the event of situations arising which create a threat to peace, the parties will seek to make immediate contact with a view to coordinating their positions in the interests of eliminating the threat which has arisen or restoring peace (Article 11).

Other articles stated common general foreign policy principles related to global and regional issues, such as promoting disarmament and struggling against imperialism. However, there was no mention of a struggle against 'reaction'; this may have been part of the compromise in Aden, in order that the regime could claim more plausibly that the treaty was not directed against any other country. It may also have been due to the compromise, or perhaps to Soviet reluctance, that the treaty did not make any claim that the USSR-PDRY relationship was on a different ideological level from that which the Soviets had with their other Third World treaty partners.[26]

The Treaty accomplished some of its intended objectives. The PDRY was tied more closely to the Soviets and their activities; thus on January 14, 1980, when the United Nations General Assembly voted to condemn the Soviet invasion of Afghanistan, the PDRY was the only Middle Eastern state to vote with the USSR. The Treaty (and a 50 percent increase in the Soviet Indian Ocean squadron) also reassured Aden, nervous at the stationing of a second U.S. carrier task force in the Arabian Sea following the seizure of the U.S. Embassy in Teheran on November 4 and the invasion of Afghanistan at the end of December. However, the signing of the treaty also had unintended negative effects for both countries. It heightened Washington's concern about the PDRY's intentions, and alarmed South Yemen's neighbors. Compounded by the Grand Mosque incident in Mecca[27] and the invasion of Afghanistan, it made Saudi Arabia and Oman more suspicious of the PDRY and susceptible to U.S. overtures (especially Oman, where the United States was trying to negotiate expanded facilities). South Yemeni attempts to arrange a visit by Ismail to explain that the Treaty was not directed at Saudi Arabia and, some suggested, to carry a message from the Soviets, were rebuffed. The Saudis could not have been reassured by the claim by Abd al-Fattah Ismail and Mikhail Suslov that the treaty "marks a new stage in the development of our relations."[28]

Ismail's position in the regime appeared for a time to have been strengthened by the treaty. Despite reported unhappiness among his opponents at the extremely close ties with the Soviets (Aden did not ratify the Treaty for four months), the PDRY signed Treaties of Friendship and Cooperation with East Germany in late November and Ethiopia in early December.[29] In February the Arab press reported a number of moves by Ismail to diminish Muhammad's control over the State Security Committee and Ali Antar's standing in the army.[30] He used his stronger position to draw Moscow and Aden closer. South Yemeni spokesmen strongly and consistently supported the Soviet rationale for the invasion, in the United Nations and elsewhere. The PDRY participated in the attempts by the Steadfastness and Confrontation Front states to deflect the anti-Soviet anger that blossomed in the Arab world and to postpone the meeting of the Islamic Conference Organization, called by Saudi Arabia to condemn the invasion. When the attempts failed, South Yemen was one of only two Arab states to refuse to participate.

Nevertheless, in its other relations with its Arab neighbors, the PDRY seemed to be adopting a more moderate stance. The Foreign Minister travelled to the UAE, Qatar, and Bahrain, and welcomed Kuwait's efforts to mediate between Aden and Muscat.[31] Ismail continued to proclaim his desire for normal relations with Saudi Arabia and his willingness to visit Riyadh,[32] and his Foreign Minister paid a visit to Saudi Arabia, which was hailed by the Saudi press as "creating a new atmosphere," marking the "beginning of a new phase" in relations.[33] (At the time the Saudis appeared to be contemplating a rapprochement with the Soviets because of the changed power balance in the Gulf region.)

The tentative feelers toward Saudi Arabia and the Gulf states stood to benefit Soviet interest and may (as some have suggested) have been urged by the Soviets. They were just as likely to have originated in the power struggle then coming to a head in Aden and in South Yemen's concerns about its isolation at a time of high tension and rapidly growing U.S. military power in the region. Had the South Yemenis been merely following a Soviet line, they would have helped in Moscow's campaign in 1980 to show that Islam and Marxism-Leninism were compatible and that the USSR was a good and constant friend of Muslim peoples (despite the contradictory evidence of Afghanistan).[34] Nevertheless, Aden's pronouncements neither supported the Soviet claim nor attempted to restore the PDRY's credentials as an Islamic country, a position from which the PDRY could better support Moscow in the Islamic world.

In the military sphere, South Yemen and the Soviet Union grew closer in early 1980. Arms were delivered at roughly the same extremely high level as in 1979, including 20 T-62 main battle tanks, and another consignment of 20 MiG-21s; Arab sources also claimed that MiG-23s and MiG-25s, probably with Soviet or Cuban pilots, had arrived. New missile systems were reported being installed, including surface-to-surface missiles.[35] The number of Soviet military advisers was doubled to approximately 1,500.[36] Most important to Moscow was its continued access to the port and in particular to the Soviet-built airfield outside Aden for maritime reconnaissance aircraft. With the invasion of Afghanistan and the enunciation of the Carter Doctrine, the United States stationed two aircraft carriers in the Indian Ocean, and sought facilities in Kenya, Somalia, and Oman for its Rapid Deployment Force. Aden's importance to the Soviets for maritime reconnaissance flights grew accordingly. The number of ship days the enlarged Soviet squadron spent in Aden doubled. This was probably more for reasons of political impact than logistic necessity; the Soviet Navy's biggest supply ship had been stationed in the area to take care of the expanded replenishment needs. To augment the political impact, its modern amphibious assault ship, the *Ivan Rogov*, with 500 naval infantrymen aboard, was sent to the Gulf of Aden.[37]

However, in the economic aid sphere, Moscow was no more prepared than before to open its purse strings. The South Yemeni economy was in serious difficulty; agricultural production was stagnating, prices were rising, the trade deficit was increasing. The economy was underwritten by remittances from the 200,000 South Yemenis working in Saudi Arabia and the Gulf. In Aden there were power failures, few goods could be found in the stores, and food was in short supply.[38] The economic situation was undoubtedly a major reason for the intensification of the power struggle within the regime. Abd al-Fattah Ismail held the two most powerful positions and was thus open to blame for the conditions. In addition, he was closely allied to the Soviets, and the Soviets could be held responsible (fairly or not) for the food shortages (South Yemeni agriculture had been reorganized along Soviet lines) and the power shortages (the Soviets had not finished building the power stations promised for Aden). Moreover, despite the PDRY's being the only Marxist country in the Middle East, despite its being designated a 'country of socialist orientation' (a category including only a handful of Third World states which were considered closest to the USSR and most reliable), despite its signing a Treaty, the PDRY had never received the volume of aid which it needed and to which South Yemenis felt entitled. Ismail, with his insistence on a close Soviet connection, was vulnerable when the connection did not live up to expectations. His opponents, especially Ali Nasir Muhammad, were considered to be less dogmatic, more willing and able to loosen the ties to the USSR and dip into the coffers of South Yemen's wealthy neighbors.

Another factor in the intensification of the power struggle was South Yemen's isolation in the Arab world. Not only were the conservative Arab states still hostile, but Iraq was stepping up its opposition to Aden as part of its move away from the Soviet Union, as well as because of the continued welcome of Iraqi exiles in South Yemen; in March 1980 Iraq sponsored a front of groups wishing to overthrow the Aden regime. At the same time, it was recognized that an improvement in inter-Yemen relations would help to reduce Aden's isolation. A reduction in military support for the antigovernment forces in the North, a group which Ismail strongly supported, would assist this process. The removal of Ismail himself, who was still suspect in the North for his Marxism and his presumed connection with al-Ghashmi's assassination, would be a major boost toward good relations, or even unification.

All of these factors overlay the basic fact of South Yemeni politics: a continuous power struggle in the Yemeni Socialist Party. All professed to be Marxists, and as was soon to become obvious, all were pro-Soviet. The 'in' faction, led by Ismail, was more overtly ideological in its motivation; more importantly, it contained many who were North Yemeni by birth; most importantly, it was actively trying to concentrate power in its own hands, and to reduce or destroy the positions of the 'out' factions. The latter, southerners all, united for the moment under the more popular, reputedly more pragmatic and moderate Ali Nasir Muhammad, perceived their chance to move first. While Ismail was attending a Steadfastness Front meeting in Libya, the 'out' factions managed to put together a majority in the Politbureau which forced him to resign his posts for "health reasons." On April 20 an emergency session of the YSP voted by a narrow margin to accept the resignation.

FROM APRIL 1980 TO THE TRIPARTITE
PACT (AUGUST 1981)

Moscow did not support the ouster of Abd al-Fattah Ismail. As dogmatic as he was, and as difficult as he was periodically to deal with, he was still a reliable ally at a time when and in a region where these were scarce. The Soviet Ambassador was said to have attempted to convince Politbureau members first that Ismail should stay, and then (more successfully) that he should not be executed.[39] Soviet air traffic into Aden increased around the time of the palace coup, perhaps in an effort to discourage it. However the Soviets found they lacked the means to influence the situation. The YSP (their favored instrument) had removed Ismail, the armed forces apparently approved, and his supporters did not attempt armed resistance. No one appealed for Soviet intervention, and Moscow, mindful of its difficulties in Afghanistan and of the fact that *its positions in the PDRY were not being threatened*, saw no advantage in trying heavy-handed tactics.[40] Ismail was ousted from all his positions. He was not executed; this was probably due less to Soviet intervention that to the continued strength of his supporters in the party. Moscow, mindful of its interests, made the best of the situation. The obligatory congratulatory message to Ali Nasir Muhammad from Brezhnev was correct, promising to continue Soviet support for South Yemen's "struggle for social progress and against the intrigues of imperialism and reaction" and reminding him that PDRY support of the Soviet Union was enshrined in the YSP Program and the Treaty of Friendship and Cooperation.[41]

The Soviet leadership was by no means hostile to Ali Nasir Muhammad. They had, after all, dealt with him for many years without serious disagreement, and at the end of 1979 had awarded him the Order of Friendship Among Peoples. In all likelihood, however, they were wary of him as sole leader because of his reputed pragmatism and willingness to move away from a close embrace with the USSR. In fact Ali Nasir, recognizing his vulnerability to a counterattack from other factions (including Ismail's supporters), moved quickly to establish his pro-Soviet credentials. On the day after his appointment as general secretary of the YSP, in a speech commemorating the 110th anniversary of Lenin's birth, he emphasized that the PDRY would adhere to the path of scientific socialism and that "militant friendship" with the Soviet Union was a "fundamental component of the revolutionary process" in South Yemen.[42] He returned to this theme in his speech to the session of the Supreme People's Council at which he was elected Chairman of the Presidium. Reflecting anger and concern at the abortive U.S. raid into Iran the previous day, he stressed that the PDRY would

> continue strengthening and developing the links of militant and fruitful cooperation with the Soviet Union and the GDR on the basis of the treaties of friendship and cooperation signed with those countries. We shall continue strengthening our links with other countries of the socialist community on the basis of proletarian internationalism. It is necessary to raise these links to a level that would reflect the identity of purpose and socialist principles for the sake of which we are fighting against imperialism and reaction, for peace and socialism.[43]

Following up these encouraging words, Muhammad sent Politbureau member (and long-time Communist) Ali Abd ar-Razzaq BaDhib to Moscow with a message for Brezhnev. Although Brezhnev did not receive him, his well-publicized meetings with Kirilenko and Ponomarev were described as taking place in a "warm atmosphere of comradeship";[44] before leaving he received an invitation for Ali Nasir to visit Moscow.

Despite these messages of continuity directed toward Moscow, Muhammad was having some success persuading other Arab rulers that he would pursue a more moderate course. Almost immediately there was a noticeable relaxation of some of the tight controls over South Yemeni society. Envoys were quickly sent to the YAR, Saudi Arabia, Kuwait, and the UAE with messages that the PDRY wished to improve relations. Ali Nasir stated that he wanted "normal, goodneighborly relations" with Saudi Arabia and that he would be happy to visit Riyadh if invited.[45] The invitation was duly offered and accepted. A high-level North Yemeni delegation was welcomed in Aden in mid-May. Muhammad's more extreme pro-Soviet pronouncements were not broadcast in full by Aden radio; its reports of his speeches emphasized other aspects.[46] The PDRY agreed to participate in the second Islamic foreign ministers' conference in May.

However, the lack of any concessions or even substantial changes in South Yemeni foreign policy brings into question the conclusion that Ali Nasir Muhammad wanted to do more than seek a relaxation of tensions with some of his neighbors (not an unimportant objective in itself) through a façade of dialog, without reducing the level of ties with the Soviet Union. Thus at the Islamic foreign ministers' meeting and elsewhere, the PDRY continued to support the USSR's right to "assist" the Afghanis. South Yemen continued to be adamantly opposed to the Sultan of Oman.

The process of establishing Ali Nasir's *bona fides* was completed with a visit to Moscow May 27-29, 1980. He was met at the airport by Brezhnev and Kosygin, a sure sign that the Kremlin was anxious to ensure a continuation of the old ties. In all his speeches Muhammad gave fulsome praise to the Soviet Union and to Brezhnev for Soviet foreign policy in general and Soviet assistance to the PDRY in particular. He pledged to continue to strengthen relations.

The communiqué was long and detailed,[47] describing the talks as held in "an atmosphere of cordiality and complete mutual understanding" (downgraded from Moscow radio's description during the talks of "an atmosphere of complete unity of views").[48] There were indications of continuing disagreement on the subject of a peaceful settlement in the Middle East, and interestingly, on "questions of further development and consolidation of the relations of close friendship and comprehensive cooperation between the USSR and PDRY." One of the questions was the strengthening and further development of CPSU-YSP ties. The Soviets made it clear that the "entire range of Soviet-South Yemeni relations" would be affected by progress on this issue; Muhammad, mindful that the YSP had been Ismail's main power base, resisted this pressure. The other question was almost certainly economic aid. The South Yemenis "rated highly" the level of economic assistance (a much less enthusiastic rating that the "profound gratitude" they expressed for Soviet military and political assistance), but they clearly wanted, and needed, more. Apparently they were not satisfied with the Soviet response; Moscow may even have begun to demand repayment of Aden's debt. However, the visit did produce a loan of 36 million rubles, and an unspecified amount earmarked for financial assistance.

On all other questions the two sides were in complete agreement. The South Yemeni side endorsed the legitimacy of the Soviet presence in Afghanistan and the illegitimacy of the U.S. presence or attempted presence in the Indian Ocean/Persian Gulf region. The Soviets explicitly supported peaceful relations between the Yemens (something which Ali Nasir was said to want, as opposed to Ismail), and the two sides expressed the wish for good-neighborly relations in southern Arabia. (PDRY-Oman relations were probably excepted from this wish; although Oman was not mentioned, both sides severely criticized the "creation of new foreign military bases" in the region, and Oman and the United States signed a military access agreement just a few days later.)

Contacts between South Yemen and the socialist countries continued at an unusual rate throughout the summer and early fall. Delegations from the PDRY Armed Forces Political Directorate visited the Soviet Union twice; this may have been connected to the extensive purge of Ismail's supporters from the armed forces. In June Defense Minister Ali Antar visited Eastern Europe and the Soviet Union, where he held "successful and fruitful" discussions with Soviet Defense Minister Ustinov; their contents were not revealed, but it is likely that they dealt with ways to respond to the new U.S.-Oman agreement. He was back in Moscow in mid-July "for a rest." This visit may well have been prompted by the internal political situation in Aden. Some of those who had supported the palace coup, as well as Ismail's supporters, were uneasy with the Ali Nasir Muhammad's rapid and apparently unchecked accretion of power (even more power than Ismail at his height, for he had retained the post of Prime Minister along with his other positions). The Soviets, too, may have been uneasy at the prospect of having to deal with a single South Yemeni leader, without rival factions to manipulate, a leader who was perhaps not totally reliable. It was probably with an eye to this situation that the Soviets had welcomed Abd al-Fattah Ismail into exile in Moscow in early July (where he lives still, in a manner befitting a retired head of a friendly country). According to Saudi Arabian sources, Ali Antar met Ismail during this trip, and the two came to an agreement on opposing Muhammad.

Perhaps to offset the growing opposition by demonstrating his reputed pragmatism, probably to try to reduce the isolation of the PDRY in the Middle East, and certainly in the hopes of generating economic aid, Ali Nasir cancelled a scheduled tour of Eastern Europe in July, and embarked on a round of visits to Arabian Peninsula countries. In these countries he cultivated the image of moderation, expressing his desire for normal relations and stability on the Peninsula. He appeared to have some success, but his mission ultimately foundered on the rocks of the Soviet presence in the PDRY, and the U.S.-Oman agreement. In particular, the Saudis (with whom he had "fraternal, frank and cordial" talks in a low-key meeting[49]) were unwilling to promise aid while Aden was so closely tied to Moscow and so hostile to the Sultan. South Yemen however saw the U.S.-Oman deal as a danger to its security; and although Muhammad was quoted in the Kuwait press as having promised to halve the number of Soviet experts in the PDRY if the oil-producing states gave aid, neither side trusted the other enough to take the first step.[50] The results of his visits were discouraging enough that Ali Nasir again came out strongly for the Popular Front for the Liberation of Oman (PFLO). Nevertheless, his reputation as a pragmatist survived, based largely on the mere fact of his trips and on the policy unveiled earlier in the summer of encouraging West European countries to set up joint economic ventures (presumably within the framework of the Five-Year Plan, a revised version of which was being drawn up with the help of Soviet experts, to cover 1981-85 — a period coincident with the new Soviet Five-Year Plan).[51]

If Muhammad intended to pursue his overtures to Saudi Arabia and the Gulf states, events in the second half of 1980 overtook him. With the outbreak of the Iran-Iraq war in September tension rose dramatically; Aden's decision to back Iran isolated it once again from its neighbors, a condition which was reinforced by its nonparticipation in the Arab summit meeting in Amman in November. More urgently Ali Nasir was preoccupied with challenges to his preeminent position, as Ali Antar began an attempt to consolidate his support in the armed forces.[52] This nascent struggle may have been a factor in the despatch of envoys to the Soviet Union and Eastern Europe in mid-September, including one led by Ali Salim al-Bayd (Secretary of the YSP Central Committee and one of Ali Antar's chief supporters) who carried a message from Muhammad to Brezhnev, and also held talks with Ponomarev and Brutents. (This flurry of visits may also have been sparked by regional events, especially the U.S.-Oman and U.S.-Somali access agreements and the deteriorating Iran-Iraq situation; certainly the visit of the Commander of the PDRY Air Force at the invitation of Soviet Air Force Commander-in-Chief Pavel Kutakhov dealt with these matters. However, if al-Bayd's YSP delegation also dealt with these defense and foreign affairs issues, it is strange that he should have met only Ponomarev and Brutents.)

Before the struggle got up a full head of steam, Ali Nasir Muhammad convened the second YSP Congress, followed by a session of the Supreme People's Congress, to finish some old business: ridding the party and government leadership of Ismail supporters. It was evident that Ali Antar had not succeeded in making serious inroads into Ali Nasir's strength, for the latter emerged with all his positions intact. Moscow had apparently decided to back the incumbent; the CPSU Central Committee telegram to the Congress indirectly appealed for unity in the ranks, and *Pravda's* coverage spotlighted Ali Nasir Muhammad's central role.[53]

The Soviets appear to have decided that Ali Nasir was a reliable friend who could also, if the regional political climate was right, help Soviet interests with his reputation for pragmatism. Thus they probably acquiesced as Aden attempted to cooperate with most of the conservative regimes. References to 'reaction' disappeared from South Yemeni utterances.[54] PDRY spokesmen did not rush to support Brezhnev's December 1980 proposals for neutralization of the Persian Gulf and noninterference in the affairs of local states; not until the end of January did Aden come out specifically in favor. Ali Nasir Muhammad participated in the Islamic Conference in Taif in January 1981 despite opposition at home because of the certainty that the Conference would condemn the continuing presence of Soviet forces in Afghanistan. Finally in the face of reports that the Gulf countries were moving toward a formal cooperation agreement, Ali Nasir tried to deflect this decision by promoting a summit conference of all regional states (including those in the Horn of Africa) to discuss the "question of comprehensively clearing the area of foreign bases and naval forces in order to make the whole area a zone of security and stability."[55] He enlisted the support of the Amir of Kuwait who on February 1 arrived on his first visit to Aden and was accorded a "tumultuous" welcome.

It should be noted that none of these actions were necessarily contrary to Soviet interest. Although the lack of support for Brezhnev's proposal and South Yemen's participation in the Taif Conference could be interpreted as evidence that the PDRY was loosening its ties with the Soviet Union, Moscow surely recognized that the objective — prevention of a Gulf states' defense cooperation agreement which the Soviets feared would link itself to the U.S. — was worthwhile. Furthermore, Ali Nasir's presence at the Taif Conference may have toned down its anti-Soviet resolutions and/or bolstered the anti-U.S. resolutions. Finally, although some may have interpreted the idea of the summit conference as including Soviet as well as U.S. bases and forces, there is no evidence that Muhammad ever considered the target to be anything but the U.S. 'bases' in Oman and Somalia, and U.S. naval forces; South Yemen has always denied the existence of Soviet bases on its soil.

While pursuing these ostensibly moderate policies, Ali Nasir was keeping his feet firmly in the other camp. In early September Aden had sent a delegation to Tashkent to participate in the Conference of USSR Muslims, which the Soviets had organized to divert Islamic criticism of their invasion of Afghanistan, and which the conservative states of the Peninsula had boycotted. There was no reduction in Soviet presence in South Yemen, something the Gulf states were reported to have made a precondition to their cooperation with the Brezhnev proposal.[56] A Soviet delegation arrived to talk about "the strengthening of bilateral relations." Discussions on cooperation with Ethiopia (and Libya) were underway, and shortly after the Gulf states went ahead with the creation of the Gulf Cooperation Council (GCC), the PDRY and Ethiopia were reported to have reached an agreement to form a military alliance to protect their interests in the region. That the PDRY's primary allegiance was to the socialist camp was underlined at the end of February 1981, when Ali Nasir Muhammad participated in the 26th Congress of the CPSU. Although Third World leaders were not lionized as they had been at the previous congress, Muhammad was received by Brezhnev for "warm, friendly" discussions which covered methods of confronting the United States in the region.[57] Brezhnev's report, in its rather perfunctory section on the Third World, singled out the PDRY in the Middle East as both a state of socialist orientation and a partner in a treaty of friendship and cooperation.[58]

By this time, Ali Nasir was on the verge of extending his power to become the undisputed leader of South Yemen, and Brezhnev's meeting with him left no doubt that the Soviets supported him. The moves and countermoves by him and by Ali Antar in late 1980 and early 1981 had left him with a slight edge in the military, while he could count on the support of the militia. In early spring he removed two of the Defense Minister's closest allies, al-Bayd and Muti,[59] and more of his supporters in the army. Ali Antar, feeling the noose tighten, apparently attempted to move first with a coup; however, the army did not follow him and his attempt was stillborn. Ali Antar was then dismissed from the Politbureau and from his position of Defense Minister.

As Ali Nasir consolidated his power, as U.S.-Omani relations grew closer, and as the GCC became a reality, the South Yemeni leader adopted a much more militant stance toward Oman, and a correct but suspicious attitude toward the rest of the GCC. He strongly endorsed Brezhnev's Persian Gulf and Indian Ocean proposals in mid-May, and PDRY-USSR contacts intensified. The second meeting of their joint economic and technical committee produced an agreement on further linkage between their Five-Year Plans in the traditional areas of Soviet aid. At the end of May, as the Persian Gulf leaders were meeting to found the GCC formally, with Oman pressing for a plan of coordinated action with the United States, Moscow sent a group of warships on an unusually well-publicized visit to Aden. Muhammad received its commanding officer, and himself visited the cruiser *Aleksandr Suvorov*, where he wrote in the visitor's book that the visit was an expression of the "militant collaboration" between the two peoples.[60] The visit was doubtless a morale-booster for the Aden regime; its effect on the GCC rulers cannot be known. (The GCC rejected Oman's plan, but there was never any indication that the other rulers had favored it.)

Relations with Oman continued to be bad, and fighting flared up again on the border in mid-June. Moscow quickly despatched Marshal Sokolov, 1st Deputy Defense Minister, to Aden for a first-hand look. He was said to have discussed ways of strengthening military cooperation; perhaps as a result South Yemen received a squadron of MiG-23s, another 20 MiG-21s and 20 T-62 tanks, and several fast attack boats armed with anti-ship missiles.[61] The South Yemeni Defense Minister could say in September that his military forces had been upgraded to cope with the "American threat."

Sokolov may also have discussed a project which had been in the making for half a year and which would reach fruition with the signing on August 19, 1981, of the Tripartite Pact[62] (Libya, Ethiopia, and the PDRY) in Aden. The pact promised: first, political cooperation in pursuit of radical causes; second, economic development cooperation "taking into consideration the ability of each country individually"; third, cooperation in building defense and security capabilities and in defense against attacks. There is no evidence that the Soviets forced this pact on any of the signatories. Each of the three had sufficient reasons to join; Aden, for example, wanted to break out of its isolation and respond, however symbolically, to the U.S. military build-up and particularly to the formation of the

GCC, an immensely wealthy alliance which contained its bitterest enemies. The pact was, in fact, largely symbolic: South Yemen already had economic and defense agreements with Ethiopia, and it was unlikely that in case of a regime-threatening attack on the PDRY it would look to Libya for protection. The practical advantage for Aden was reportedly a promise of $400 million in Libyan aid, including $100 million in financial aid.[63]

On the other hand, the Soviets were certainly involved in the discussions leading to the treaty, promoted it, and probably helped to draft it. They were doubtless content that three of their closest friends in the Middle East should be linked formally, and that one of them would apparently be picking up the tab; they may even have contemplated being paid in Libyan petrodollars for some of the arms delivered to Ethiopia and the PDRY.[64] Article 7, which called on the parties to "exert maximum effort. . . to strengthen and deepen their ties . . . with socialist countries," would have been particularly pleasing. However, the Soviets said little about it, a subdued treatment which was probably intended to play down the treaty's focus on the struggle against 'reaction,' in order not to alarm the GCC states and push them into Washington's outstretched arms.

The stiffening polarization in the region kept tension high for the remainder of 1981. An attempt by Ali Nasir to reduce the tension by a visit to North Yemen in mid-September failed. The South Yemeni leader's potential freedom of movement was constrained by the continuation of the power struggle; the new Defense Minister (formerly Interior Minister) Salih Muslih Qasim' was a strongly pro-Soviet radical with close ties to Libya, the PFLO, and the National Democratic Front (NDF). Nevertheless, there is no reason to assume that the power struggle involved a desire on Muhammad's part to pull away from the Soviet Union. All South Yemenis continued to be wary of the GCC,[65] an attitude which intensified when the GCC decided in November to proceed toward cooperation in defense (a decision which itself was largely a reaction to the Tripartite Pact). Aden also continued to fear and be angered by what it insisted was the creation of U.S. bases in Oman, and these feelings were heightened by the Oman phase of the 'Bright Star' maneuvers in November.

Close ties were therefore maintained with the Soviet Union and the socialist camp. High-ranking delegations from these countries, including one led by Marshal Kutakhov, attended the tenth anniversary celebrations of South Yemen's armed forces. The Foreign

Minister of Afghanistan visited in September and was received by Muhammad. Treaties of Friendship and Cooperation were signed with Czechoslovakia, Hungary, and Bulgaria. The links seemed to be getting tighter. An article in *New Times* left no doubt about the importance of South Yemen to the Soviets; Democratic Yemen, the author wrote, "plays an important role in repulsing the machinations of imperialist and pro-imperialist quarters to set up military bases. . ."[66]

FROM AUGUST 1981 TO THE DEATH OF BREZHNEV (NOVEMBER 1982)

In the second half of 1981 events in the Middle East moved the Soviets to try a more accommodating stance toward the region's moderate regimes. One of the factors influencing Moscow was the desire to encourage closer relations with Kuwait; the Soviets could see the advantage of having a friend in the counsels of the GCC, and would have been very pleased to see more economic aid flowing into Aden from the Gulf principality. Kuwait was in any case very unhappy about U.S. military relations with Oman, and several Kuwaiti actions earlier in the year had seemed to promote closer relations with Moscow.[67] Now Moscow was willing to reciprocate.

A second factor was the reappearance of a glimmer of hope for Saudi-Soviet relations. The Fahd Plan for a Middle East peace settlement, enunciated in August, was similar to Brezhnev's proposals, and Saudi spokesmen made it clear that they saw a major role for the Soviets in the realization of the plan.[68] In addition, at the GCC summit meeting in November the Saudis supported Kuwait's non-aligned line, rejecting the presence of military fleets and foreign bases in the region (although they were instrumental in the decision to move toward defense cooperation). Also, the Soviets were concerned about the impact of the U.S. sale of AWACS aircraft to Saudi Arabia, approved in late October. They may have felt that a lessening of the tension in the region would keep the Saudis from moving too far back into the U.S. camp.

In addition, the Soviets were looking toward the possibility of improving their bitterly hostile relations with Egypt after Anwar Sadat's assassination on October 6. Furthermore, relations between Aden and Baghdad and between Moscow and Baghdad were warming up — Saddam Hussain sent "warmest greetings" to Muhammad on

South Yemen's National Day, and in early November several hundred Polish tanks reached Iraq. Finally YAR President Salih paid a highly successful visit to Moscow, the first by a North Yemeni leader since 1971.

All of these developments had the effect of ameliorating South Yemen's position and making it possible for Ali Nasir gradually to assume a somewhat more moderate stance while not moving away from the Soviets. (In October, Muhammad referred to the PDRY-Soviet Treaty as "a bright milestone in our strategic militant relations";[69] in December it was reported that a large complex, protected by surface-to-air missiles was being constructed near Aden to serve as a headquarters for the Soviets in the PDRY and the region.[70]) The process began in early November with his short trip to Kuwait (where the views were said to be identical) and then after a visit to Eastern Europe, to Bahrain, Qatar, and the UAE. This was followed, after YAR President Salih visited Moscow, by a meeting in November between Muhammad and Salih in Kuwait, under the mediation of the Amir. By the end of the year, inter-Yemeni relations appeared to have warmed considerably (see p. 194). The hostility between Aden and Oman was much more intractable, as both sides traded accusations about their relationships with their respective patrons. Nevertheless, at the end of the year Muhammad took a small step toward reducing tension (see p. 144).

These tentative openings seemed to close in early 1982, mostly, it would appear, because of a fresh outburst of the power struggle in Aden expressed through new hostilities in North Yemen (see p. 195). This soured Ali Nasir's initiatives, but he seemed unable to override his domestic opposition and curtail the northward flow of weapons until the end of March. However, he continued the moderating trend as best he could; the PDRY agreed in early January to end its feud with Iraq by exchanging ambassadors. He also continued to support and apply more liberal internal economic policies such as the Investment Promotion law passed in December 1981 which encouraged South Yemenis abroad and foreigners to invest in the private and mixed sectors.[71] More construction and other commercial contracts were awarded to companies of non-Communist countries, and in the late spring the PDRY accredited ambassadors to several Western European nations.[72] The Soviets expressed guarded approval.

At the same time Muhammad protected his back by preserving his radical credentials. The PDRY participated in a meeting in Prague to consider the work of *Problems of Peace and Socialism*, a sure signal of allegiance to the socialist camp. Ali Nasir hosted a World Peace Council conference to Aden in early February; his speech was stridently anti-United States and anti-imperialist, (but did not attack the U.S.'s friends in the region[73]). In February Aden announced that a gang of saboteurs had been arrested. The unusual level of publicity given to their trial suggested that Ali Nasir was using it to demonstrate his awareness of the threat of the PDRY; (however, the fact that the publicity centered on their alleged training by U.S. citizens, not on Saudi Arabia as the location of their training, indicated that he did not wish to inflame relations with Riyadh). In mid-February, Muhammad visited Cuba.

In March the power struggle in Aden became more acute. Ali Nasir had regained the initiative, but when Sanaa launched an attack on the NDF, debate raged in Aden over the PDRY's response. For several weeks substantial forces were moved to the North Yemen border, and the possibility of open war loomed. At this juncture Moscow sent 50 more T-62 tanks to demonstrate its support. Karen Brutents was also despatched to Aden; he put the Kremlin squarely on Muhammad's side, issuing an invitation to the South Yemeni leader to visit Moscow at the end of the month. In addition, he apparently mediated between the groups in Aden, and by early April the power struggle had subsided, and with it the tension on the border.

Another event which was even more important in the subsidence of the power struggle (and the quest for better relations with the oil states) was the catastrophic flooding in late March 1982, in which the flows in the wadis in several governorates were up to six times higher than ever before recorded; the bulk of the dams and canals built (mostly by the Soviets and East Europeans) to control water for irrigation were either badly damaged or destroyed. Thousands were left homeless, and the total damage was estimated to be in excess of $900 million. In these circumstances the troops were removed from the border, and the oil states rallied to help, sending approximately $13 million (of which Saudi Arabia contributed $5 million) and supplies of food, tents, and medical supplies within a few days.[74] Western countries and funding agencies also rushed aid. The Soviets were slow to respond; no shipments of immediate flood assistance were announced, although Moscow did promise to rebuild or repair the Soviet-built projects damaged by the floods.

The flooding caused Ali Nasir's trip to Moscow to be postponed, and he did not make the visit until September; this long delay was probably due to the pressures of other events (such as Israel's invasion of Lebanon), but it may have suited Muhammad not to underline his Soviet ties at the time. The rapid response of the oil states raised South Yemeni hopes for more aid. Foreign Minister Salim Salih Muhammad visited Saudi Arabia, Iran, Bahrain, and Kuwait in April. The visits appeared to be successful; although the inclusion of Iran could not have been much to the liking of the other three, it produced a new source of crude oil for Aden's refinery. [In fact, by the end of the summer, the refinery, which was being overhauled with a loan from the Islamic Bank for Development (based in Abu Dhabi), was being used by both Iran and Iraq to supplement their war-damaged refineries.] In addition, in April the Italian oil company AGIP announced it had discovered high quality oil in significant quantities off the coast of the PDRY. This was not only cheering news; it also tended to make the South Yemenis less enthusiastic about the Soviets. The latter had been searching for oil in the PDRY for years within the framework of technical assistance loans. AGIP had found oil in a short period of drilling, and South Yemen had not had to pay a penny. The disillusionment with Soviet aid spread beyond oil exploration. Soviet aid had never been overly generous, and non-Soviet bloc sources had provided the bulk of the flood aid. The dams and projects which had been destroyed were Soviet or East European built; whether or not the construction was at fault, this added to a general perception of poor workmanship. To this was added disillusionment with the small number of projects[75] and the slow pace of aid utilization; for example, a power station and desalination unit for which a contract was signed in 1980 had still not been started by mid-1982. Agricultural stagnation and budgetary difficulties, which were of considerable concern in the spring, could all be laid at the Soviet door with some justification.

Disappointment with the Soviets did not extend to downgrading relations with Moscow, but it did apparently make it easier internally for Ali Nasir to promote his regional policy of relaxation of tensions in order to encourage Arab economic aid. In early May he made conciliatory moves toward North Yemen and Oman; soon after came the news that the Kuwait-based Arab Fund for Economic and Social Development had approved a long-term loan of approximately

$10 million for construction of a new fishing port.[76] The linkage of aid to normalization seemed obvious. However, it soon became evident that Muhammad still was not in complete command in Aden. Internal dissension in his regime forced him to postpone the meeting between PDRY and Omani representatives until July 1, when he was able to send a delegation to Kuwait for intensive discussions.

The move toward Oman and the conservatives was stalled at that point, largely because of the Israeli siege of West Beirut and the question of rescuing the Palestinian Liberation Organization (PLO). Not only was Aden preoccupied with these questions, but for a time it was catapulted into the mainstream of Arab politics and thus did not need to curry favor. In early August, Ali Nasir and YAR President Salih collaborated on a mission to various Middle East countries to urge the convocation of an Arab summit to achieve a united policy on Lebanon, and once a plan for the PLO's evacuation had been devised, Aden agreed to be one of the recipient countries.

During this time there were reports that claimed that Soviet–South Yemeni (or more particularly Kremlin-Muhammad) relations had deteriorated;[77] these, however, are not convincing. Aden continued contacts with the socialist countries during Ali Nasir's overtures to his neighbors. More importantly, Ali Nasir's was the highest-ranking (and for much of the time the only) voice defending Soviet (in)action in Lebanon, even to the point of jeopardizing those overtures. Thus on July 31 TASS quoted him as saying that:

> The assertions by reactionary Arab propagandists that the Soviet Union does not render effective help to the Arabs in the struggle against Israel is not only aimed at undermining Soviet-Arab friendship, but is also indicative of the existing connections between Arab reaction and U.S. imperialism.[78]

Radio Peace and Progress in an Arabic broadcast on August 3 said:

> A.N. Muhammad has stated to those who are demanding that the USSR enter the battlefield instead of the Arabs. . .: where is the Arab army, where are the Arab arms, and where is the Arab oil?[79]

Earlier, Aden radio defended the quality of Soviet weapons,[80] an extremely sore point in Moscow, and on August 14 *Izvestiia* reported that (for the first time) Muhammad had come out in favor of an international conference to achieve a "just and lasting settlement" in the Middle East.

Ali Nasir, then, appeared to be in very good standing with the Kremlin, and to prove it, Moscow issued to him the first invitation to visit after the Arab summit conference in Fez. Brezhnev was not at the airport, but that was probably because his health was deteriorating. (He died just two months later.) The two met the following day "in an atmosphere of friendship and full mutual understanding" for talks which were limited almost entirely to the Middle East situation, the aim of which was to stress Soviet assistance to the Arabs and Soviet approval of the peace plan adopted at the Fez summit. In his dinner speech Brezhnev lauded the "coincidence or closeness of our views and assessments of both the questions of bilateral relations and of topical problems of foreign policy,"[81] and the communiqué made it clear that there was indeed a closer coincidence of views than usual. *For the first time* in a meeting between Soviet and South Yemeni leaders the phrase "exchange of opinions" did not appear in the communiqué.[82]

The agreement was largely due to their common outrage at Israel's actions in Lebanon, their concern at the possible success of the Reagan peace plan, and their hopes for a long-awaited Arab unity. However, the level of agreement was also due to the willingness of each side to make an important concession to the other. Ali Nasir Muhammad made official his endorsement of Moscow's proposal for an international conference on the Middle East, thereby becoming the first Steadfastness and Confrontation Front member to support this long-standing and high-priority aim of Soviet Middle East policy. In return, the Soviets gave the PDRY a "big credit...on advantageous terms" for the construction in Aden of a power station (promised in 1980) which would double Aden's power supply, and a desalination plant.[83] No details were made available about the terms (although the specific mention of "advantageous terms" was so rare by this time in Soviet economic deals with South Yemen that it suggests that they were better than usual), or about the size of the credit. (British sources indicate that it was $320 million;[84] this was so much larger than any previous project as to suggest that the Soviets had elevated the maintenance of their position in the PDRY to a high priority.)

The absence from the communiqué of evidence of disagreement is the more interesting because of indications that disagreement existed. Ali Nasir referred in his dinner speech to an "exchange of opinions" (albeit a "*comradely* exchange of opinions"), and a TASS analysis also mentioned an "in-depth exchange of views."[85] The contentious issue seems to have been Ali Nasir's move toward Oman and perhaps even his desire for cooperation with Saudi Arabia and the other conservative Arabs. In his dinner speech Ali Nasir called for a "summit conference among the countries of the Peninsula, Gulf, and Horn of Africa, and including other concerned sides, in a joint effort to free the region from the threat of the imperialist presence"; not only was this not mentioned in the communiqué, it was not included in the TASS report of his speech.[86] The communiqué did mention Soviet approval of better PDRY-YAR relations, but did not refer even directly to Aden's attempts to improve relations with its other neighbors. It is possible that Moscow was worried lest the PDRY move so far in pursuit of petrodollars that the Soviets' positions there would be endangered. There may also have been differences over military aid. Military officials, including PDRY Defense Minister Salih Muslih Qasim, participated in the talks, but there was no hint that the Soviets had promised more aid. (Interestingly, Salih Muslih returned to Moscow at the invitation of Ustinov only ten days after the delegation had left.)

Differences notwithstanding, the visit was a success. The PDRY received new aid and Ali Nasir praised Soviet political, military, and (less effusively) economic assistance to South Yemen. He also expressed "profound gratitude" for Soviet support to the Arabs and condemned "attempts at discrediting the Soviet Union's policy," and awarded Brezhnev the 14 October Revolution medal. More importantly, Brezhnev was given a forum connected to the Middle East in which to say that Arab unity (not the USSR) should rebuff Israeli aggression, and to present again his peace plan (which was very similar to the Fez plan).

On his return home, Ali Nasir continued his praise (sometimes extravagant) of the Soviets. At the same time, he stressed the PDRY's economic difficulties and moved very quickly to improve relations with Oman (the *sine qua non* of better relations with the neighboring oil states). On October 25 (the eve of the anniversary of the Soviet-South Yemen Treaty!) the foreign ministers of the PDRY and Oman met in Kuwait to sign an agreement to normalize relations (see p. 147). Two weeks later the South Yemeni Minister of Interior flew to Riyadh to discuss demarcating the PDRY-Saudi Arabian border; although no agreement was reached, both sides announced the talks had been "useful" and the way seemed to be open for further normalization.

THE ANDROPOV MONTHS
(NOVEMBER 1982-FEBRUARY 1984)

A few days later, Leonid Brezhnev died. In tribute, Ali Nasir Muhammad led a high-ranking party and government delegation to Moscow for the funeral. His reception was cooler than he must have expected. Although he was ranked high in the socialist orientation camp contingent (and well ahead of any other Arab leader), Andropov did not single him out (or any Arab leader) for special talks, and there were no reports that he or any of his entourage had talks with other Soviet officials.

This (coupled with a report that Saudi Arabia had given Aden $13 million in budgetary aid after the agreement with Oman had been signed) gave rise to reports in Arab circles of deteriorating relations between the PDRY and the Soviet Union. Both sides sought to dispel this impression. Moscow, for the first time since 1970 sent a delegation (but not a high-ranking one) to the celebrations of the PDRY's national independence (its 15th anniversary). At the same time, the Soviet media paid much greater attention than usual to this celebration, with great praise for South Yemen's political, social, and economic transformations, its foreign policy, and Soviet assistance in its development.[87] The Soviets also played to South Yemenis' sense of insecurity by sending the *Minsk* into the Indian Ocean for anticarrier exercises and by conducting a vehement campaign (in which Aden participated) against the newly created U.S. Central Command which was said to be the instrument of Washington's drive for control of the region.

For his part, Ali Nasir affirmed that Aden-Moscow ties were still close. He travelled to Moscow for the 60th anniversary celebrations of the founding of the USSR and praised Soviet support for the Arabs; as for mutual relations, he said, there existed a "close militant internationalist union of the Yemeni and Soviet peoples."[88] He had a "warm and friendly" talk with Ustinov and members of the Soviet General Staff. However, he did not meet Andropov, and he pointedly did not praise Soviet support for South Yemen. His discussion with Ustinov was said to be a "useful exchange of opinions on bilateral relations. . . , on the situation in the region [the PDRY-Oman agreement] and other questions of mutual interest."[89]

The issues that clouded the relationship, and continued to do so throughout the spring of 1983, were probably the following: the continuing PDRY-Oman rapprochement; Soviet pressure on Aden to expand the training camps for the PLO in South Yemen;[90] Soviet pressure for repayment of some of the PDRY's debt; and the continuing low level of Soviet aid in the face of a general decline in South Yemen's economic situation.[91] It is likely that the Soviets were also unhappy over Aden's decision to offer oil concessions to other Western companies (after AGIP's success).[92] Several Soviet and other communist countries' delegations travelled to Aden; all were given perfunctory treatment in the South Yemeni media. A Soviet delegation arrived in February to negotiate a new scientific and cultural cooperation agreement. The Soviet media gave it substantial publicity, stressing that the agreement would expand Soviet assistance greatly; Aden played it down as simply a routine meeting of a joint committee, and did not mention expanded assistance.

The coolness seemed to come to a head with the visit of Admiral Gorshkov in late March to "bolster and expand relations between the armed forces" of the two countries. The visit did not go very well; his discussions were said to have been an "exchange of views" held in an "amicable atmosphere"[93] (an almost glacial situation considering the close ties between Moscow and Aden). While in Aden, he received the PDRY's friendship medal and heard Ali Nasir Muhammad praise Soviet military aid, but he was allowed to talk with the South Yemeni leader for only 15 minutes. The Gorshkov visit was disturbing enough that Moscow immediately sent a party-government delegation, led by Brutents and the First Deputy Foreign Minister. In discussions with Ali Nasir, they were apparently able to bring relations back on an even keel (helped, it seemed, by a speech by President Reagan which contained references to the PDRY which Aden felt were threatening); however it did not appear that these Soviet envoys had been able to restore the previous warmth to the relationship.

At this point, Ali Nasir embarked on an effort to improve relations with the other peninsula states, sending PDRY Foreign Minister Abd al-Aziz ad-Dali on a two-week tour in April. It began auspiciously, with Saudi Arabia reportedly promising to give South Yemen $60 million (the remainder of the $100 million promised in

1976),[94] but no other progress was reported. Furthermore, this initiative was soured by Qabus' simultaneous friendly trip to Washington. A Supreme People's Council meeting in early May endorsed Muhammad's efforts in the peninsula, but in lukewarm fashion; considerable opposition was mustering in Aden, and in mid-May the border talks with Oman were abruptly postponed indefinitely. A month later a party-government delegation was despatched on a two-week tour of East Europe and the Soviet Union.

The debate in Aden over foreign policy orientation[95] raged throughout the summer. PDRY envoys made several trips to the UAE (during one of which mutual diplomatic recognition was arranged), and in late July Aden and Riyadh were reported to have exchanged Ambassadors for the first time since 1977.[96] However, PDRY-Omani relations continued to deteriorate, and Aden moved to improve relations with Moscow. The tenth session of the YSP Central Committee at the end of August, strongly declaring its support for the foreign policy of the USSR and criticizing Oman, signalled that the pro-Soviet line had won out. Salih Muslih Qasim (generally considered to be the leader of the faction which was more pro-Soviet) received the 14 October Revolution medal, and a Soviet military expert the 'medal of sincerity' in honor of the efforts of Soviet advisers in building the PDRY's armed forces.[97] Shortly thereafter, a YSP delegation was sent to Moscow, and PDRY Foreign Ministry officials consulted with their Soviet counterparts.

At the end of September Ali Nasir flew to Moscow for his first meeting with Andropov. The Soviet leader by that time was seriously ill, and their meeting was brief. The communiqué[98] indicated that the discussion concentrated on the Lebanese crisis, on which Ali Nasir had no trouble supporting the Soviet line. Nonetheless, there was some evidence that, in general, he was still not happy with the relationship. Although *Pravda* referred to a "warm comradely" atmosphere,[99] Aden radio was cooler; both mentioned an exchange of opinions. On the subject of USSR-PDRY ties, the *Pravda* report was more emphatic in favor of strengthening them.

Moscow continued to pursue warmer relations. In mid-October 1983, the 20th anniversary of the Radfan uprising and the concurrent fifth anniversary of the founding of the YSP were marked with great attention for the second consecutive year. (Significantly, the two events chosen to symbolize Soviet assistance were the laying of the cornerstone for a new YSP Central Committee building, the gift of the CPSU and other communist parties, and the opening of a repair station for irrigation equipment.) Moscow sent the third highest ranking delegation it had ever sent to the PDRY,[100] led by M. Solomentsev, candidate member of the Politbureau and Chairman of the Party Control Commission, and including Brutents and the Navy's Deputy Commander-in-Chief. The delegation was received by Muhammad, and conveyed to him the Politbureau's personal "cordial, comradely greetings." The Soviet attentions were partly the result of their concern over Ali Nasir's decision to renew his pursuit of warmer relations with Oman; they probably also stemmed from the need to repair relations at a time when their relations with their other Arab friends, particularly Syria, were strained. The treatment appeared to be achieving results; in his anniversary speech, Ali Nasir stressed his approval of the general Soviet foreign policy line and thanked the Soviets for their security assistance and "great and generous aid."[101]

He also reaffirmed his rapprochement with other Arabian Peninsula countries and in the following months continued to pursue that policy; ambassadors were exchanged with both Oman and the UAE. However, on the whole, South Yemeni policy had shifted closer to the Soviet Union by the end of 1983. This may have been because Arab aid once again did not live up to expectations; it may have been due to Aden's concern at U.S. military construction activities in Oman; or it may have been caused by another upsurge in the factional struggle in Aden. (Ali Nasir reportedly postponed the YSP Congress scheduled for October.[102]) A South Yemeni delegation to Syria affirmed the PDRY's support for Assad; and Aden increased its criticism of the United States. A party-government delegation visited Moscow and had "warm, comradely" talks with Brutents and Ryzhov, although again there were signs of disagreement, with an "exchange of views" said to have taken place over "certain international problems, questions of relations between the CPSU and the YSP, and between the PDRY and the USSR."[103]

As Konstantin Chernenko took up the reins in Moscow, USSR-PDRY relations were closer than they had been for over a year. There were still, of course some difficulties, stemming mainly from Aden's continuing economic problems. However, relatively little Arab aid was being offered, tension seemed to be growing on the Saudi Arabian border, and the YSP Central Committee was expressing anxiety over U.S. activities in Oman; out of all of this, the power struggle within the regime surfaced again. Ali Nasir Muhammad, the consummate survivor, knew wherein lay his advantage.

For their part the Soviets also knew the value of their assets in South Yemen. Their potential military assets were enhanced in early 1984 with (Soviet-financed) runway improvements at Khormaksar and with the construction of an airport at al-Ghaidha in the east, which could if necessary take Il-38 reconnaissance planes, thus improving Soviet capabilities. Moscow's political assets, such as the consistent support given by Aden to the USSR's global and European foreign policy lines, and to most Soviet policies in the Middle East region, had again been demonstrated in January as the PDRY delegation walked out of the Islamic Conference Organization summit conference to protest the readmittance of Egypt. The Kremlin was willing to accept some tension in the Soviet-South Yemeni relationship to preserve these assets.

NOTES

1. *Pravda*, October 13, 1978. The phrase 'Marxism-Leninism' is never used in PDRY documents.
2. *FBIS/MENA*, October 16, 1978, p. C3.
3. To gain entry to this group, a country had to have an economy dominated by the state sector, and to have initiated agrarian and social reforms. However the most important criteria seem to be the creation of a ruling 'vanguard party' which includes local communists, the pursuit of an antiimperialist foreign policy, and above all, "all-sided cooperation and close friendly relations with the socialist states." K.N. Brutents, *Osvobodivshiesia strany v 70-e gody* (Moscow: Politizdat, 1979), pp. 53-54; R.A. Ulianovskii, "O stranakh sotsialisticheskoi orientatsii," *Kommunist*, no. 11 (November), 1979, pp. 118-20; G. Starushenko, "O gosudarstvakh sotsialisticheskoi orientatsii," *Agitator*, no. 14 (July), 1979, pp. 59-60.
4. F. Halliday, "Yemen's Unfinished Revolution: Socialism in the South," *MERIP Reports*, no. 81 (October 1979): 13.
5. *FBIS/MENA*, November 14, 1978, p. C1.
6. *FBIS/MENA*, November 17, 1978, p. C3.
7. *FBIS/MENA*, December 28, 1978, p. C7; *MECS 1978-79*, p. 725; *The Military Balance 1979-80* p. 105.
8. *Arab Report and Record*, December 1-15, 1978, p. 901.
9. Stockholm International Peace Research Institute, *World Armaments and Disarmament 1980* (Stockholm: SIPRI, 1981), p. 162.
10. In December 1978 the U.S. State Department estimated there were 300 Soviet and 300 Cuban military advisers in the PDRY. At the end of 1979 the numbers were reported by the CIA to be 1,100 and 1,000, respectively, with a slightly larger number of Soviet economic technicians. U.S., CIA,

Communist Aid Activities in Non-Communist Less Developed Countries 1979 and 1954-79 (McLean, VA: CIA, 1980), p. 15. Other sources put the number of Cubans much higher. Cf. *MECS 1978-79*, p. 726; *Strategic Mid-East and Africa* 5(April 25, June 13, 1979).

11. U.S., Arms Control & Disarmament Agency, *World Military Expenditures and Arms Transfers 1971-80* (Washington, D.C.: ACDA, 1983), p. 114.
12. *FBIS/USSR*, June 5, 1979, p. A2; *Pravda*, August 21, 1979.
13. *New York Times*, May 27, 1979.
14. *FBIS/USSR*, July 3, 1979, p. H3; *Pravda*, June 30, 1979.
15. *FBIS/MENA*, August 13, 1979, pp. C4-5.
16. *MECS 1978-79*, pp. 719-20.
17. The conflict had begun the previous June with the murder in Aden by Iraqi agents of an Iraqi communist professor at the University of Aden, an episode which ended with the South Yemeni security forces storming the Iraqi Embassy to capture the gunmen; each country then sealed off the other's embassy in reprisal and filled the airwaves with recriminations. *Keesing's Contemporary Archives*, April 18, 1980, p. 30200; *FBIS/MENA*, June 4-13, 1979.
18. *FBIS/USSR*, September 20, 1979, pp. H4-7.
19. *FBIS/USSR*, October 15, 1979, pp. H4-5, in which the PDRY was called "the vanguard of the national liberation movement."
20. *MECS 1978-79*, pp. 67, 723.
21. *FBIS/USSR*, October 25, 1979.
22. *FBIS/USSR*, October 30, 1979, pp. H1-5.
23. *FBIS/USSR*, October 29, 1979, pp. H2-5.
24. For a comparison of Soviet-Third World treaties, cf. Z. Imam, "Soviet Treaties with Third World Countries," *Soviet Studies* 35 (January 1983): 53-70.
25. This is the standard clause for Soviet treaties with noncommunist Third World states. It is much weaker than the corresponding clause in the Soviet-Afghanistan treaty which was used to justify Soviet military intervention. A.Z. Rubinstein, "Afghanistan: Embraced by the Bear," *Orbis* 26 (Spring 1982): 137.
26. For example, the Soviet-Mozambique treaty claimed they were "natural allies"; the Soviet-North Korean treaty was said to be based on "socialist internationalism." Z. Imam, op. cit., p. 60.
27. It was initially reported that the group which had occupied the Grand Mosque for two weeks at the end of November had been armed and trained in South Yemen; although the Saudis later denied that, it appears the Omanis continued to believe it. *New York Times*, December 10, 1979.
28. *FBIS/MENA*, November 5, 1979, p. C2; *Pravda*, December 12, 1979, p. 2.
29. *FBIS/MENA*, December 4, 1979, p. C6; this treaty, which was almost identical to Soviet-Third World treaties, was perceived in the region as a Soviet-inspired move.
30. Cf. *MECS 1979-80*, p. 659.
31. *FBIS/MENA*, January 14, 1980, p. C11.
32. *FBIS/MENA*, March 4, 1980, p. C10.
33. *FBIS/MENA*, April 2, 1980, p. C6.

34. Cf. I. Beliaev, "Islam and Politics" *Literaturnaia Gazeta*, January 16 1980, in *FBIS/USSR*, January 25, 1980, pp. H3-6; *FBIS/USSR*, February 5, 1980, pp. H2-3; A. Vasilev, "Islam: I politicheskaia borba," *Pravda*, April 14, 1980.

35. *FBIS/MENA*, February 27, 1980, p. C3.

36. *The Military Balance 1980-81*, p. 12.

37. B.W. Watson, *Red Navy at Sea* (Boulder: Westview Press, 1982), pp. 216, 218; L.T. Walsh, "Bab el-Mandab: The Gateway of Tears for the U.S.?," *Armed Forced Forces Journal International*, September 1980 P. 74. An *Al-Anba* (Kuwait) report that the Soviets were building a submarine base in Aden was denied by both Soviets and South Yemenis, and has not been substantiated by any other source.

38. F. Halliday, *Threat From the East? Soviet Policy from Afghanistan and Iran to the Horn of Africa* (New York: Penguin Books, 1982), p. 97. The shortages had been evident for some time; cf. J. Gueyras, "South Yemen: Cuba of Arabia," *Le Monde*, February 28, 1979.

39. F. Halliday, *Threat From the East?*, p. 144 fn. 15.

40. L. Mylroie, *Politics and the Soviet Presence in the People's Democratic Republic of Yemen* (Santa Monica: Rand, 1983), pp. 23-26. The *New York Times* on April 27, 1980 opined that the Soviets had been deterred from military intervention to keep Ismail in power by the fear that the United States might invoke the Carter Doctrine and overreact. However, for the reasons given here, it is extremely unlikely that the Soviets contemplated intervention, either by themselves or by Cuban troops in Ethiopia.

41. *Pravda*, April 23, 1980.

42. *FBIS/MENA*, April 23, 1980, pp. C3-5.

43. *FBIS/USSR*, April 29, 1980, p. H4.

44. *FBIS/USSR*, May 6, 1980, p. H2.

45. *MECS 1979-80*, p. 666.

46. Cf. for example, Aden radio's report of his speech to the Supreme People's Council on April 26, in *FBIS/MENA*, May 1, 1980, p. C5.

47. *FBIS/USSR*, June 3, 1980, pp. H1-5.

48. *FBIS/USSR*, May 29, 1980, p. H1.

49. *FBIS/MENA*, July 1, 1980, p. C4.

50. *FBIS/MENA*, July 10, 1980, p. C5. It is likely that this offer was not made without consulting Moscow; in tandem with Muhammad's efforts, the Soviets were floating another trial balloon concerning reestablishing Soviet-Saudi relations. Cf. I. Beliaev's article in *Literaturnaia Gazeta*, July 9, 1980.

51. P. Alkhimov, "Sodeistve SSSR v razvitii ekonomiki NDRI," *Vneshniaia Torgovlia*, no. 9 (September), 1981, p. 35 states that the revised Second Five-year Plan is "coordinated" with those of the CEMA countries.

52. *MECS 1980-81*, pp. 715-20 contains an excellent description on the power struggle.

53. *FBIS/USSR,* October 21, 1980, pp. H1-3.

54. Cf. The YSP Central Committee report in *FBIS/MENA*, January 21, 1981, pp. C3-7.

55. *MECS 1980-81*, p. 722.

56. *An-Nahar Arab Report & MEMO*, 4 (December 22, 1980): 2.
57. *Izvestiia*, March 4, 1981; *14 October*, February 25, 1981.
58. *CDSP* 33 (March 25, 1981): 7.
59. Muti, former Politbureau member and Foreign Minister, had been under arrest since August, accused of subversive dealings with Saudi Arabia. He was put on trial in March and two weeks later was said to have been shot while trying to escape.
60. *FBIS/USSR*, June 9, 1981, p. H3.
61. *FBIS/MENA*, June 26, 1981, p. C2; *The Military Balance 1981-82*, p. 59; MiG-23s had been reported in the PDRY for several years, but always with Soviet or Cuban pilots.
62. The text of the treaty can be found in *FBIS/MENA*, April 28, 1982, pp. BB1-3.
63. C. Kutschera, "South Yemen: a slow move towards the West," *The Middle East*, no. 94 (August 1982): 21. Libyan aid in these proportions has not materialized.
64. Total arms aid to the PDRY in 1981 has been estimated at $935 million. U.S., Arms Control & Disarmament Agency, op. cit., p. 114. Total arms aid to Ethiopia has been estimated at $1 to 2 billion." M. Ottaway, *Soviet and American Influence in the Horn of Africa* (New York: Praeger, 1982), p. 116.
65. At the same time, Ali Nasir appeared to start an attempt to split the GCC by pointing out the differences between Oman and at least some of the other members. Cf. his interview in *FBIS/MENA*, September 9, 1981, pp. 3-7.
66. A. Guskov, "A Solid Foundation," *New Times*, no. 43 (October), 1981, p. 14.
67. Deputy Prime Minister Shaikh Sabah's highly successful visit to Moscow in April, when he identified Kuwait with Brezhnev's proposals on a Middle East settlement, and on zones of peace in the Persian Gulf and the Indian Ocean; the despatch of a Kuwaiti military mission to the USSR on an arms buying mission; Kuwait's angry criticism of the United States over the Israeli bombing of Beirut in July.
68. J. Muir, "The Saudis set their sights on Fez," *Middle East International*, no. 162 (November 13, 1981): 2; *FBIS/USSR*, November 6, 1981, p. H1.
69. *Pravda*, October 25, 1981, p. 1.
70. *FBIS/MENA*, December 11, 1981, p. C9.
71. *Middle East Economic Digest* 26 (February 19-25, 1982): 51-2. The Soviets approved of this measure; one analyst wrote that "the leftist excesses of the early 1970s have been finally overcome." V.V. Naumkin, "Democratic Yemen: concerning the appraisal of the results of development," paper delivered to the International Symposium on Contemporary Yemen, Exeter University, July 1983, p. 17.
73. *FBIS/MENA*, February 1, 1982, pp. C4-7.
74. *An-Nahar Arab Report & MEMO* 6 (April 12, 1982): 5.
75. Soviet sources claim only that 50 projects have been or are being built in the PDRY. This is not an impressive figure for 12 years of aid to a

reliable friend. A. Guskov, "Dynamics of Development," *New Times*, no. 49 (December), 1982, p. 26.

76. *MECS 1980-81*, p. 679.

77. This especially refers to the reported ash-Sharjabi-Ismail meeting in Bulgaria, with Soviet connivance, to plot a coup, reported first in *The Observer*, August 22, 1982. However, cf. also V. Rybakov's article in *World Marxist Review* 25 (August 1982): 42-50, which painted a rather bleak picture of party development and socioeconomic progress in South Yemen, and did not mention Ali Nasir Muhammad.

78. *FBIS/USSR*, August 2, 1982, p. H7.

79. *FBIS/USSR*, August 4, 1982, p. H9.

80. *FBIS/USSR*, July 27, 1982, p. H1.

81. *FBIS/USSR*, September 16, 1982, p. H1.

82. The communique was published in *FBIS/USSR*, September 17, 1982, pp. H1-4.

83. *FBIS/USSR*, September 17, 1982, p. H5; A. Guskov, "The Sound Foundations of Soviet-Yemeni Friendship," *International Affairs* (Moscow), no. 12 (December), 1982, p. 73.

84. U.K., Foreign and Commonwealth Office, International Division, *Soviet, East European and Western Development Aid 1976-82* (London: FCO, 1983), p. 22.

85. *FBIS/USSR*, September 16, 1982, pp. H3, H5.

86. FBIS reported it in Aden radio's text of the speech, in *FBIS/USSR*, September 17, 1982, p. H6.

87. A. Guskov, "Dynamics of Development," *New Times*, no. 49 (December), 1982, pp. 26-8; V. Peresada, "Postup revoliutsii," *Pravda*, November 29, 1982; *FBIS/USSR*, November 30, 1982, pp. H1-2; *FBIS/USSR*, December 13, 1982, pp. H1-2.

88. *Pravda*, December 23, 1982.

89. *Pravda*, December 24, 1982.

90. Yasir Arafat, cited in *Foreign Report*, March 24, 1983, p. 4; Aden had not reduced its commitment to the PLO, and its reluctance probably stemmed from financial considerations.

91. One might speculate that Aden was also not happy with the Warsaw Pact's unilateral declaration that it would not involve itself in the Persian Gulf region (*Pravda*, January 6, 1983) at a time when the United States was consolidating its military commitment there.

92. In October 1983 Aden announced an agreement in principle to award a concession to B.P. *Middle East Economic Digest* 27 (October 21-27, 1983): 63.

93. *FBIS/MENA*, March 28, 1983, pp. C4-5.

94. It should be noted, however, that *Middle East Economic Digest* 27 (July 29-August 4, 1983): 43, states that Saudi Arabia had not provided any new aid.

95. Probably not included in the debate was the attempt by Muhammad and Salih to use their long-standing support of the Palestinians to mediate

between Arafat and his opponents (which both Soviets and peninsula countries supported).
    96. Middle East Economic Digest 27 (July 29-August 4, 1983):43.
    97. *FBIS/MENA*, September 1, 1983, p. C5. *FBIS/MENA*, September 2, 1983, p. C4.
    98. *FBIS/USSR*, October 3, 1983, pp. H3-5.
    99. *Pravda*, September 30, 1983.
    100. The top two were the Kosygin visit in October 1979 and the visit of the Chairman of the Presidium of the Supreme Soviet in November 1970.
    101. *FBIS/MENA*, October 14, 1983, p. C5.
    102. *Defense and Foreign Affairs Weekly* 9 (December 12-18, 1983): 1. The Congress had still not been held by mid-July 1984.
    103. *Pravda*, December 17, 1983.

5

MOSCOW, THE PDRY, AND OMAN: THE LIMITATIONS OF INFLUENCE (1967-84)

MOSCOW, ADEN, AND THE DHOFAR REBELLION

The Dhofari rebellion, which began with the creation and activities of the Dhofar Liberation Front (DLF) in June 1965, owed nothing to the Soviet Union. The DLF was inspired in part by Arab nationalism, but mainly by the desire to overthrow the oppressive rule in Oman of Sultan Said ibn Taimur. It did not become a movement to be taken seriously until the end of 1967, after it had been taken under Chinese patronage[1] and been given a secure sanctuary and logistical and ideological support by the newly independent PRSY. Revitalized by these new conditions and by the radicalization of Arab nationalism elsewhere in the Middle East, the DLF itself was radicalized, and at its Second Congress in September 1968 adopted a Marxist-Leninist revolutionary program (with the example before it of the NLF's new program adopted at its Fourth Congress in March); in addition to internal social and political goals based on "scientific socialism," the program linked the Front with the NLF in a wider revolution by the masses of Arabia against "imperialism, colonialism, Arab reaction, and the rotten bourgeoisie."[2] Reflecting this wider goal, it renamed itself the Popular Front for the Liberation of the Occupied Arab Gulf (PFLOAG).

After the conference Chinese and South Yemeni support increased. A Dhofari delegation was sent to China for political and military training, and its members took up influential positions in the Front when they returned. Beijing and Aden gave valuable publicity to the struggle, elevating its intensity to a level where it appeared to be in the vanguard of the fight against imperialism. The PRSY set up political and military training camps and supply depots near the Omani border, where Chinese personnel were active and to which Chinese arms were sent to be distributed in Dhofar. By the end of the 1960s, almost all of the PFLOAG's weapons were Chinese, light weapons mostly, but also some artillery and anti-aircraft guns.

The Soviets were slow off the mark in Dhofar. They must have been concerned by the head-start the Chinese had in the area, and feared that in a limited guerrilla war like this they could not compete ideologically, and that their quantitative and technological edge in weaponry would be valueless. Moscow must also have feared that too much activity on its part would disturb the Shah, with whom the Kremlin was intent on establishing good relations, or cause Britain to cancel its proposed withdrawal from the Gulf, or precipitate a U.S. decision to fill the vacuum. Finally, the Soviets were limited by their perceptions of events in South Yemen; they were slow to make a real commitment to the young PRSY lest it collapse, or until it stabilized, and they would not get involved in Dhofar until they had taken that step. Once that commitment had been made, in mid-1968, and after the PFLOAG had been created in September with its revolutionary flags flying, the Soviets began to take an interest. Indeed, they had little choice by then. Had they continued to ignore the PFLOAG, and neglect the needs of the NLF, they risked losing potential allies in Aden to internal or external enemies; they also risked being attacked by the Chinese for not carrying out their internationalist duties; more importantly, they risked losing to Beijing the chance to influence revolutionary movements which might succeed in spreading revolution to other parts of the Peninsula and forfeiting important strategic positions on the Indian Ocean.

Having decided to involve itself in the Dhofar rebellion, Moscow did not forget the constraints on too enthusiastic an involvement. Action was to be low-key (and low-cost); one way of fulfilling these conditions was to work through the South Yemeni regime, supporting its regional ambitions, and not to attempt a major direct initiative. The first sign of Soviet interest was the publication of a few articles on the rebellion in early 1969 and then a major series by *Pravda* correspondent A. Vasilev, who had been spirited into Dhofar in the first half of the year.[3] Vasilev's task was to popularize the rebellion for his readers and in doing so to signal Soviet approval of support for the cause. Thus he wrote in graphic terms of British brutality, the Sultan's wickedness (not forgetting to titillate his audience with stories about the old Sultan amusing himself with his harem and pornographic films), and the PFLOAG's popularity among the oppressed people. He dwelt on how joyfully his group, the first Soviets to visit Dhofar, had been received, and how proudly people had worn the Lenin and Kremlin badges he had handed out; he did not mention the pervasive Mao badges and little red books which were the mainstay of political indoctrination classes.[4]

Officially, the Vasilev articles were as far as Moscow was willing to go in support of the PFLOAG at the time. Earlier in the year, during Qahtan as-Shaabi's visit in January, Soviet leaders had had the chance to come out in favor; however, the communiqué mentioned only that the existence of the PRSY was in itself a "major contribution to the cause of the Arab peoples' struggle for abolition of colonialism in that area."[5] ("Socialism in One Country"?) This could have been a reflection of as-Shaabi's distaste for the Marxism-Leninism of the PFLOAG, but Soviet reluctance could be seen in the failure of any speech or accompanying article to allude to the Dhofaris' struggle in any way. In their arms deal with the South Yemenis in January 1969, the Soviets may have included some light arms for Dhofar, but very little, if any, reached the PFLOAG. In September its political office in Aden said that most of its weapons were Chinese; of the Soviet Union, it said: "We do not say that the Soviet Union has totally discarded us. We are still hopefully trying in this direction."[6]

Throughout 1970 China continued to be the PFLOAG's main patron; Moscow remained at arm's length, probably because of this close relationship and because of its uncertainty over the PRSY's orientation (uncertainty that was accentuated by Salim Rubay Ali's successful visit to China in August). The Soviets did not react to the appearance in June of a new revolutionary group in central Oman, the National Democratic Front for the Liberation of Oman and the Arab Gulf (NDFLOAG). They did, however, pay some attention to the overthrow in July of the old Sultan by his son Qabus with London's support; this they regarded as another British move in its attempt to shore up its positions in the Gulf region while pretending to leave, and as a move to tighten the reactionaries' noose around the PRSY (now that a conservative government had been installed in Sanaa, and émigré groups threatened Aden from both the YAR and Saudi Arabia). Moscow doubtless linked these conditions with the decision in London and Washington in December 1970 to establish a military base on Diego Garcia in the Indian Ocean.

The Soviets began to take a greater, more open, interest in Dhofar,[7] and possibly more Soviet arms reached the guerrillas via Aden. Nonetheless, it was not until mid-1971, when the Chinese had begun to change their policies in the direction of accommodation with the conservative states of the region (particularly Iran and Kuwait), and the PFLOAG had moderated its radical Marxism-Leninism to try to offset the weakening of its position by Qabus' reforms and amnesty, that Moscow could be seen to have substantially increased its involvement. The development was signalled in June by congratulations to the PFLOAG leadership on the sixth anniversary of the beginning of their fight, from the Soviet Afro-Asian Peoples' Solidarity Committee (AAPSO), and by another series of articles in *Pravda* by Vasilev in August.[8] Then in September for the first time a PFLOAG delegation arrived in Moscow, at the invitation of the Committee. It was evident that the Kremlin was still reluctant to admit complete and open support for the PFLOAG's struggle; thus the invitation by AAPSO, not by the CPSU or the government. At the same time, however, the Kremlin undermined this façade by allowing the delegation to meet openly with the Central Committee's Secretary for Foreign Relations. (Aden radio claimed that the delegation had also had talks with members of the Politbureau, but Moscow did not admit that.[9]) Both sides were satisfied with the meetings. The PFLOAG endorsed the Soviet Union as a friend of the world's oppressed peoples, and the Soviets said they "absolutely" supported the revolution and would give "all possible help" to it.[10] Several weeks later the head of the delegation revealed that the Soviets would double their assistance to the PFLOAG.[11]

Soviet motives for increasing their support were the same as those for increasing their support for the PDRY (see pp. 30-31), particularly the expansion of U.S. naval activity. Added to these were reports of closer Omani-British and Omani-Saudi Arabian relations. By the end of 1971 Moscow was also encouraged by the steep decline in Chinese aid for the Dhofar rebels, and by the unification of the two movements into the Popular Front for the Liberation of Oman and the Arab Gulf (PFLOAG still). The change of name signified that the movement would concentrate more on Oman than the Gulf, something that the Soviets favored.

It was likely the Gulf situation that held Moscow back from complete support. The British withdrew on schedule, the new states in the southern Gulf proclaimed their independence, and the UAE even indicated that it would establish diplomatic relations with the USSR. Moscow wanted good relations with them, and ignored South Yemeni requests that it not recognize them; it wanted good relations with Iran, the dominant power in the Gulf. Thus it could not go too far in support of the guerrilla movement; indeed, it did not follow South Yemen in opposing Oman's successful bid for United Nations membership, although it stopped short of extending full recognition to the Sultan's government. Although they had opened the door for closer relations with PFLOAG in September, the Soviets did not allow that organization to be mentioned during Ali Nasir Muhammad's visit three weeks later; the communiqué alluded only briefly to the "peoples of the Arabian Gulf who are struggling for the complete elimination of . . . colonialism and neocolonialism."[12] There is no doubt that Muhammad wanted a greater commitment, for the Aden regime was united behind the PFLOAG's struggle, and with the Chinese withdrawing, it was carrying the burden of supporting the struggle alone. As 1972 began, Moscow was willing to provide Aden with generous portions of extra weapons to pass on to the PFLOAG, but wished to be a silent partner.

In the first half of 1972 the Soviets gradually let their relationship with the Dhofari movement warm up. In March a broadcast announced for the first time that the "Soviet people . . . supports the just struggle of the people of Dhofar for freedom, independence, and a happy future";[13] however, the reference to "Soviet people" and not the Soviet government, and the fact that it was the 'unofficial' station (Radio Peace and Progress) that was used, indicated that Moscow was not willing to take the final step. The improvement in the relationship was influenced by reports of developing U.S. involvement in Oman, by the signing of the Soviet-Iraqi Treaty in April (which seemed certain to allow Moscow a greater role in the Gulf now that the British had withdrawn), and by the tightening of

Soviet-PDRY relations after the Fifth NF Congress in March. It received a further boost when, at the time of émigré attacks from Saudi Arabian and YAR territory, fighting broke out on the Oman-PDRY border. The Soviets (as the South Yemenis) doubtless saw this fighting, and the fighting which broke out again in the fall, as a manifestation of imperialist and reactionary Arab attempts to crush the PDRY; since Moscow was developing a greater interest in preserving the Aden regime, it was natural for it to encourage the PFLOAG.

At the same time, that group needed and sought much closer ties to the Soviets, for visits to Beijing in July by both Abd al-Fattah Ismail and a PFLOAG delegation had made it clear that China no longer supported the guerrillas;[14] furthermore, a major PFLOAG attack on Mirbat in eastern Dhofar in July was beaten back with devastating losses. In the fall of 1972, Moscow signalled much closer ties by bringing three PFLOAG delegations to the USSR, including one for the 55th anniversary of the October Revolution, but again all three were said to have been invited by unofficial organizations. The group that attended the anniversary celebrations was not given any publicity, and was not reported to have met any Soviet officials; however, it is likely that they had talks with both Soviet officials and Salim Rubay Ali, who was in Moscow at the time. The Soviet-PDRY communiqué on this occasion for the first time came out strongly in support of the national liberation struggle in the Arabian Peninsula, but did not mention the PFLOAG by name.[15] This omission was rectified to some extent when the communiqué of a Soviet party and government delegation's visit to Aden did mention support for the PFLOAG (for the first time in an official Soviet document).[16] The Soviets continued to supply arms to the PFLOAG through its expanded shipments to the PDRY, and in November the Dhofari movement's relations with the socialist community received a significant boost when Ismail signed an agreement with Castro for Cuban officers to train PFLOAG units in South Yemen.

The Soviets accompanied this greater level of indirect involvement[17] with increased publicity in 1973 about the PFLOAG's struggle and reaffirmations of the "Soviet people's" solidarity. Their continuing reluctance to put themselves officially behind the Dhofari movement was perhaps sharpened by the realization that it was being pushed back in the field, and that it was making no headway in spreading its organization even into the rest of Oman. In particular the Soviets were worried by the decision of the Shah, with whom they were assiduously cultivating good relations, to intervene in the Dhofar struggle. This development caused the Soviets to reinterpret (on their own initiative) PFLOAG's objectives, to de-emphasize revolution in the Arab Gulf. Thus, on the occasion of a visit in September by a PFLOAG delegation (on the invitation of the Afro-Asian Solidarity Committee), the Front was said to be pursuing the goal of freeing Oman from "foreign mercenaries" and the "military-imperialist presence."[18] As there was a struggle under way in the PFLOAG's leadership over this very issue, Moscow was evidently indicating its preference for a restricted objective and throwing its support to the more moderate faction.[19] Aden was in no hurry to follow suit; at the end of 1973 Ali Nasir Muhammad pledged complete support for the "struggle of the people of Oman and the Arab Gulf under the leadership of PFLOAG."[20]

However, conditions in the region were changing. The October War had brought the PDRY and the conservative Arab countries closer, and the possibility of large-scale aid appeared. The threat of U.S. reaction to disturbances in the Gulf alarmed both radicals and conservatives, as Washington announced plans to increase its naval presence in the Indian Ocean and to expand the base at Diego Garcia. In December, the Shah, concerned about the security of the Straits of Hormuz and determined to become the policeman of the Gulf, sent an expeditionary force (initially 1,500 men, quickly built up to 4,000, with artillery, helicopter gunships, and transport aircraft) at the Sultan's request; the Iranians provided the foreign forces (mainly British) with the numbers to succeed in gradually confining the Dhofar war to the border area and in cutting supply lines from the PDRY over the next two years.

In Aden these new conditions promoted Salim Rubay Ali's more flexible and moderate tactics (see pp. 53 ff.). In particular, the Iranian intervention focussed attention on Oman, and allowed the PDRY quietly to drop its support of revolution in the Arab Gulf; from the beginning of 1974 it posed as the champion of Arabism, of Omani nationalism against the foreign invaders. In the interests of its new moderation, Aden also strove to create the image of distance between itself and the PFLOAG. In April South Yemeni leaders declared the Dhofar revolution to be strictly an internal Omani matter — the PDRY did not export its revolution.[21] (This declaration had two advantages for Aden: first, it allowed the regime the pretense of noninvolvement, which might help its quest for Arab economic aid; second, this meant that the PDRY could 'legitimately' avoid cooperating with the Arab League's efforts in the spring to mediate an end to the struggle.)

In Moscow, the new conditions presented the Kremlin with a dilemma regarding its relations with Iran, but in general confirmed its policy of keeping the PFLOAG at arms length and of emphasizing that the strugglers were Omani patriots fighting against foreign intervention. (As much as possible, however, the Soviets played down Iran's role, and referred to "foreign intervention" or the British.) The arms-length policy allowed Moscow to deny (on its own and on Aden's behalf) the Sultan's allegations that the PFLOAG was based on imported (communist) ideology. It did not prevent the Soviets from continuing to aid the guerrillas.[22] For the most part, however, the paucity of references to the PFLOAG in its increasingly desperate struggle (including the failure not only to refer to it in the communiqué of Abd al-Fattah Ismail's visit in July, but even to reciprocate his passing reference to it) left the impression of declining Soviet interest in Dhofar. Even the decisions of the Second Congress of PFLOAG in July to devote itself to the struggle in Oman against the Sultan and his foreign helpers, to admit the possibility of other forms of struggle than armed conflict, to de-emphasize scientific socialism and mobilize "all national forces, individuals and classes," and to change its name to the Popular Front for the Liberation of Oman (PFLO),[23] did not raise the level of political support from Moscow, although it favored these moves and may have encouraged them.

Aden's relations with the PFLO in the second half of 1974 depended on the balance of power within the regime between the Ismail and Rubay Ali factions. Ismail kept up his support and doubtless argued for more assistance from both Aden and Moscow; it was perhaps due to his influence that the Voice of Oman was able to increase its broadcast time on Aden radio in September to one hour per night. However, it was Salim Rubay Ali, with his policy of flexibility, moderation, and quest for aid, that was in the ascendancy. Saudi Arabia and the Gulf Arab states were holding out the prospect of hundreds of millions of dollars in aid; one of their conditions was apparently cessation of support for the PFLO, and the PDRY President moved to accommodate them. From October, many of the PFLO's statements were made via Iraq News Agency, an indication that the Voice of Oman was being restricted. As Dhofari fighters came under greater pressure, the PFLO stepped up its appeals for Arab support, and began to criticize Arab states for not opposing Iranian intervention; the only Arab state to be specifically excluded from these attacks was not the PDRY, but Iraq.

Throughout 1975, as the rapprochement with the conservative Arab states progressed, Aden kept its political support of the PFLO at a low level. Ismail spoke in support of the PFLO at a press conference in March, at the time of the NF's Sixth Congress. In May the PFLO appealed publicly to Aden for support. (The fact that the appeal was reported by Aden radio indicates that the regime was split on the issue.) There was no response; although Ismail spoke in support of them again in June on the PFLO's anniversary, Aden radio did not report his speech.

Support did seem to be developing in October as the Unification Congress (itself a victory for Ismail) specifically praised the PFLO. In addition, captured documents[24] indicated that South Yemeni soldiers were in Dhofar in a support function, and PDRY and PDRY-based PFLO artillery began to fire into Dhofar to back up the fighters.

This was, however, a last-ditch response, and as Omani government and allied forces cut the PFLO's last supply lines from the PDRY and began what would be the final offensive in the fall (and as PDRY-Saudi Arabian negotiations were approaching their climax), the Aden regime again distanced itself from the PFLO. PDRY Foreign Minister Muti assured the Arab Foreign Ministers Conference in October that South Yemen would not intervene in the conflict. By this time, Rubay Ali had regained the political initiative, and may have hoped that the Saudis would be successful in their diplomatic efforts to prise the Iranians out of Oman. It also appears that Aden may have been concerned lest the Shah and Sultan take their anticommunism seriously and give their forces the green light to pursue the PFLO into South Yemen.[25] (Iranian planes had attacked the guns firing into Oman.)

Soviet public reaction to the PFLO in 1975 differed from Aden's, sometimes sharply. This was due partly to Moscow's concern about Rubay Ali's more moderate line and its desire to maintain close ties with Ismail. (In any case, public support for the PFLO was an issue on which there must have been pressure from the ideologues in the Kremlin to keep the faith.) However, the different reaction was due more urgently to the visit of Sultan Qabus to Washington in January, during which the United States offered to expedite the sale of anti-tank missiles, and asked for occasional access to the RAF base on Masirah Island.

Moscow seized on rumors in the Arab world (promptly denied by Omani officials, a denial that was accepted in later Soviet reports) that Qabus had actually signed a secret agreement, and launched a media-wide propaganda campaign which lasted into the spring. The campaign had two main themes: first, the alleged U.S. deal was linked to the expansion of Diego Garcia, the MIDLINK naval exercises in November 1974, the reactivating of CENTO, and the Kissinger comments on intervening in the Gulf oil fields, to try to arouse the fears of the Gulf Arab states and Iran and to convince them to abandon the Sultan. The second theme, which produced a remarkable outburst of reports in January and February 1975, was the struggle of the Dhofari patriots against the puppet Qabus, propped up by foreign intervention forces (often now acknowledged to be Iranian, but surprisingly, often claimed to be from the United States as well). The reports invariably claimed that the PFLO fighters were inflicting heavy losses on their opponents, but occasionally, when they quoted a PFLO communiqué directly, it was obvious the fight was going badly, for it was steadily moving closer to the PDRY border.[26] It was clear that the Soviets recognized it was a losing cause, for however much they would have liked to use the PFLO somehow to prevent the Sultan and Washington from joining forces, they did not offer more assistance, nor did they admit Soviet government support. A PFLO delegation visited Moscow in February, again on the invitation of the Afro-Asian Peoples' Solidarity Organization, but despite their critical need, they were not able to claim more support. A long article in *Krasnaia Zvezda* in April excoriated the Sultan and his friends, and praised the PFLO for its social and military accomplishments, but could say only that its struggle "meets with the understanding and support of the peoples of the socialist community."[27]

There followed a hiatus in Soviet publicity until late fall 1975. In the interval, the PFLO received more weapons, including SAMs, but these were apparently provided by Libya.[28] In October, when the PFLO's supply lines had already been cut, and their fight all but ended, the Soviet media launched a brief but intense campaign, ostensibly to show that the Dhofari struggle was continuing ever more successfully, but in fact to trumpet the danger of an attack on the PDRY. The imperialists and reactionaries, they said, wanted nothing better than to destroy the example of progressive social transformation on the Peninsula; Oman was being turned into a base for aggression against democratic Yemen.[29] The Soviets reportedly demonstrated their concern, and their determination to support the PDRY, by allowing Soviet advisers to be directly involved in the artillery attacks from South Yemen.[30]

MOSCOW, ADEN AND OMAN 1976-82: DIVERGING GOALS

Widespread fighting in Dhofar ended, although barrages from PFLO artillery on PDRY soil (apparently without Soviet participation) and occasional guerrilla raids continued. Despite the brave words of the previous months the Dhofari patriots were indeed alone in their struggle. Salim Rubay Ali had completed his approach to Riyadh, and was reported to have agreed to stop Dhofaris from crossing the border and to have accepted Saudi mediation to end the rebellion.[31] The Soviets were slower to abandon the fight, occasionally reporting fierce combat, while also admitting that the insurgents were in an "extremely difficult situation."[32] They were said to have given a small sum of money to the Front, and the Voice of Oman (but not any of the Soviet media) reported that Arab groups in the USSR had founded the "All-Soviet Committee for the Support of the Oman Revolution." A Soviet trade union delegation visiting Aden in March declared its support for "the Omani people under the leadership of the PFLO."

However, after this, Moscow's attention waned. It continued to be concerned about the Iranian forces in Oman and the reported agreement for U.S. forces to use Oman facilities, but did not devote much effort to attacking them. In fact, a broadcast on July 19, 1976, the 19th anniversary of the beginning of the Imam of Oman's rebellion (not the Dhofari rebellion) was very careful not to ascribe to the PFLO any support from the Soviet people, much less the Soviet government; it merely said that the Soviet people expressed "firm conviction that the patriotic Omani forces will emerge victorious."[33]

South Yemen's official policy toward the Dhofari movement continued to be unhelpful for the most part, although the exigencies of the power struggle in Aden hindered consistency and some assistance was rendered to the PFLO. The Front was allowed to hold a mass rally in Aden on its anniversary in June, and a few days later (although significantly not at the rally) Rubay Ali affirmed the PDRYs support of the "just cause of the Omani people" (but not of the PFLO); the "just cause" was not revolution, but expulsion of the foreign invaders.[34] However, in October after the Omani and South Yemeni delegations to the United Nations had engaged in recriminations, Abd al-Fattah Ismail made a fiery attack on the Sultan and pledged Aden's support for the PFLO; there could be, he said, no understanding nor any relations between Oman and the PDRY.[35] An incident in late November illustrates the divergencies in Aden's policies. As the Gulf Foreign Ministers met in Muscat to discuss a Gulf defense arrangement, PDRY forces shot down an Iranian reconnaissance plane (not the first one to have flown over PDRY territory, but the first one to have been shot down). These seemed, on both sides, to be provocative acts; however, Aden damped down its propaganda response to the Iranian action, and a week later quietly turned over the pilot and the wrecked plane to the Saudis.

In the next 18 months, the propaganda positions (and sometimes the actual policies) of the PDRY and the Soviet Union *vis-a-vis* Oman and the PFLO varied considerably. This was due to the ebb and flow of the power struggle in Aden; Rubay Ali in his desire to normalize relations with Saudi Arabia and the Gulf states was apparently willing to sacrifice the PFLO completely and come to terms with the Sultan, while Ismail was opposed on all counts.

For its part, Moscow abandoned the PFLO, except for occasional references to it to preserve the illusion that there was a national liberation movement alive which could be reactivated. The Soviet focus was now the Sultan of Oman, who was reported variously as having given or having decided to give the United States permission to establish a military base on Masirah Island which Soviet commentators claimed could house nuclear submarines and, in time, B-52s.[36] In the first three months of 1977, Soviet concern on this issue led to a feverish attack, both as part of the campaign against U.S. military moves in the Indian Ocean, and as a specific theme. There were many reasons for Soviet concern. First, the weapons they believed could be stationed at Masirah were strategic, threatening the USSR. Second, Soviet involvement in the Horn of Africa was growing more complicated, and the Kremlin was anxious about a further growth in U.S. power in the region. Third, the Sultan, out of conviction and also the need to attract and hold powerful patrons, constantly preached the dangers of communist expansion via Soviet naval presence in the Indian Ocean and positions in the PDRY. For Moscow this was more than an annoyance; there was the possibility that he would be able to convince the other Gulf states and persuade them to join in a Gulf defense agreement (as he had attempted to do at the Gulf Foreign Ministers' conference the previous November). Fourth, there was the danger to Soviet interests of Saudi success in wooing the PDRY and bringing Aden and Muscat together; part of the Soviet strategy for preventing this was to emphasize the threat to Aden from a U.S. base on Omani territory.

This line of reasoning appeared to have little impact on Rubay Ali as he moved toward accommodation. In the communiqué issued after Fidel Castro's visit in March 1977,[37] only the Cuban side expressed support for the PFLO; the South Yemeni side did not even join in the denunciation of foreign bases. A week later (just prior to the Taizz Conference on the Red Sea) Sudan's President Numairi reported success in mediating between Oman and the PDRY, and a report out of Muscat claimed that a senior South Yemeni official would visit to discuss normalization of relations.[38] At this point the Ismail faction was apparently able to intervene. The South Yemeni delegation was not despatched to Muscat and on April 5, 'a responsible source in the Government of the PDRY' firmly denied any intention to normalize relations as long as Oman harbored Iranian forces and foreign military bases.[39] In May during PDRY Foreign Minister Muti's visit to Moscow, both sides supported the "anti-imperialist struggle being waged by the peoples of the Arab Peninsula and the Arab Gulf for political and economic independence";[40] this was probably farther than Rubay Ali wanted to go, but the Soviets doubtless demanded it, partly to sabotage PDRY-Saudi relations. Both sides were content not to express explicit support for the PFLO.

Within South Yemen the Rubay Ali faction was able to keep the wraps on the PFLO; while they allowed a small group of fighters to continue to train under Cuban advisers, and continued to provide broadcasting facilities for the Voice of Oman, they effectively discouraged guerrillas from crossing into Dhofar.[41] At the same time, forces in Aden were working to prevent any further reduction in tensions. In June 1977 both Ismail and Muhammad spoke of "material and political" support for the PFLO. In July Muhammad accused Oman and Iran of carrying out military maneuvers near the border, a direct provocation, he said, and a threat to South Yemen's security.[42] The situation in the region was also contributing to rising tension. Aden was increasingly involved in support of Ethiopia. Despite Salim Rubay Ali's visit to Riyadh at the end of July, relations between the two countries did not develop; the hoped-for Saudi aid was diverted to Oman[43] as the Saudis became disillusioned about their ability to change Aden's orientation. Oman and the PDRY again traded accusations in tough speeches to the United Nations General Assembly in October. Abd al-Fattah Ismail pledged continued support for the Omani national liberation movement during his visit to the Soviet Union in early November.

The Soviet airlift to Ethiopia, and Aden's participation, ended the faint hopes of normalization of PDRY-Omani relations. Both sides became more strident in their comments, and South Yemeni leaders (including Rubay Ali) resumed their pledges of support for the PFLO and their demands for the expulsion of the 'Iranian aggressors.' In reply, the Sultan applauded Sadat's trip to Jerusalem and hosted the Shah's first visit to Oman, during which the two countries agreed to conduct joint naval surveillance in the Straits of Hormuz.

In the first half of 1978, both PDRY and Soviet support for the PFLO and hostility to the Sultan remained high. However, it appeared that the Soviets, heavily committed in the Horn of Africa, were reluctant to vocalize that support, to avoid involvement. The communiqué and reports of Ali Nasir Muhammad's visit to Moscow did not mention the PFLO, either directly or under the rubric of the national liberation movement, although earlier in East Berlin he had proclaimed strong support for it. A *New Times* article on Oman, published during the visit, did not even mention the PFLO, and accepted uncritically the Sultan's statement that he would not give base rights to Washington.[44] Even when the Sultan established diplomatic relations with Beijing in May, with the two sides making it clear that this was in response to what the Chinese called "Soviet hegemonism" in the region, Moscow barely responded.

From the PDRY, however, the PFLO began to expand its activities. Not only did its political communiqués and 'diplomatic' activities in other countries increase, but reports of small-scale military activities again began to appear. As the power struggle approached its climax, the South Yemeni regime underlined its support at a mass PFLO anniversary rally in June; Muhammad made a hard-line speech in support of "the valiant heroic struggle of the brotherly Omani people, led by the PFLO."[45] Two days later, five British citizens (variously described as technicians, engineers, or contract officers) were killed by PFLO guerrillas. Alarmed voices in the Peninsula began to lend credence to PFLO claims that the rebellion was flaring up. The Soviets did not admit this possibility. Aside from publishing a PFLO statement on the anniversary, they ignored both Oman and the PFLO for the rest of the year, even when the Sultan publicly supported the Camp David agreements. In a December meeting of the South Yemeni and Soviet Foreign Ministers, it was Gromyko who appeared to be more anxious for development of good-neighborly relations in the interests of normalizing the situation in the southern Peninsula.[46] (However, an article in a military journal in November listed Oman among the few remaining "active or potential" centers of national liberation war.[47])

In the PDRY as well, support for the PFLO seemed to wane after the resolution of the power struggle in June with the victory of Abd al-Fattah Ismail; a PDRY envoy in the Gulf was reported to have said that Aden was prepared to abandon the PFLO and establish relations with Oman, and in early August, Aden radio suspended the transmission of programs hostile to Oman.[48] This was unexpected, for Ismail was known to be a PFLO supporter. It is possible that the Soviets exercised some restraint here, in view of their interest in making an approach to Riyadh in the fall, and of the Shah's domestic problems. It is more likely that the restraint was due to opposition within the new Aden regime and to Ismail's need to tend to more pressing business. As he consolidated his power, the PDRY again began to support the PFLO; thus the Yemeni Socialist Party in its first congress in October came out in support of the PFLO's struggle. However, PFLO guerrilla activity did not resume.

Moscow's policy of moderation regarding the PFLO seemed to be changing in 1979 as a result of the cataclysmic changes in the region, particularly the fall of the Shah in January and the weakness demonstrated by Saudi Arabia in the war between the Yemens in March. These events seemed to increase the potential for unrest and instability in the Gulf, nowhere more so than in Oman, from which the remaining Iranian troops were removed in February. The Soviets had to tread a fine line, for they wanted to take advantage of this situation, yet they also wished to reassure Kuwait that the Soviet Union wanted Gulf stability, and they still hoped to develop relations with Saudi Arabia. In addition, they did not want the Sultan to be pushed into an even closer relationship with the United States, which expanded its naval presence and went ahead with plans for a rapid deployment force (for which Omani bases would have been ideal).

In light of these contradictory objectives, Soviet policy remained cautious. The propaganda campaign against Qabus was intensified. PFLO communiqués received somewhat more publicity, and the occasional Soviet article claimed that it had "stepped up" its operations. At the end of April, the Soviet Afro-Asian Peoples' Solidarity Committee played host to a PFLO delegation in Moscow. During the highly publicized visit, the Soviet committee expressed "firm support for the just struggle being waged by the Omani patriots" and the Omani side praised Soviet "full solidarity and support";[49] however, no new assistance was promised. In Aden, Abd al-Fattah Ismail was more dedicated to the cause, as was Libya's Colonel Muammar Qadhdhafi; these two donated arms and money, and South Yemeni artillery attacks on Omani positions were reported again. In the first half of 1979 the PFLO apparently was able to mount several small-scale attacks in Dhofar. However, the military operations, combined with the military build-up in South Yemen after the March border war, were counterproductive. Sultan Qabus, more than ever convinced of the communist threat from the Soviet Union and the PDRY, requested arms aid from the United States and began to urge Washington to play a more active role in the Gulf region; the United States responded favorably on arms, and in September sent a military mission to assess Oman's requirements. Qabus also developed a plan, the wisdom of which he was ultimately unable to convince his fellow Gulf rulers, to use the Omani and Western navies to ensure the security of navigation in the Straits of Hormuz. The Soviets reacted with shrill indignation, but, interestingly, did not invoke the threat of the PFLO's struggle;

instead they raised the stakes a notch by referring to Washington's policies in the region as a threat to the security of the PDRY *and the Soviet Union*.[50]

Aden's reactions to the Sultan's moves were affected by an upsurge in the power struggle. Hard on the heels of the PFLO military action in June, Ali Nasir Muhammad's faction was able to secure an agreement for Kuwaiti mediation toward the normalization of PDRY-Omani relations; however, this collapsed with the insistence on preconditions by both Aden (withdrawal of all foreign troops, the Sultan's reconciliation with the PFLO, and an end to his support of Sadat) and Muscat (suspension of PFLO propaganda and activities).[51] Ismail reasserted his authority on this issue in late September with the declaration that Aden would continue to support "the Omani revolution" until these conditions were met. At about this time, the Voice of Oman was allowed to change its name to the Voice of PFLO, a move which seemed to indicate a renewal of Aden's support for the Front. The Soviets probably approved this hard-line stance, in keeping with their concern over growing Omani-U.S. relations, although it was by no means certain that they believed the PFLO could be reactivated. However, it was evident from the failure of the communiqués of both Kosygin's visit to Aden in September 1979 and Ismail's visit to Moscow in October to mention Oman, that there was a divergence of opinion in Aden over tactics. The Muhammad faction appeared to want to explore a more moderate approach.[52]

Regional events cancelled any hope of this. All factions in Aden were concerned by the continuous stationing of two U.S. task forces in the Indian Ocean after the hostage crisis began in Teheran. The invasion of Afghanistan, followed by the enunciation of the Carter Doctrine and Washington's related decision to seek access to facilities for prepositioning material for the Rapid Deployment Force, completed the repolarization of the Peninsula. Alarmed by the invasion, by the dramatic increase in great power military presence in the region, by the Soviet-PDRY Treaty, and the subsequent upgrading of South Yemen's armaments, Sultan Qabus announced in early spring 1980 his intention to offer Washington access to Omani military facilities in return for U.S. arms.[53]

Moscow responded with an extensive and bitter propaganda campaign aimed at the fears of Oman's neighbors, the burden of which was that Qabus was cooperating with the United States to enable Washington to gain control of the Persian Gulf and its resources and to threaten the Soviet Union. The South Yemeni response was similar, both before and after Ali Nasir Muhammad's takeover in April. In addition, the Aden regime restated its support of the PFLO; one of the first visitors Muhammad received after he took control was a member of the PFLO's Executive Committee, to whom he "pointed out the importance of developing militant relations between the PFLO and the YSP."[54] Interestingly, Moscow joined in invoking the PFLO for a few days after Oman signed its military access agreement with the United States in June; the PFLO was quoted and discussed, and the Afro-Asian Peoples' Solidarity Organization expressed the "invariable solidarity" of the Soviet people with the Omani patriots struggle.[55] However, the Soviets quickly abandoned this tack when they realized that the agreement was less than they had feared,[56] and that it (and the United States' unauthorized use of Masirah Island in its abortive effort to free the hostages in late April) had disturbed Oman's friends on the Peninsula as much as its enemies.

In Aden, however, the PFLO's allies prevailed; the YSP expressed its support at its session at the end of June 1980 for "the struggle of the heroic Omani people, led by the PFLO."[57] Although Ali Nasir appeared to be pursuing a more moderate policy when he visited most of the peninsula countries in early July, the failure of this tactic threw him back on the attack. Rejecting the possibility of further Kuwaiti mediation because of the Sultan's agreement to allow the United States "to use Omani territory as a military base," he called on all Arabs to adopt a "resolute common stand against the agent regime in Oman."[58] Once again he received the chairman of the PFLO Executive Committee; while reiterating Aden's support for the PFLO, he discussed

> the relations between the YSP and the PFLO concerning their struggle, and methods of developing them further, in promotion of the common struggle of the fraternal Yemeni and Omani peoples.[59]

A month later he referred to the Sultan's regime as "intolerable."[60]

Soviet and South Yemeni policies toward Oman continued to work in tandem in the first four months of 1981, but neither altered its attitude toward the PFLO. Both countries were worried about the inclusion of Oman in the Gulf Cooperation Council, fearing that the Sultan might succeed in overriding Kuwait's objections to U.S.

military access to other Gulf facilities, or even in formally linking the GCC to the United States in a defense agreement. Their worries were underlined by the U.S.-Omani exercises in February to test communications facilities for a deployment of forces in the Gulf zone.

The Soviets responded to the GCC's formation with mildly negative notices, and to Oman and its military cooperation with the United States with vigorous antagonism. Interestingly, though, they chose not to use the PFLO as an instrument of attack. Although the U.S.-Omani exercises took place during the 26th CPSU Congress, the PFLO delegation was not given a chance to speak, nor indeed any publicity. It is likely that the Soviets had decided that supporting the PFLO could only add to suspicions about the USSR in the region, and that diplomacy and propaganda would give them a better chance at foiling Muscat's and Washington's plans. Thus after the GCC rejected the Sultan's proposal for military cooperation with the United States and other Western countries, the Soviets muted their criticism of the Council. Soviet criticism of Oman remained strong, but the brunt of Moscow's anger was directed at the United States for its activities in bolstering positions in Egypt, Somalia, and Oman, increasing its naval forces in the Indian Ocean, and expanding its Diego Garcia base.

The PDRY also attacked the formation of the GCC and Oman's inclusion, and attempted to sponsor a regional conference to forestall the event. When this tactic failed, Ali Nasir Muhammad threatened in mid-February 1981 to resume aid to the PFLO. Aden hosted a meeting of liberation movements to generate support for the PFLO and the PDRY, and generally gave more publicity to the Front. Tension built between the countries, but when fighting broke out on the border in February it involved not the PFLO but PDRY regular troops. There were several incidents in the second half of February and again in late March; both sides protested to the Arab League about alleged border incursions, and Aden declared it to be "the duty of all Arabs to eliminate the treacherous regime" in Oman.[61] It was widely felt that these incidents were exaggerated by both sides to further their respective interests; consequently, there was little reaction.

The Soviets did not report the clashes despite their hostility toward the Sultan; one analyst has speculated (based on reports of the visit of Kuwait's Foreign Minister to Moscow in late April 1981) that they had decided to shift tactics and would encourage Aden to ease the tension with Oman and come to some sort of *modus vivendi* with the Sultan.[62] The Kuwaiti Foreign Minister had suggested that this tactic would work because Qabus had pledged to cancel his agreement with the United States if the conflict with the PDRY were resolved. It is doubtful that Moscow would have taken the Sultan at his word on this issue, especially as he was showing no signs of relaxing his determined anti-Soviet campaign.[63] However, since the Soviets had implied to the Kuwaitis that if the Gulf states established relations with the USSR, Moscow would seek to relieve PDRY-Omani tensions,[64] it seems likely that they saw some hope of improving relations and decided to try to nourish it.[65] There was also, as always, the concern that too much tension with the PDRY would push the Sultan further into Washington's embrace. [At the same time there was no question of reducing support for Aden; the highly publicized naval visit during the GCC's founding conference in May, as well as the (almost certain) participation of the Soviets in the discussions of the PDRY, Libya, and Ethiopia which led to the Tripartite Alliance, were proof of that.] Nothing came of Soviet moves (if indeed any had occurred) behind the scenes, or of Kuwaiti-UAE mediation in the spring. Fighting flared up again on the border in mid-June. Moscow again did not comment on the fighting, but apparently abandoned its (none-too-visible) 'carrot' approach; opting for the surer prospect of an agreement between its friends, it supported the signing of the Tripartite Alliance in August.

The signing of this pact immediately raised tensions and suspicions on the peninsula, leading a GCC summit conference in November 1981 to agree to Oman's call for defense cooperation. Nevertheless, in retrospect it can also be seen as the beginning of Aden's abandonment of the PFLO,[66] and of Ali Nasir's move toward accommodation with Oman. Throughout the fall, he concentrated on reassuring the other members of the Council about the nonaggressive nature of the Tripartite Alliance. Kuwait resumed its attempt to mediate between Oman and the PDRY, and the South Yemeni leader rewarded it by lowering tensions in late December by denying that mediation efforts had failed and insisting that South Yemen was ready to negotiate all outstanding issues[67] (a remarkable statement, considering the PDRY's long-standing intransigence over the issue of foreign presence); the usual preconditions were not mentioned. This was the more extraordinary since in early December Aden had accused Oman of conducting a helicopter raid into the PDRY, and just after that Omani forces had participated in amphibious landing maneuvers with 1,000 Marines as part of the United States' 'Bright Star' military exercises in the Middle East. Although Aden was clearly angered and worried by the exercises, South Yemeni (and PFLO, interestingly) propaganda was not as virulent or pervasive as might have been expected.

Ali Nasir's restraint regarding Oman was not matched by Moscow. The Soviet media launched a burst of vituperation about Oman's participation in 'Bright Star,' and again in early February 1982 about U.S. Secretary of Defense Weinberger's visit to Oman; they stressed the size and cost of U.S. 'bases' in Oman and the Sultan's willingness to do Washington's bidding.[68] On the other hand, Ali Nasir did not mention Weinberger's trip, even in his speech to the World Peace Council conference in Aden at the same time; in that speech he thoroughly castigated the United States for its military activities and bases in the Indian Ocean region, but did not once mention Oman. In early March he travelled to the UAE to discuss the Oman-PDRY dispute and the security situation in the Gulf. On his return he received a PFLO delegation; although they were reported to have discussed the "militant relations" between the PFLO and YSP,[69] Ali Nasir neither reiterated support for the Front nor attacked the Sultan, and it seems more likely that the meeting was to inform them of Aden's decision to pursue a normalization agreement with Oman.

The way to this agreement was opened by the catastrophic flooding in the PDRY in late March 1982. The desperate need for aid and the generous emergency relief of the oil states reduced domestic opposition to Ali Nasir's more pragmatic policy. His foreign minister visited the Gulf states in April. In early May, after a round of mediation visits by the foreign ministers of Kuwait and the UAE, it was announced that the PDRY and Oman had agreed to meet in Kuwait on June 5. On the eve of the meeting, however, Aden asked for a postponement *sine die*, claiming that Oman had downgraded its representation and was concentrating military forces along their border.[70] The Kuwaitis did not accept those excuses, and it appears that renewed opposition within the regime was behind the delay. (Evidence of this came a few days later with Aden radio's broadcast on the PFLO's anniversary, in which a PFLO representative praised the PDRYs unqualified support of the "Omani revolution.") At the same time the PFLO's Third Congress in Aden expressed the Front's "determination to carry on the struggle for the liberation of Oman from feudal oppression and imperialist domination, from the corrupt regime of Qabus. . . ."[71] Interestingly, however, this conference was not publicized in Aden, not even by Voice of PFLO, until mid-August.

By the end of June, Ali Nasir had regained sufficient strength to win acceptance for his Omani initiative. On July 1 the Kuwait talks began, and after five days of discussion on noninterference, on foreign military presence, on the cessation of propaganda campaigns, and on the establishment of diplomatic relations, the two sides agreed to meet again at a later, unspecified date. While this may not have seemed like a breakthrough, events showed that Aden had adopted a more accommodating policy. At the end of July, whether because of Aden's desire for a new vehicle with which to apply political pressure on Muscat or because the Front could see that Aden was abandoning it, the PFLO announced that it was sponsoring the formation of a new organization, the United Omani National Front (UONF), a nationalist organization which abandoned revolutionary Marxist language and focussed on the attainment of democracy and especially on the rejection of "foreign dominance" in economic, political, and military matters; it stopped short of calling for the Sultan's overthrow.[72] However the UONF never took hold, and the PFLO continued its broadcasts (a situation which indicated that it still had powerful friends in the Aden regime).

Moscow's policy toward Oman during this period was not coincident with Aden's, nor did it give any indication that the Soviets agreed with Ali Nasir's course. At the end of May (at the time when Ali Nasir was having problems over the proposed Kuwait meeting), a delegation from the Organization of Omani Youths attended the 19th Congress of the Komsomol and returned with pledges of support.[73] In mid-June TASS publicized the PFLO's Third Congress and its praise for the friendship and cooperation of the Soviet Union. The few references in the Soviet media to Oman in the summer and early fall were hostile, and dwelt on the alleged U.S. bases and on Oman's willingness to participate in the United States' fall maneuvers, code-named 'Jade Tiger.' Moscow did not mention, either directly or indirectly, the PDRY-Omani talks.

It is significant that the subject was also ignored in the speeches and documents pertaining to Muhammad's visit to Moscow in September 1982. This was a highly successful visit which seemed to put Ali Nasir in the front rank of the USSR's Third World allies. Although the talks concentrated on the Lebanese and PLO crises, their content was wide ranging and each side praised the other's policies; it would have been a natural time for the Soviet leaders to praise the PDRY's move toward peaceful relations with its neighbors, as they did with reference to inter-Yemeni affairs. Nevertheless, the topic was not mentioned in the communiqué.[74] Nor did Muhammad refer to it in his speeches. He thus ignored a policy which could have great significance for conditions in the Arabian Peninsula and Indian Ocean and for the positions of both the PDRY and the Soviet Union in the region; he ignored a policy which he was actively pursuing despite internal opposition, a policy for which Soviet support would have undercut his opponents. It seems reasonable to conclude that his omission was due to Soviet unhappiness about his policy. This conclusion is borne out by a Moscow radio broadcast just four days after the end of the visit; Oman, it declared was a "satellite" of the United States, a "loyal stooge," which under the pretext of the "Soviet threat" would participate in the 'Jade Tiger' exercises.[75]

Aden chose to ignore Omani participation in 'Jade Tiger' and other evidence of close Oman-U.S. ties;[76] the Sultan, helpfully, was trying to smother publicity about the exercises, while the Soviets and the United States persisted in publicizing them. Negotiations between the two Peninsula countries continued; they came to a head on October 25 with the signature by their foreign ministers of a formal agreement (1) to demarcate their border, (2) not to allow "any hostile act" to emanate from their territory, or foreign forces to use their territories for attacks on the other, (3) to cease propaganda attacks, and (4) to exchange diplomats.[77]

THE ANDROPOV MONTHS (NOVEMBER 1982 TO FEBRUARY 1984)

The agreement was received with apparently unanimous approval in Aden. The media praised it, despite the Sultan's failure to fulfill any of South Yemen's former preconditions. Even Oman's participation in the 'Jade Tiger' exercise, which included U.S. aircraft landings at the Thumrait airfield in Dhofar, generated only a mild reaction from Aden, which blamed Washington not Muscat; it did not prevent Muhammad from sending a friendly reply to Qabus' message on the PDRY's national day. The Voice of PFLO, which might have been used to express opposition, for a week devoted itself to music and theoretical discussions, and then went off the air completely.[78] Ali Nasir's policy of moderation, springing from a concern that regional instability could bring greater U.S. involvement in Oman,[79] and from South Yemen's desperate need for aid, was dominant.

Moscow recognized this and acquiesced, albeit with rather poor grace. As the agreement was being signed, *New Times* printed a rare article on Oman, attacking Sultan Qabus for turning his country into "a dangerous beachhead of American militarism."[80] *Pravda's* announcement of the agreement was brief, and contained no praise for the normalization of relations; nor did any other Soviet report. Instead, Moscow broadcasts harped on the 'Jade Tiger' exercises and on the United States' alleged desire for military control of the Indian Ocean and Persian Gulf region, in fulfillment of which Oman was said to be providing permanent bases. The threat from the Rapid Deployment Force (RDF) was particularly stressed.

The cause of Soviet disquiet was not obvious. Moscow may have been worried at the idea (expressed by a Kuwait Foreign Ministry Undersecretary) that both South Yemen and Oman would refrain from depending on "world powers" for their protection.[81] While (if true) this held the promise of great opportunities, it also carried a threat to Soviet positions in South Yemen, should Muhammad go too far. In all likelihood the Soviets preferred the security of existing positions.[82]

Relations between Moscow and Aden remained cool as South Yemeni and Omani delegations began to meet in Abu Dhabi in an 'atmosphere of friendliness and understanding' to implement the normalization agreement, starting with border demarcation. South Yemeni spokesmen refrained from criticizing the continuation of close Omani-U.S. ties, and it was expected that the exchange of ambassadors would take place momentarily. However, in mid-April 1983 Sultan Qabus paid a very friendly visit to Washington, during which he was reported to have agreed, under "very specific conditions," to grant U.S. forces access to the Omani facilities being developed by the U.S.[83] He reaffirmed this agreement on several occasions, indicating that the United States was a friend on whom to fall back if the need arose. This appeared to strengthen the hardliners in Aden; the border demarcation committee meeting in May was postponed indefinitely. The door was not completely closed; the Supreme People's Council meeting in early May approved the PDRY's moderate policy; even Oman's support of the Israel-Lebanon agreement and public declaration favoring nonbelligerency with Israel, and the announcement that U.S. forces would conduct military exercises ('Bright Star 83') in Oman in August did not cause a final break. However, the border talks were postponed again.

The Soviets said nothing about PDRY-Oman relations, or even, strangely, about Qabus' visit to Washington. They did, however, let their irritation show at Oman's continuing anti-Soviet statements,[84] and publicized the 'Bright Star' exercises. The lack of reference to Oman in the communiqué issued after Muhammad's brief visit to Moscow in September, even though Soviet-PDRY relations had improved, and even though Ali Nasir had already decided to move ahead with normalization, seems to indicate that Moscow had serious reservations.

Nevertheless, Ali Nasir did proceed, ignoring the obvious refusal of the Sultan to loosen his ties with Washington and the failure of the border demarcation committee to achieve substantive progress; on October 27, Aden and Muscat announced they had established diplomatic relations and would exchange ambassadors. Muhammad's reasons were as usual not articulated, but may have been related to concern over evidence of increasing GCC cohesion in defense matters (the GCC held its first joint army maneuvers in October) and willingness to commit major funding for military aid to Oman;[85] they may also have been related to the possibility of Saudi economic aid commitments.

After the establishment of diplomatic ties, PDRY-Oman relations remained stable. Omani spokesmen continued to insist that Moscow had in the past interfered in Oman's internal affairs and must assure Oman that it would not do so again. Aden did not reciprocate with attacks on Washington, even when the United States declared its interest in cooperating in the defense of the Straits of Hormuz. On their national days in 1983 both Ali Nasir and Qabus wished each other "robust health and, happiness" and their "fraternal" peoples progress and prosperity, ending with the hope that relations would be further developed.[86]

NOTES

1. Cf. H.S.H. Behbehani, *China's Foreign Policy in the Arab World 1955 - 1975* (London: Kegan Paul International, 1981), pp. 176-86.
2. Cf. F. Halliday, *Arabia Without Sultans* (New York: Penquin Books, 1974), chs. 10-11; J.B. Kelly, *Arabia, the Gulf and the West* (New York: Basic Books, 1980), pp. 134-48.
3. A. Vasilev, "Buntuiushchie gory Dofara," *Pravda*, September 29, 1969; "Partizanskimi tropami Dofara," *Pravda*, October 4, 1969; "My ne raby," *Pravda*, October 12, 1969; the first two articles can be found in *CDSP* 21 (October 22, 1969): 5-6.
4. In his book about his experiences (published in 1974 after the Dhofari movement was firmly in the Soviet camp), Vasilev acknowledged seeing Mao badges and little red books, but claimed rather defensively that they had not had any impact on the movement. A.M. Vasilev, *Puteshestvie v 'Araviia Feliks'* (Moscow: Iz. Molodaia Gvardiia, 1974), pp. 35-36.
5. *FBIS/USSR*, February 10, 1969, p. A35.
6. S. Page, *The USSR and Arabia* (London, Central Asian Research Centre, 1971), p. 116.
7. TASS interviewed a PFLOAG representative in Aden in January, and a Soviet film crew allegedly shot a documentary ("The Hot Wind of Freedom") on location in Dhofar in April.
8. *CDSP* 23 (August 31, 1971): 15-16. Cf. also A. Vasilev "Rebels against Slavery," *New Times*, no. 38 (September), 1971, pp. 27-30.
9. *FBIS/MENA*, September 17, 1971, p. B1.
10. *FBIS/USSR*, September 24, 1971, p. B1.
11. *USSR and Third World* 1 (September 20 - October 24, 1971): 528.
12. *FBIS/USSR*, October 12, 1971, pp. B17-19.
13. *FBIS/USSR*, March 24, 1972, pp. B6-7.
14. H.S.H. Behbehani, op. cit., pp. 185-6.
15. *FBIS/USSR*, November 29, 1972, p. B10.
16. *FBIS/MENA*, December 8, 1972, p. B3.
17. In July 1973 the first and only Soviet direct action in support of the Dhofar war took place; this was a sealift of PFLOAG units from Aden to the eastern PDRY (probably to Hauf) whence they crossed into Dhofar. It may well have served in part as an exercise for Soviet naval units, as well as assistance to the movement. It was not publicized by any of the parties, and not repeated; thus it did not represent a leap in Soviet involvement. Cf. B. Dismukes and J.M. McConnell (eds.), *Soviet Naval Diplomacy* (New York: Pergamon Press, 1979), p. 137.
18. *FBIS/USSR*, September 20, 1973, pp. F5-6.
19. H.M. Hensel, "Soviet Policy towards the Rebellion in Dhofar," *Asian Affairs* 13 (June 1982): 195-6.
20. *FBIS/MENA*, November 30, 1973, p. B2.
21. *FBIS/USSR*, April 19, 1974, p. F5; interestingly, the latter part of this statement was not broadcast in Aden. *FBIS/MENA*, April 10, 1974, p. C2.

22. Cf. D.L. Price, *Oman, Insurgency and Development* (Conflict Studies no. 53) (London: Institute for the Study of Conflict, 1975), pp. 7, 16-17; PFLOAG fighters probably began to go to the USSR for training in early 1974.

23. The National Program of the PFLO, in The Gulf Committee, *Documents of the National Struggle in Oman and the Arabian Gulf* (London: The Gulf Committee, 1974), pp. 95-104.

24. *FBIS/MENA*, July 3, 1975, p. C2; *FBIS/MENA*, October 30, 1975, p. C2.

25. *FBIS/MENA*, December 29, 1975, p. C3. Cf. statements on Teheran radio, October 20, 1975, in *FBIS/MENA*, October 21, 1975, p. B1 and *Kurier* (Vienna), April 22, 1975, in *FBIS/MENA*, April 23, 1975, pp. C1-3.

26. Compare Radio Peace and Progress, January 21, 1975, in *FBIS/USSR*, January 23, 1975, pp. F4-5, with *Pravda*, January 22, 1975, and *Pravda*, October 21, 1975.

27. *FBIS/USSR*, April 28, 1975, pp. F6-8.

28. A. Haselkorn, *The Evolution of Soviet Security Strategy 1965-1975* (New York: Crane, Russak, 1978), p. 78 fn. 97.

29. *USSR and Third World* 5 (July 7 - December 31, 1975): 382; *FBIS/USSR*, November 10, 1975, pp. F4-5.

30. J.E. Peterson, "Guerrilla Warfare and Ideological Confrontation in Arabian Peninsula: The Rebellion in Dhufar," *World Affairs* (Spring 1977): 289.

31. *FBIS/MENA*, March 16, 1976, p. C1; Sultan Qabus, interviewed in *Le Monde*, November 19, 1976.

32. A. Filippov, "Patrioty nanosiat udary," *Pravda*, April 6, 1976, p. 5; *FBIS/USSR*, January 15, 1976, pp. F7-9.

33. *FBIS/USSR*, July 20, 1976, p. F7.

34. *FBIS/MENA*, June 22, 1976, p. C5.

35. *FBIS/MENA*, October 18, 1976, p. C4.

36. *FBIS/USSR*, January 12, 1977, pp. F4-5. The Sultan denied the reports, but then refuelled the suspicion by saying that "if the U.S. or any friend asked for transit rights or refuelling facilities, we are disposed to grant it." *Washington Post*, January 24, 1977.

37. The communiqués can be found in *FBIS/MENA*, March 14, 1977, p. C6.

38. *FBIS/MENA*, March 25, 1977, p. C1, *Arab Report and Record*, March 16-31, 1977, p. 222-3.

39. *FBIS/MENA*, April 7, 1977, p. C1.

40. *FBIS/USSR*, May 16, 1977, p. F1.

41. *Arabia and the Gulf* 1 (May 9, 1977): 10-11. The PFLO issued no military communiqués between July 1977 and the end of February 1978.

42. *Arabia and the Gulf* 1 (June 27, 1977): 15; *Arab Report and Record*, July 1-15, 1977, p. 564. Iran, by this time, had reduced its contingent to approximately 1,000 men, mostly in support services.

43. *Arab Report and Record*, July 16-31, 1977, p. 603.

44. Iu. Tiunkov, "Joyous Morning Has Yet to Come," *New Times*, no. 5 (February), 1978, pp. 26-8.

45. *FBIS/MENA*, June 9, 1978, p. C3.
46. *FBIS/USSR*, December 5, 1978, p. F1.
47. Col. E. Rybkin, "The 25th CPSU Congress and Wars of Liberation of the Contemporary Era," *Voenno-Istoricheskii Zhurnal*, no. 11 (November), 1978, pp. 10-17, in *Strategic Review* 8 (Winter 1980): 80.
48. *FBIS/MENA*, July 10, 1978, p. C1; *FBIS/MENA*, August 15, 1978, p. C3.
49. *FBIS/MENA*, April 30, 1979, p. C1.
50. *Izvestiia*, October 5, 1979; *FBIS/USSR*, June 5, 1979, p. A2.
51. *FBIS/MENA*, July 3, 1979, p. C1; *FBIS/MENA*, October 29, 1979, p. C1; *MECS 1979-80*, p. 416.
52. In January 1980, the PDRY Foreign Minister Salim Salih Muhammad welcomed Kuwait's mediation efforts; *FBIS/MENA*, January 14, 1980, p. C11. However, Aden did not relax its preconditions.
53. *FBIS/MENA*, February 22, 1980, pp. C1-9.
54. *FBIS/MENA*, April 25, 1980, p. C7.
55. *FBIS/USSR*, June 9, 1980, p. H1; *FBIS/USSR*, June 10, 1980, pp. H1-2; *SWB*, SU/6441/A4/2.
56. The agreement did not allow automatic access to facilities, nor did it include storage facilities for prepositioned supplies for the RDF.
57. *FBIS/MENA*, June 27, 1980, p. C4.
58. Quoted in *MECS 1979-80*, pp. 667, 700.
59. *FBIS/MENA*, July 17, 1980, p. C3.
60. *FBIS/MENA*, August 29, 1980, p. C4.
61. *MECS 1979-80*, p. 721.
62. A. Yodfat, *The Soviet Union and the Arabian Peninsula* (New York: St. Martin's Press, 1983), p. 137.
63. Cf. *FBIS/MENA*, May 5, 1981, p. C2; *FBIS/MENA*, July 2, 1981, pp. C1-2.
64; This was reported by the Saudi Foreign Minister. Cited in A. Yodfat, op. cit., p. 137.
65. Moscow may have been trying to take advantage of the Bekaa Valley missile crisis, during which the Saudis had come out in support of Syria, and the strain in U.S.-Saudi relations over congressional opposition to the sale of AWACS to Riyadh.
66. The communiqué accompanying the signature of the pact attacked Oman, but did not mention the PFLO, despite Qadhdhafi's recent strong support of that organization. *FBIS/MENA*, August 28, 1981, p. Q3.
67. *MECS 1981-82*, p. 677.
68. *FBIS/USSR*, February 11, 1982, p. H1; V. Vinogradov, "Forpost agressii u Persidskogo zaliva," *Krasnaia Zvezda*, January 21, 1982.
69. *FBIS/MENA*, March 11, 1982, p. C12.
70. F. Halliday, "Aden and Muscat still far apart," *The Middle East*, no. 93 (July 1982): 12.
71. *FBIS/USSR*, June 21, 1982, p. H5.
72. *FBIS/MENA*, July 30, 1982, p. C4.
73. *FBIS/MENA*, May 28, 1982, pp. C2-3.

74. Cf. *FBIS/USSR*, September 17, 1982, pp. H1-4.
75. *FBIS/USSR*, September 21, 1982, pp. H10-11.
76. Cf. *Time*, October 25, 1982, pp. 47-8.
77. The text is in *FBIS/MENA*, November 16, 1982, p. C3.
78. Editorial note in *FBIS/MENA*, November 9, 1982, p. ii
79. Cf. The interview given by the PDRY's Ambassador to the U.N. al-Ashtal to *The Middle East*, no. 98 (December 1982): 18-19.
80. D. Zgersky, "Oman's 'Open Door'," *New Times*, no. 44 (October), 1982, p. 15.
81. *FBIS/MENA*, November 3, 1982, p. C2.
82. It has also been suggested in Western intelligence circles that the Soviets saw some advantage to normalization, in that it might facilitate Soviet overtures to the Gulf states, but that the Kremlin was annoyed because it felt that Aden had not consulted it sufficiently. I have not found evidence of this in Soviet sources.
83. *Middle East Economic Digest* 27 (April 15-21, 1983): 57.
84. *FBIS/USSR*, July 19, 1983, pp. H4-5.
85. *Defense & Foreign Affairs Weekly* 9 (September 5-11, 1983): 1; the aid and the maneuvers were directed at the perceived threat from Iran, but the South Yemenis (who were supporting Iran in the Gulf War) could not but be nervous at the prospect of a much stronger, hostile Oman.
86. *FBIS/MENA*, November 21, 1983, p. C2; *FBIS/MENA*, November 30, 1983, p. C2.

PART III

MOSCOW AND THE YAR: THE PROGRESS OF RELATIONS AND THE YEMENI UNITY ISSUE

6

MOSCOW AND THE YAR: RELATIONS AT LOW EBB (1970-77)

FROM THE NATIONAL RECONCILIATION (1970) TO AL-HAMDI'S COUP (JUNE 1974)

By mid-1970, the conservatism of Northern Yemen's society had prevailed; although the Yemen Arab Republic (YAR) still existed, its potential as a radical force in the peninsula had been smothered by the renewed power of the tribes, the machinations of Riyadh, and the pressing need for Saudi financial aid. By then an alternative had presented itself in the south, a radical regime which would pursue policies compatible with Soviet interests in the region (including access to better military facilities), and Moscow quickly shifted its focus southward.

The shift, although inevitable because of the conservative trend of the Sanaa regime and the affinity between the PRSY and the USSR, made it more difficult for Moscow to pursue its objectives in the YAR[1] and in the Red Sea region. The two Yemen regimes quickly fell into the antagonism of the conservative and the radical, fed by Aden's revolutionary pronouncements and by border attacks mounted by émigré forces against South Yemen, some of which emanated from YAR territory. More and more, Moscow was forced to choose between the two. After mid-1969 Soviet military aid to the PRSY grew rapidly, while supplies to the YAR were curtailed. Economic aid was continued within existing programs (partly because the Soviets did not want to leave the field open to the Chinese, who were running very effective economic and medical aid programs), but new credits went to South Yemen. The Soviets scaled down their objectives in the north: to develop as good state-to-state relations as were possible in these changed circumstances; to try to persuade Sanaa not to move closer to the West (or China); to encourage good relations between the Yemens, at the very least to keep YAR territory from being used by the 'imperialists and their agents' to attack South Yemen. Soviet objectives in the Red Sea region were not changed by the shift; they were better served by Moscow's expanding activity and military presence in Egypt and the Sudan. In the Indian Ocean the addition of South Yemen's facilities to those being prepared in Somalia was a major boost to Soviet policy in the region, far outweighing the deterioration in relations with the YAR.

There was always, of course, the possibility that the latter could be reversed. In both Yemens, cultural, religious, and tribal ties in some regions have for decades lent validity to the myth that southwest Arabia constitutes a single Yemeni state; there seems to be substantial popular support for the unification of the two parts, and both regimes gain internal legitimacy from their espousal of Yemen unity.[2] A united Yemen might present the Soviets with the opportunity to reestablish themselves in the north, in a state which would be the largest (in population) on the peninsula and which would occupy a strategic position on the Red Sea littoral.

The mystique of Yemeni unity has clearly been (and remains) a powerful motivation for nationalists in both North and South Yemen. In the 1960s it was given fresh impetus by the 1962 North Yemen revolution and the vociferous support for it in Aden, by the YAR's support of the struggle to expel Britain from the south, by the NLF's use of North Yemen territory for supply and sanctuary during its early fights in the border shaikhdoms, and by the despatch of PRSY troops to help defend Sanaa.

Unity talks were begun in Sanaa in 1968, but came to nought. Mistrust blossomed quickly, as thousands fled South Yemen to become émigré forces which were financed and armed by Saudi Arabia to bring down the radicals in Aden. There is no evidence that the Sanaa government encouraged these activities; indeed its writ did not reach into parts of the YAR. However, the fact of its growing conservatism and its eventual reconciliation with Saudi Arabia in early 1970 were enough to convince Aden that it had forsaken the ideals of the revolution and joined the imperialist camp.[3] On the other hand Sanaa felt threatened by the radical pronouncements of the NLF's Fourth Congress in March 1968, by the victory of the radicals in June 1969, and by rebellious leftist North Yemeni military personnel who fled into the PRSY in early 1968, set up camps in the border areas, and proceeded with their own raids and mine-laying forays. Finally, one should not discount the factor of power. Both groups had gained power after arduous struggle, and neither was willing to relinquish control and play a junior role in a system abhorrent to it.

Moscow was in an impossible situation: unification would be in its interest only if the NLF dominated the new state, and this was improbable given the forces in the YAR and Saudi Arabia arrayed against it. The Soviets therefore ignored the unity issue and indicated its preference between the two states by cutting off military aid to the YAR and increasing its involvement in the PRSY. However, despite growing tension on the Yemen border throughout 1970, 1971, and 1972, and the tightening of YAR-Saudi Arabia ties and development of YAR-West relations,[4] the Soviets maintained as friendly relations as possible with Sanaa. The Sanaa regime as well had a stake in preventing a total disintegration of relations. The armed forces still used Soviet weapons and were not eager to switch; the Soviets might be useful in reining in the radicals in South Yemen; and no North Yemeni wants to be tied too tightly, much less exclusively, to Saudi Arabia. Therefore, Soviet economic aid projects continued, and approximately 100 Soviet military advisers stayed in the country training military units.[5] YAR religious delegations visited Soviet Central Asia; they praised the "freedom of religious liberty" in the USSR and thanked the Soviets for their assistance to the Arab people.[6] On the anniversary of the October Revolution, YAR Prime Minister Muhsin al-Ayni sent a friendly telegram which reaffirmed that Soviet-YAR ties of friendship and cooperation would remain strong.

However, more and more these relations were hostage to the condition of North-South Yemeni relations and to events in South Yemen. Progress toward unity seemed to be gathering momentum in the fall of 1970 with the establishment of joint committees; however, it was abruptly halted when the PRSY's new constitution changed its name to the People's Democratic Republic of Yemen, thus laying claim to Aden's legitimate control over a unified, socialist

Yemen. The YAR, not unnaturally, rejected this idea; its constitution, which was adopted a few weeks later, affirmed the sacred goal of Yemen unity, but set out the idea of a traditional state based on Islamic values. Relations deteriorated, and military incidents on the border grew more frequent and serious in 1971.

Partly because of this, relations between Sanaa and Moscow did not improve. The Soviets were beginning to place a higher value on their South Yemeni friends, and although they were careful publicly to blame only Saudi Arabia and the imperialists for the émigré attacks, the fact that some of these originated on North Yemeni territory obviously made Sanaa suspect. With the choice of a conservative three-man Republican Council to head the state, and the appointment of a conservative as Prime Minister, the government of the YAR became less palatable to Moscow; the arrival of more Saudi economic aid and weapons to bolster North Yemen's aging Soviet stocks served to quicken this process. For its part, Sanaa was unhappy with growing evidence of Soviet support for the PDRY. In mid-January, 1971, Chairman of the Republican Council, Abd al-Rahman al-Iryani announced in an interview that he would like North Yemen to have economic relations with the United States. In the first six months of 1971 North Yemeni media barely mentioned Soviet aid, but *Ath-Thawrah* on May 24 contained effusive praise for the Chinese.[7]

At the beginning of June the YAR Prime Minister, in a major speech to the YAR Consultative Assembly, expressed the desire for relations "with other countries" and unity with the south; he omitted any attacks on "imperialism and colonialism," and he had no kind words for the Soviets. In mid-June, al-Iryani visited Riyadh; although the communiqué mentioned "frankness" as well as "brotherhood," the Saudis promised aid "in all fields," and the Yemenis reaffirmed their adherence to Islamic values and their rejection of "destructive tendencies that totally or partially contradict its basic values, beliefs and traditions. . . ."[8] In Aden this was perceived to be directed against South Yemen, as was the appointment to the YAR Cabinet of Abdullah al-Asnaj, a prominent South Yemeni foe of the NF.[9]

Nevertheless, in the second half of 1971 there were pressures for reconciliation between the YAR on the one hand, and the USSR and the PDRY on the other. The YAR was weak militarily and politically, and was being swept (to the dismay of many North

Yemenis) into the embrace of Saudi Arabia. It needed not only Saudi economic aid, but also updated weapons and a powerful interested party to offset the Saudis. Discussions were therefore begun with the Soviets, with the result that they agreed to provide spare parts for the engineer corps' equipment, and invited al-Iryani to visit Moscow. Moscow's incentive for reconciliation grew as new conditions in the Red Sea (see pp. 30-31) convinced the Soviets that they should not abandon their position in North Yemen. They may have seen in the appointment in September of moderate leftist Muhsin al-Ayni as Prime Minister an indication of North Yemen's desire for better relations. As a sign of their renewed interest they sent a military delegation led by a Deputy Minister of Defense to the anniversary celebrations of the September 26 revolutions (the first Soviet delegation to be sent to attend these celebrations).

Aden as well may have seen al-Ayni's appointment as a favorable sign (although his retention of al-Asnaj in his Cabinet was not encouraging). However, the military pressure on the borders continued to be troubling; despite attempts at reconciliation, particularly heavy battles were fought in the Bayhan region of the border between the Yemens in mid-October, during which the NF claimed (for the first time) that the YAR was actively cooperating with the émigrés.[10] The South Yemenis appear to have won a decisive victory (at least part of which was on YAR territory) and in November sent a delegation to Taizz for talks with al-Iryani; they were reported to have offered to help the YAR police its territory to rid itself of the émigrés.[11] The meeting was described as "brusque," and al-Iryani agreed only to resurrect the economic unity committees; once again they failed to meet. Apparently after this Aden decided to step up its subversive activities in the YAR.

It was against the backdrop of these conditions that YAR President al-Iryani and Prime Minister al-Ayni visited Moscow for ten days in December 1971. The North Yemenis had high expectations for this visit; the Soviet military delegation in September had stayed for several weeks and must have led Sanaa to believe that substantial military aid would be forthcoming.[12] In that respect, the visit was far from successful. The Yemenis received only a gift of $15 million worth of obsolescent weapons.[13] They fared somewhat better in the economic field, as Moscow promised a new $35 million loan for the expansion of existing projects; even so, a TASS report spoke of an "exchange of views on expanding cooperation," a sign that the YAR delegation was not satisfied. The communiqué[14] said only that the two sides had "discussed questions of further developing friendly relations and cooperation between the USSR and the YAR in various spheres." There were other signs of serious differences. Soviet Premier Kosygin did not appear. The North Yemeni side did not associate itself with Soviet attacks on imperialism, and the word 'reaction' was not mentioned. The Soviet side did not praise YAR foreign policy, despite the Yemenis' acceptance of ritual Soviet fulminations on Indochina, racism, disarmament, etc.[15]

Nevertheless, for the most part the wording of the communiqué indicated that relations were correct, not unfriendly. The atmosphere was described as one of "friendship, frankness and mutual understanding." This was the same wording as was used during Ali Nasir Muhammad's visit two months previously, but a comparison of the two communiqués shows a closer Soviet-South Yemen relationship, a greater tendency on Aden's part to accommodate the Soviets; thus, for example, Ali Nasir had joined them in an attack on "reaction." Further, the South Yemenis had expressed "great gratitude for Soviet aid," whereas the North Yemenis merely "noted" that the Soviets had helped in constructing a number of important economic projects.

Moscow continued its policy of maintaining correct relations with Sanaa throughout 1972. Tension on South Yemen's borders grew, some of it generated as before from YAR territory. However, the Soviets, despite a growing interest in Aden's survival, blamed not the YAR but Saudi Arabia and the imperialists, who were judged to be poisoning inter-Yemeni relations in order to weaken the 'progressive forces' on the peninsula. On the other hand, Sanaa's friendship was at the very least suspect, and there was no question of Moscow's recommending Yemeni unity. No Soviet commentator went further than to advocate cooperation or collaboration between the two Yemens.

To avoid driving the North Yemenis irrevocably into the Western camp, Moscow was reluctant to criticize the YAR[16] even when it was obvious that Sanaa was moving in directions contrary to Soviet interests, closer to Saudi Arabia and the West, and to China. In May a Saudi military delegation visited Sanaa, presaging direct military cooperation to accompany the financial aid and tribal subsidies which appeared to be tying the YAR tightly to Riyadh.

The Saudi connection led to a great improvement in Sanaa's relations with Washington. On July 2, Secretary of State Rogers arrived unexpectedly at the end of a trip to Riyadh for a short visit during which diplomatic relations were restored and U.S. economic aid was promised. The Soviets saw this as another move to encircle the PDRY (which it certainly was), and after Sadat's expulsion of Soviet advisers in mid-July, worried about possible U.S. plans to organize an anti-Soviet security bloc in the Red Sea;[17] this concern was inevitably heightened by the convening at the end of July of a Red Sea economic conference in Jiddah, to which the PDRY was not invited.

This must have been a period of considerable anxiety for Moscow with regard to the region. Its Red Sea strategy was in tatters, the positions carefully cultivated in the late 1960s in the Sudan and Egypt destroyed, and those in the YAR on the verge of disappearing. (It was persistently rumored that the approximately 100 Soviet military advisers were kept virtually isolated so that they could not pass information to Aden, and that Sadat was urging the North Yemenis to follow his lead and expel them altogether.) To make matters worse, South Yemen was in turmoil and apparently under acute threat on all its borders. The Soviets poured arms into Aden to avoid losing its last strategic foothold in the region. Still, the Soviets refused to turn against the YAR. Moscow did not follow the lead of the PDRY Foreign Minister in describing the Sanaa regime as "hostile" to the PDRY.[18] In late September the Soviet Union and YAR exchanged visits. Podgornyy's anniversary cable expressed confidence that relations of friendship and cooperation would continue, and wished the YAR progress, well-being, and peace.

By that time, war had already broken out. For some time the PDRY had been sponsoring the infiltration of groups into the YAR to plant mines and carry out other terrorist activities. In late summer PDRY forces had begun interdictory raids to try to counter and disrupt the intensified émigré raids on South Yemen. The YAR armed forces then became involved, and a limited war ensued which lasted three weeks and seems to have taken place on the soil of both countries near the frontier. The émigré forces were soundly defeated, but the YAR forces gave a good account of themselves (and corrected a colonialist anomaly by capturing undefended Kamaran Island, off the coast of the YAR, north of Hodaydah, and almost 200 miles north of the PDRY).

The war again put Moscow in the difficult position of trying to be friends with both sides, and it tried to remain neutral. It did, however, express its preference by shrill media attacks on the imperialists and reactionaries for their intrigues against the PDRY. Relations with the YAR deteriorated in any case. Sanaa was angered by reports that Soviet pilots had flown missions against YAR positions[19] and was again reported to be considering expelling the Soviets. Al-Ayni complained that the Soviet Union had not delivered any arms to North Yemen for two years,[20] while South Yemen had been receiving unlimited military aid from the Soviets. No doubt Ali Nasir Muhammad's October 6 declaration of Soviet protection, although never confirmed by Moscow, also angered Sanaa, and may have been the cause of a peremptory summons to the Soviet Ambassador to meet al-Ayni.

The inter-Yemen war ended on October 19, 1972, after diplomatic intervention by other Arab states, and al-Ayni and Muhammad went to Cairo to discuss peace. A week later, to the amazement of all, there emerged not just an agreement for troop disengagement and cessation of all types of hostile activities, but also an agreement to unify within one year![21] This startling result was confirmed a month later at a meeting between Presidents al-Iryani and Rubay Ali, at which time joint committees were set up to work out the technical details. Moscow greeted the ceasefire and the Cairo normalization agreements with relief, and even claimed some of the credit for the cessation of hostilities.[22] The unity agreement evidently caught it by surprise; Soviet references to it were sparse and cautious, welcoming it, but stressing the fact of different social, economic, and political positions in the two countries. Salim Rubay Ali went to Moscow immediately prior to signing the unity agreement; presumably one of his tasks was to explain it and solicit Soviet approval. The Soviets did not respond; Kosygin referred only to the settlement of the conflict, not to the unity plan, and stressed the progressive changes in South Yemeni society. The communiqué mentioned only the normalization of relations between the two states.[23] Salim Rubay Ali himself made surprisingly few references to Yemeni unity, and it may be that both he and the Soviets were skeptical, or even worried, about its outcome.

Moscow could take comfort from some parts of the unity agreement text: socialism (but not scientific socialism) was said to be the aim of the state; a single political organization was to run the state, a provision which obviously favored the NF. However, arrayed against these clauses was the declaration not just that Islam would be the religion of the unified state, but that the Islamic Sharia would be the source of legislation. Soviet fears about the reversal of progressive changes in the PDRY and about their positions were made clear in a Radio Peace and Progress broadcast on January 15, 1973:

> Reactionaries like King Faysal of Saudi Arabia. . . are interpreting the agreement on unity. . . as demands for a capitulation of the progressive regime in Aden. They demand that the Democratic Yemen abandon scientific socialism, agrarian reform and the growth of the state sector. . . . The main condition for unity would be a break with the USSR. . . .[24]

Moscow need not have worried. Aden made it clear that unity would have to be on a "progressive" and "revolutionary" basis;[25] that is, on its terms. The South Yemenis had achieved a major goal, an end to émigré pressure against their western border; they could wait for unity. In the meantime Sanaa appeared to be willing to sacrifice South Yemeni goodwill in the interest of hanging on to Kamaran Island. In any case, the Saudi king was not trying to reinterpret the unity agreement — he was determined to scuttle it before it could lead to a possible anti-Saudi state with twice the population of his kingdom. The shaikhs of the northern Zaydi tribes (traditionally friends and/or clients of Saudi Arabia and the dominant political force in North Yemen) were in any case opposed to a deal which seemed likely to subject them to the rule of the 'communists' or the southern Shafii tribes. Supported by Riyadh, they forced the resignation of al-Ayni and the appointment of a conservative, Abdullah al-Hajari, as Prime Minister.

With a staunchly conservative government in place in Sanaa, the unity movement never really gained momentum, although the various joint committees functioned for a time in the spring of 1973. Border tension was again reported in January. Relations with Saudi Arabia grew closer (just as the PDRY and Soviet Union were developing closer ties), especially after al-Hajari's visit to Riyadh in March when he reaffirmed the 1934 Taif treaty in which the Saudis had taken three Yemeni provinces. Saudi development and budgetary aid began to increase significantly, and in mid-1973 the Saudis began to pay their tribal subsidies directly to the YAR Central Bank. This gave Sanaa a greater potential for controlling the tribes, but the financial support was large enough also to give Riyadh considerable influence over Sanaa's policies.[26]

The PDRY also contributed to the failure of this phase of the unity movement by encouraging the disaffection which built up in the southern regions of the YAR (mainly, it appears, over the resurgence of Zaydi power and the growth of Saudi influence), and by sending teams of saboteurs to lay mines and assassinate local leaders. There were several such incidents in the spring, but Sanaa appeared to regard them as local internal matters until the assassination of a member of the Republican Council, which Sanaa laid directly at the door of Aden. After that, there were constant reports from Sanaa of sabotage and terrorism in the southern region, all of which were blamed on the PDRY. Tensions on the border grew accordingly, and by September troops were said to be massing. However, the outbreak of the October War distracted everyone, and the troops were withdrawn.

These developments, in conjunction with the closer Soviet-PDRY ties, led to a further cooling of relations between the Soviets and the YAR. The latter was openly critical of Moscow's failure to provide even the small gift of arms promised in December 1971, and al-Iryani complained that the Soviets were still implementing the projects to which they had committed themselves in 1964.[27] Sanaa must also have been displeased that Yemeni students in Moscow had again been allowed to take over the YAR Embassy (see footnote 16), this time over the results of al-Hajari's trip to Riyadh.[28] For their part, the Soviets in the few references made about the YAR, were mildly critical of its backwardness, its repression of the "progressive forces" in the south, its threat to the PDRY, and its ties to Saudi Arabia.

Nevertheless, neither side was willing to allow a total breakdown in relations. A Soviet parliamentary delegation visited in April 1973. The YAR Commander-in-Chief visited Moscow (but came away empty-handed). Several hundred YAR students continued their studies in the USSR, and 60 new scholarships were awarded. In August a YAR delegation led by Abdullah al-Ahmar (who led the Hashid federation of northern tribes which was instrumental in undermining the unity agreement, and who had recently visited the United States) visited the Soviet Union. The delegation expressed itself happy to see the freedom of the Muslim religion in the Soviet Union,[29] and thanked the Soviets for their assistance in the economic, cultural, and health fields.

The October War opened the way for better relations as Arab countries of all stripes rallied against Israel and the United States. North Yemen took part, at least symbolically, in the closure of Bab al-Mandab to Israeli shipping; the prospect of the reopening of the Suez Canal gave Moscow an extra stake in improving its positions in the Red Sea; finally, the oil embargo led the Soviets to hope for a breakthrough in Saudi-Soviet relations, and improved Soviet-YAR relations might be of some use im promoting this. For a few months both sides made public relations gestures. Telegrams were sent expressing support and gratitude; religious delegations were exchanged. The Soviets talked of providing more medical and educational aid, and agreed to expand the port facilities at Hodaydah, and to sell wheat to the YAR at low prices. In March 1974 (the tenth anniversary of the Soviet-YAR Friendship Treaty) TASS referred to the YAR's "anti-imperialist foreign policy" and the "identity or proximity of the stands held by the USSR and YAR on many pressing foreign policy issues" which "creates favorable conditions for the further expansion of all-round cooperation between our two countries."[30]

The difficulty for Moscow was, of course, that the October War worked to the long-term advantage not of the Soviet Union and most of the radical Arab states but of Saudi Arabia. The staggering leap in its oil revenues gave Riyadh a chance to exert a moderating influence in the Middle East on some issues, and even to wean away some of Moscow's friends. In the competition for influence in the YAR, it was no contest. As the Saudis grew wealthier and more able to dominate Sanaa, they at the same time grew more dependent on the YAR for their labor force; this made them more determined to keep the Soviets and South Yemenis in a minor role (at most) in the YAR and the Red Sea. New offers of aid were made, including large quantities of oil at prices below the new world levels. At the end of May, it was announced that Riyadh had given $25 million in budgetary aid alone, and had agreed to increase their contribution by 50 percent, as well as to supply more development aid.

MOSCOW AND AL-HAMDI (JUNE 1974 - OCTOBER 1977)

Moscow's hopes for Sanaa received a further setback in mid-June 1974 with Lieurenant-Colonel Ibrahim al-Hamdi's assumption of power. Al-Hamdi was generally considered to be Saudi Arabia's man, and indeed the army's return to power came as a result of disaffection with al-Iryani from those northern tribes most closely in touch with the Saudis.

The Soviets recognized the danger in this, for Saudi Arabia had recently signed agreements with the United States on economic cooperation and arms purchases. Moscow reacted by promising more arms to Aden, but also by making overtures to Sanaa's new Prime Minister, Muhsin al-Ayni (an encouraging appointment), and applauding the new regime's declaration that the joint committees would continue to work toward Yemeni unity.[31] This was the first time Moscow had mentioned unity in 18 months; it may have indicated a decision to support unity in the face of an expected increase in Saudi pressure on the YAR. The Saudis themselves came under increasing attack from the Soviet media (although, interestingly, South Yemeni propaganda attacks on Saudi Arabia virtually ceased at this time). It was to no avail, however. Al-Hamdi's first trip was to Riyadh, and he announced no plans to visit Aden.

A breakthrough seemed possible a few months later. In October al-Hamdi hosted several meetings with PDRY officials, reportedly including Salim Rubay Ali.[32] A Soviet military mission was due to visit Sanaa. In November 1974, the two Yemens, extolling their closure of Bab al-Mandab as "perhaps one of the decisive factors in the October War," submitted a joint appeal to the Rabat summit conference for relief from high oil prices. However, the opponents of closer Yemeni ties with both the Soviet Union and South Yemen were too strong. The Soviet mission was postponed; in its place came U.S. and Saudi missions to begin working on a Saudi-financed arms deal. When the Soviet delegation was allowed to visit at the beginning of November, their proposal to sell MiG-21s (which the South Yemenis had just received) was rejected.[33]

This was due in part to Sanaa's hopes for substantial U.S. aid, to Saudi pressure, and to the unhappiness of conservative Yemeni forces, which manifested itself in demonstrations during the Soviet visit. Al-Hamdi responded by putting a more conservative face on his government, mainly by replacing al-Ayni in January 1975 with an apolitical technocrat, Abd al-Aziz Abd al-Ghani. From his later moves, it is apparent that the North Yemen leader had in fact decided to try to curb the power of the northern tribes, and to strive for unity as his most important foreign policy objective. Although the Saudis were becoming more willing to see the Sanaa government's power increased vis-a-vis the tribes, and were themselves beginning the dialog with Aden which would result in relations being established in a year's time, they were likely to be wary of his attempts; thus, al-Hamdi sought to protect himself by cutting off the Soviets and turning to Riyadh and Washington for his defense needs.

U.S. Navy ships visited Hodaydah twice; on the second occasion the commander of the small U.S. force stationed in the Persian Gulf was involved. This must have caused considerable concern in the Kremlin and Soviet military circles. The Suez Canal was reopened in June; it did not take an overactive imagination to assume that Washington was attempting to get a base or at least access to facilities at Hodaydah. (The Soviets themselves were probably not interested in acquiring facilities in that port, since both Berbera and Aden were far superior to it in both port facilities and location; they were, however, very interested in the U.S. Navy's not acquiring any new facilities in the region.) Of further concern was Washington's developing policy of large arms sales to Riyadh and of encouraging the Saudis to concentrate on the Red Sea. This the latter were not loath to do, and began to define the Red Sea as an "Arab Lake," from which all foreign forces should be excluded. Reports began to appear in the Arab press, noted by the Soviets, of a U.S. agreement to sell $140 million of military equipment (all of it World War II vintage) to the YAR.[34] The reports were finally confirmed in August by al-Hamdi, who said in addition that

> military relations with the Soviet Union are frozen at the moment, although the Russians are trying to get them moving again. . . . If the proposed U.S. arms sale is approved, the Yemen Arab Republic will end its 20-year arms supply relationship with the Soviet Union.[35]

Chief of Staff Ahmad Al-Ghashmi had earlier insultingly referred to Soviet weapons in the YAR as "museum pieces" and threatened to terminate the Soviet military mission.[36] The YAR appeared to fall further into Riyadh's orbit with a new aid agreement in August reportedly worth $250 million in aid, loans, and petroleum.[37]

The Soviets did not respond in any way to this annoyance, largely because they had no effective response; they had little access to al-Hamdi's domestic opposition, cessation of their aid programs would hardly have been noticed in economic terms, and, most important, their regional allies in Aden were unwilling to put pressure on Sanaa. Nevertheless, they doubtless took some comfort in the apparent movement in the unity issue; the personal representatives of the two presidents met often in 1975, the economic committee achieved some progress, and the other committees continued to meet. Both presidents declared themselves strongly in favor of unity, and although there were occasional incidents on the border, these were resolved without apparent tension.

In November 1975 Moscow attempted to improve relations with Sanaa by receiving a YAR military mission led by Abdullah Abd al-Alim, confidant of al-Hamdi. He had "warm and friendly" talks with Grechko on "questions of mutual concern,"[38] which would certainly have included the question of resuming Soviet military aid. The Soviets did offer a substantial aid package,[39] proof that they were anxious to reestablish their presence in North Yemen at a time when Aden was opening relations with Riyadh. However, it was rejected, for al-Hamdi knew he could not afford to antagonize the Saudis on this issue, and was merely engaged in the traditional game of playing off the suitors, trying to force Washington's and Riyadh's hands. In this he succeeded, for in January 1976 the United States finalized its offer of a ten-year modernization program, with the Saudis initially paying $140 million for U.S. and $80 million for French equipment; the total aid for the first five years was expected to come to $500 million, and would include U.S. F-5s. This stunning rejection of a major Soviet military aid program was moderated six months later by Sanaa's acceptance of a small number of obsolete tanks. At the same time, however, Chief of Staff al-Ghashmi again declared that the Soviet military mission would be terminated. In the end it was not, but it was reduced by half.[40]

The Soviets were apparently in retreat before the onslaught of petrodollars, from North Yemen, from South Yemen, and from Egypt. They were expelled from Egypt (April 1976) just as the reopening of the Suez Canal had encouraged them to assert their growing interest in the Indian Ocean. Thus, they concentrated on the southern end of the Red Sea, on Somalia, and increasingly on Ethiopia. Partly in response, Riyadh wooed Somalia with offers of aid, helped the Eritrean liberation movements, contracted to build a naval base on its Red Sea coast, and began seriously to discuss the idea of a security arrangement in the Red Sea. This idea, often encapsulated in the slogan "The Red Sea is an Arab lake," was aimed at now-radical and anti-U.S. Ethiopia and at the Soviet Union; it discussed with some interest by Arab governments in 1976. The Saudis also appeared to have used promises of aid to buy a rapprochement with the PDRY, and the Soviets worried that their positions in Aden might be threatened (see p. 57, 58, 60).

The YAR was the least important to the Soviets of the three countries in which they suffered setbacks in 1976, but they were not willing to abandon it. Al-Hamdi was known to be a strong nationalist, and the Soviets could imagine as well as anyone that he would not be comfortable so tightly bound to Saudi Arabia. Saudi money by this time was balancing Sanaa's budget and reducing the balance of payments deficit; however, Riyadh was also helping to prevent al-Hamdi's central government from extending its control, having resumed its subventions to the northern tribes. Saudi money was reequipping the YAR's armed forces, but at a stiff price — Riyadh insisted that the United States remain at arm's length from Sanaa, routing all arms through the Saudi military mission (which was governed at least in part by a desire not to allow the North Yemeni armed forces to become too strong); the Saudis also insisted that they control all military retraining, and tried to use that control to exclude those who had been trained in the USSR (by 1976 approximately 1,100 officers in a 32,000 man army[41]). Furthermore, the political situation was still very unstable. There had been several attempted coups in al-Hamdi's 18-month rule. The Soviets were excluded from contact with his main opposition, the northern tribes, but it was perhaps no coincidence that in 1976 the main leftist organizations in the southern YAR banded together to form the National Democratic Front (NDF). There is no indication that Moscow had anything to do with this directly, but its main allies in South Yemen's UPONF, Abd-al-Fattah Ismail's faction, were instrumental in the NDF's creation, and gave it support and sanctuary. A common aim of all three was to stop what appeared to be a drive for a Saudi-dominated, anti-Soviet, anti-radical grouping in the southern Arabian Peninsula.

Al-Hamdi himself attempted to reduce his country's dependence on Saudi Arabia. As he had done in 1975, he visited or sent delegations to Arab countries to try to expand North Yemen's friendships and diversify its sources of aid. In April 1976 he visited Oman, another country which was nervous about Saudi intentions and the Saudi-South Yemen rapprochement, and the two leaders recommended that the YAR join Gulf summit deliberations. In December he visited China, and was rewarded with a $25 million loan. Relations with the Soviets were not broken off. A small arms shipment arrived in the summer. At the end of January, the Soviets agreed to begin hard currency purchases of YAR salt. (This was a political decision, to take advantage of Japan's cancellation of its salt purchases in 1975; economics played a part, however, for some of the deliveries were used to begin paying off Yemen's debts to the USSR.) The Soviet Navy paid unpublicized working visits to Hodaydah, at much higher rate than in previous years (or in succeeding years).[42] The number of North Yemeni students in the Soviet Union increased from 400 to 700. Most important, however, was Sanaa's acceptance of a Soviet military delegation for the September 26 celebrations; al-Hamdi recognized the usefulness of the Soviet connection both in attracting Saudi Arabia and the United States and in keeping them at bay, and he did not intend to cut it. To keep the game alive, however, he invited a U.S. military delegation to participate in the celebrations as well.

His other option, closer ties with South Yemen, did not develop in 1976 as long as there appeared to be a real chance of normal relations developing betwen Aden and Riyadh. This lack of movement seemed to be in everyone's interest: Saudi Arabia because it preferred to deal with two weak states, the Soviet Union because it feared that the 'progressive' PDRY might be swamped by 'feudal remnants' in the YAR, and the two Yemens because they did not have enough mutual trust to risk all in the creation of a new state (if indeed that were possible, given the immense social and economic differences between the two). It was only at the end of the year, when Rubay Ali was feeling threatened by his failure to attract large-scale Saudi aid, and al-Hamdi frustrated by Saudi heavy-handedness, that the two leaders met. They made small progress, but expressed the hope that rapid measures would be taken to unify the two countries. By that time al-Hamdi was being subjected to increasing pressure from the northern tribes because of his attempts to curb their power and signs of his willingness to negotiate with the NDF. Despite the pressure, or because of it, the North Yemen leader invited Salim Rubay Ali to a meeting in Taizz in February 1977, where in an 'historic meeting' they created a council to pursue unity more actively. The Soviet media paid no attention.

At the same time Riyadh was making another attempt to draw Aden into its orbit (see p. 63-64) and was continuing its pressures on

Sanaa, through encouraging the tribes, manipulating the supply of U.S. arms which began to arrive in February, and increasing its aid. (Budgetary aid alone grew to $98 million, an increase of 20 percent over 1976.) Saudi efforts had been reinvigorated at the end of 1976 after a small Soviet-Ethiopian arms agreement opened the prospect of the Soviets' gaining a foothold on the Red Sea shores. This danger (in Saudi eyes) was magnified by Soviet attempts to defuse the explosive situation on the Horn[43] (by encouraging the creation of a federation of radical states — Ethiopia, Somalia, the PDRY), and thus reconcile its interest in the new radical government in Addis Ababa with its substantial positions in Somalia — Soviet military personnel were operating naval and air facilities that Soviet propagandists would have labelled a 'base' had any other power been involved, and the President, Siad Barre, was loudly committed to 'scientific socialism' and had signed a Treaty of Friendship and Cooperation with Moscow.

For the Soviets, the risks in getting involved with both sides in the dispute on the Horn of Africa were great, but the prize was great, too: Soviet presence on both sides of the Bab al-Mandeb and on the shores of the Indian Ocean adjacent to the oil shipping routes from the Persian Gulf, with the attendant pressures that that presence would put on Egypt, Saudi Arabia and the other oil states, and the oil consuming countries.

However, Saudi Arabia with its rapidly accumulating oil revenues was capable of and vitally interested in exerting counterpressure. Encouraged by Washington to focus its attention on the Red Sea (the 'twin pillar' policy) Riyadh had begun to promote the concept of a Red Sea security pact to be joined by all the Arab countries on the Red Sea littoral (including Eritrea, Somalia, and the PDRY). Planning went on at a feverish pace in January and February 1977, with Saudi Arabia choosing to remain behind the scenes as much as possible. Sudan and the YAR were the most vocal of the advocates, the latter motivated perhaps partly by Saudi pressure, and probably also by a desire to consolidate relations with other regional states in the hope of reducing Saudi pressure. Sanaa did not appear to be as concerned about the Soviets in the Red Sea as it was about its dispute with Ethiopia over ownership of some of the Red Sea Islands and about recent Israeli air activity.[44]

To all intents, however, the idea of a Red Sea security pact fizzled out with the Taizz Conference March 22-23, 1977, which was attended by the heads of state of the YAR, Sudan, Somalia, and the PDRY, but not of Egypt or Saudi Arabia (those governments apparently waiting until the waters had been tested). Somali President Barre returned home disgruntled, apparently because he could get no significant support for his Ogaden adventure; Salim Rubay Ali would agree only to the declaration of the Red Sea as a zone of peace, free of Zionist and imperialist aggression; the North Yemenis did refer to the Red Sea as an Arab Lake[45], but softened it by assurances that this was not directed against anyone. Red Sea security was discussed occasionally during the remainder of the year, but nothing ever came of it; the massive Soviet and Cuban intervention in Ethiopia after November effectively put an end to it.

However, in the spring Moscow took it seriously, for it seemed to threaten Soviet positions in both Somalia and the PDRY as well as possible positions in Ethiopia. The 'Arab Lake' concept seemed also to deny to the USSR any role in a region which, as Soviet commentators frequently pointed out, was of strategic and commercial importance, not least for the Soviets.[46] A barrage of propaganda denounced the Saudis for trying to "knock together a closed military and political grouping" (i.e., anti-Soviet and anti-Ethiopian), but, more significantly, for "making generous promises of aid" in

> attemptimg to draw into the conservative camp which it heads countries such as Somalia and South Yemen. . . . The heightened interest which Riyadh is displaying in unification trends in the two Yemens. . . should also be regarded in this light.[47]

The propaganda, containing this very obvious concern that Saudi aid and the unification issue could pull the PDRY away from the Soviet Union, petered out in late spring, following the South Yemeni Foreign Minister's visit to Moscow in May. The rapid disappearance of the broadsides made it clear that Muti had told his hosts that the chances of success of the Red Sea security plans and of Yemeni unity were nonexistent. The latter part of the message was borne out in al-Hamdi's September 26 anniversary speech, when (despite another meeting with Rubay Ali in August) the only progress he could point to was the decision to prepare a joint Yemeni history curriculum.[48]

With this reassurance, and with its attention in the region taken up with the deteriorating situation in the Horn and the need to ensure

South Yemeni's cooperation, the Soviets had little time to spare North Yemen. Relations continued on the same low but correct level of the previous year. The number of Soviet economic technicians declined by one-quarter (to 155), but the number of Yemenis studying and training in the USSR increased substantially.[49] Moscow wanted nothing to aggravate this cool relationship; thus even the expulsion of the TASS correspondent in August for "misusing his position" rated only a few lines in *Pravda* under the heading "Unfriendly Act."

There were also promising signs in the summer of 1977 for the Soviets. Al-Hamdi faced down the tribes in July, and in September it was reported that the two sides had reached an agreement which left the tribes in a weaker position. Working from this position of greater strength, he apparently saw the possibility of legalizing the NDF and using it to reduce the influence of the tribes even more.[50] His government also joined with Aden in a declaration of their determination to keep the Red Sea a zone of peace, protected from "imperialist and Zionist ambition" (Aden's phrase at the Taizz Conference); al-Hamdi himself apparently increased his contacts with Rubay Ali and announced his intention to make his first visit (and the first ever by a North Yemeni leader) to Aden in mid-October to pursue the elusive chimera of unity.

NOTES

1. For a detailed examination of Soviet involvement in Yemen prior to 1970, cf. S. Page, *The USSR and Arabia: the development of Soviet policies and attitudes toward the Arabian Peninsula* (London: Central Asian Research Centre, 1971).

2. J. Peterson, *Yemen: the search for a modern state* (Baltimore: John Hopkins University Press, 1982), p. 60. Cf. S. Nagi, "The Genesis of the Call for Yemeni Unity," paper presented to the Symposium on Contemporary Yemen at Exeter University, July 15-18, 1983.

3. Stookey points out that the Saudi press made it quite explicit that Riyadh sponsored the national reconciliation that ended the civil war in the YAR to gain an ally for a joint military action against the Aden regime. R.W. Stookey, *South Yemen: A Marxist Republic in Arabia* (Boulder: Westview Press, 1982), p. 101.

4. From 1970 the Saudis began to give project and budgetary aid to Sanaa, while continuing to subsidize the tribes which exerted a strong conservative influence on the regime. Diplomatic relations were established with Saudi Arabia, France, and Britain in 1970, and with the United States in 1972.

5. U.S., Department of State, Bureau of Intelligence and Research, *Communist Governments and Developing Nations: Aid and Trade in 1973* (Washington: Department of State, 1974), p. 13.
6. *FBIS/USSR*, July 22, 1970, p. A33.
7. *FBIS/MENA*, June 1, 1970, p. B1.
8. The communiqué is to be found in *FBIS/MENA*, June 17, 1971, pp. B1-2.
9. This was not unusual. During the civil war the YAR National Assembly allocated seats for South Yemen, and there were many North Yemenis (such as Abd al-Fattah Ismail) active in South Yemeni politics.
10. J.B. Bell, *South Arabia: Violence and Revolt* (London: The Institute for the Study of Conflict, 1973), p. 10.
11. *FBIS/MENA*, November 18, 1971, p. B1. Ali Nasir Muhammad had recently returned from a trip to Moscow, and this initiative may have been at Soviet urging.
12. On the eve of the visit the Deputy Supreme Commander of the Yemeni Armed Forces expressed "high hopes. . . especially as regards our armed forces. . . . We very much hope that the Soviet Union will meet all our remaining requirements." N. Novik, "On the Shores of Bab al-Mandab: Soviet Diplomacy and Regional Dynamics," *Crossroads*, no. 2 (Winter 1979): p. 67.
13. *Arab Report and Record*, February 16-29, 1972, p. 97; Sanaa radio indicated Yemeni displeasure by referring only to a gift of "some arms." *USSR and Third World* 2 (January - February, 1972): 46.
14. The communiqué is to be found in *FBIS/USSR*, December 22, 1971, pp. B3-5.
15. One reason for Soviet coolness may have been the issuance during the visit of criticism of the Soviet Union from within the YAR regime, and the suggestion that relations with the United States should be resumed. *FBIS/MENA*, December 13, 1971, p. B1.
16. However, the occupation of the YAR Embassy in Moscow by North and South Yemeni students in the USSR should be taken as Soviet criticism; this sort of event does not happen at random in the Soviet Union, and it was no accident that it was the YAR and not the PDRY Embassy that was occupied.
17. *FBIS/USSR*, July 19, 1972, pp. B10-11; *FBIS/USSR*, July 25, 1972, p. B15-16. A later book asserted that Sanaa had reached an agreement with Saudi Arabia on splitting the PDRY in half, with the Saudis to have the east (and the rumored oil deposits) and the North Yemenis the west. O.G. Gerasimov, *Iemenskaia revoliutsiia 1962-1975 gg.: problemy i suzhdeniia* (Moscow: Iz. Nauka, 1979), p. 183.
18. *FBIS/MENA*, July 11, 1972, pp. B1-2. The Soviets, in fact had reason to be encouraged; in July the government instructed a Sanaa periodical to cease publishing articles critical of Moscow. *Arab Report and Record*, July 16-31, 1972, p. 362.
19. *Financial Times*, October 4, 1972.
20. In an interview with *Al-Hawadith*, January 18, 1973, al-Iryani confirmed that the Soviets did not deliver even the gift of arms promised in December 1971. *Arab Report and Record*, January 16-31, 1973, p. 42.
21. For the text, cf. *FBIS/MENA*, November 29, 1972, pp. B1-3.

22. A.N. Kosygin during Salim Rubay Ali's visit at the end of November. He did not say what the Soviets had done. *Pravda*, November 22, 1972.
23. *Pravda*, November 22, 1972; *Pravda*, November 26, 1972.
24. *USSR and Third World* 3 (January 15 - February 18, 1973): 105.
25. *FBIS/MENA*, December 5, 1972, p. B6; *FBIS/MENA* December 29, 1972, p. B3.
26. J. Peterson, op. cit., p. 144.
27. *FBIS/MENA*, August 1, 1973, p. B2.
28. *Arab Report and Record*, April 1-15, 1973, p. 167.
29. *USSR and Third World* 3 (September 3 - October 21, 1973): 502.
30. *FBIS/USSR*, March 22, 1974, pp. F5-6.
31. *FBIS/USSR*, July 16, 1974, pp. F7-8.
32. R.W. Stookey, *Yemen: The Politics of the Yemen Arab Republic* (Boulder: Westview Press, 1978), p. 275.
33. Al-Hamdi quoted by *International Herald Tribune*, August 4, 1975.
34. *FBIS/USSR*, April 14, 1975, p. F3; DMS, *Foreign Military Markets - Middle East/Africa* (Greenwich, CT: DMS, Inc., 1982), p. 4.
35. *International Herald Tribune*, August 8, 1975.
36. *FBIS/MENA*, June 18, 1975, p. C7; *FBIS/MENA*, July 24, 1975, p. C1.
37. *FBIS/MENA*, August 7, 1975, p. C2.
38. *FBIS/USSR*, November 18, 1975, p. F6.
39. The package was worth $500 million, and included two squadrons of MiG-21s, patrol boats, ground-to-air missiles, and enough equipment to modernize the army. U.S. Congress, House, Committee on International Relations, *United States Arms Policies in the Persian Gulf and Red Sea Areas: Past, Present and Future* (Washington: Government Printing Office, 1977), p. 80.
40. Ibid.
41. U.S. Central Intelligence Agency, *Communist Aid to the Less Developed Countries of the Free World 1976* (McLean, VA: CIA, 1977), p. 6.
42. B.W. Watson, *Red Navy at Sea* (Boulder: Westview Press, 1982), p. 218; *MECS 1976-77*, p. 662.
43. The most serious problem in the Horn was Somalia's irredentist claims to the Ogaden sector of Ethiopia, and its increasingly open use of its Soviet-armed and -trained army in support of the liberation movements there. The Soviets were also concerned that Eritrea would win its war of independence, and cut Ethiopia (and perhaps the Soviets) off from its ports on the Red Sea. For an explanation of Soviet strategic interest in Ethiopia, cf. R. Remnek, *Soviet Policy in the Horn of Africa: The Decision to Intervene* (Alexandria, VA: Center for Naval Analyses, 1980).
44. In November 1976, the YAR claimed that Israeli planes had overflown its air space near the Bab al-Mandab. It is hard to say whether Sanaa was really worried about it or whether it was seen simply as an effective issue for generating more military aid.
45. *Middle East Intelligence Survey* 4 (March 16-31, 1977): 191-2.
46. V. Kudriavtsev, "Teni nad Krasnym Morem," *Izvestiia*, April 16, 1977; Iu. Tsaplin, "The Red Sea in Reaction's Plan," *New Times*, no. 17 (April) 1977, pp. 20-1.

47. *FBIS/USSR*, April 22, 1977, p. F7; V. Kudriavtsev, op. cit.

48. In light of a January agreement between the YAR and Saudi Arabia to work toward unifying their total school curricula, this appears a meager result of two summit meetings.

49. In 1977, the number of Yemeni students in the USSR was 850, more than double the number in 1975.

50. P. Rondot, "La Mort du Chef d'Etat du Yemen du Nord," *Maghreb-Machrek*, no. 79 (January-March 1978): 13.

7
MOSCOW AND THE YAR: DISASTER AND RECOVERY (1978-84)

FROM OCTOBER 1977 TO THE AUTUMN OF 1979

Two days before the visit, Ibrahim al-Hamdi was assassinated. Responsibility for the deed was never revealed, but there was a long list of motives, ranging from ideological differences (either with Saudi Arabia or the NDF), to tribal disgruntlement (either northern or southern tribes), to personal ambition.[1] However, there was no doubt in Moscow about the identity of the assassins; the Soviets put the blame squarely on Saudi Arabia, whose motive, they alleged, was to halt al-Hamdi's move toward South Yemen.[2] Whatever the accuracy of these allegations (and it should be noted that the Soviets were angered and concerned at the time by Saudi encouragement to Somalia to break its ties with Moscow and by the possibility, however remote, of a Saudi-instigated Red Sea security pact), Saudi interest did appear to be furthered by the succession of Lieutenant-Colonel Ahmad al-Ghashmi, who had close ties to the northern tribes and to the Saudis. He was not a popular or respected figure throughout the country, and was, in fact, widely suspected of being responsible for al-Hamdi's murder. Thus his dependency on the northern tribes and on Riyadh was likely to remain great.

Moscow's attention focussed on the new North Yemeni situation only briefly. Within weeks the Soviets had mounted an airlift through Aden to Ethiopia, and were involved in a shooting war against Somalia and a verbal war against Saudi Arabia. The Saudis and South Yemenis withdrew their Ambassadors and began to engage in border skirmishes for the first time in six years. Under these conditions, the Soviets obviously wanted to avoid pushing North Yemen irrevocably into the Saudi camp. They ignored al-Ghashmi's repression of the NDF and retreat from rapprochement with Aden, al-Asnaj's statements that the Soviets' interest in the Horn of Africa was to gain positions from which to threaten the oil states of the Arabian Peninsula, and evidence of developing relations between the YAR and the United States.[3]

In addition, both sides gave positive signals that they did not wish relations to deteriorate. On the 60th anniversary of the October Revolution, al-Ghashmi sent a friendly telegram expressing his conviction that good relations between the YAR and the Soviet Union would continue to develop. Moscow offered a $38 million Soviet loan in late April 1978 for the expansion of the Soviet-built Bajil cement plant. Several delegations were exchanged, the most important being that of the YAR Chief of Staff at the beginning of April; he was reported to be seeking heavy artillery, which the Soviets, mindful of the deterioration of relations between the Yemens, were reluctant to promise. Nevertheless, the Soviet media gave the visit considerable publicity. The real goal for the Soviets of this visit (and that of a military delegation to Sanaa on the anniversary of the June 13 Corrective Movement) was to insert a wedge of even the smallest size between the YAR and Saudi Arabia; the latter was causing Moscow some concern for its potential ability to complicate Soviet policies in the Horn and Red Sea, and more realistically for its ability to threaten the PDRY. As the failure of the April visit showed, however, the Soviets stopped short of actions that could harm the PDRY. For al-Ghashmi, the goal of the visits was partly to reestablish some semblance of the traditional balance in Yemeni foreign policy; this was largely illusory, for the Saudis were pouring ever more money into the coffers of both the central government[4] and the northern tribes, and a Saudi military delegation arrived in Sanaa immediately on the return of the Chief of Staff from Moscow, for the purposes of "military coordination." Al-Ghashmi may also have hoped to persuade the Soviets to influence Aden not to support the NDF in the border regions, to leave the YAR army free to try to cope with continuing tribal unrest in the north.

The North Yemeni leader may have had some success. In April al-Alim's paratroops rebelled, and appealed to Aden for support. Despite the deterioration of relations between the two Yemens, the PDRY apparently did not respond. There could of course be several reasons for this; however, it is interesting to note, together with the marginal improvement of Soviet-YAR relations, that al-Ghashmi had a publicized talk with the Soviet Ambassador, and that Ali Antar (the PDRY Defense Minister) made a quick trip to Moscow at the height of the suppression of the rebellion. Nevertheless, the main factor in the PDRY inaction was probably the internal political struggle in Aden which was approaching its climax. The more radical forces, led by Ismail, had not yet won. Rubay Ali may have used his remaining authority to prevent assistance being given to the North Yemeni rebels; it is known that, in a rearguard action, he began contacts with al-Ghashmi in a desperate attempt to develop a plan to undermine the growing strength of his opponents.

As we have seen in Chapter 3, the attempt failed. Al-Ghashmi was killed on June 24, 1978 by a bomb sent, in all likelihood, by the Ismail faction in Aden in order to destroy any possibility of the PDRY working closely with the YAR under Saudi influence, and to bring down Rubay Ali at the same time; the latter attempted to strike back, but was defeated and executed two days later. If this is the correct scenario for the deaths of the two Presidents, then the East Germans in the Security Service probably played a part, and the Soviets were likely at least to have been aware of Ismail's intentions. Their acquiescence (although the decision to send the bomb appears to have been made on extremely short notice and the Soviets might not have had an opportunity to affect it) might be explained by the end of the crisis in the Horn of Africa with Ethiopia's victory, by their eagerness to see Ismail and his vanguard party come to power, and/or by their concern lest a Rubay Ali - al-Ghashmi plan succeed, to the detriment of their positions in South Arabia.

In the crisis that followed, Moscow left no doubt that it would sacrifice its relationship with Sanaa to its greater interest in Aden. It supported unconditionally the South Yemeni version of these events, laid the blame for both killings firmly at the feet of the Saudis and the imperialists, shrilly accusing them of planning to attack the PDRY, and left the impression that it would come to South Yemen's assistance if that happened. (See p. 78.) However, the Soviets did not go out of their way to antagonize the North Yemenis; at no time, even during Sanaa's bitter threats to "punish" the Aden regime, did the Soviets criticize the YAR. When the two sides traded accusations of troops massing on the border, Moscow accepted Aden's version, but again laid the blame on Saudi Arabia for trying to provoke a North Yemeni attack, and urged Sanaa to settle its differences with Aden peacefully. Even al-Asnaj's call for "support for the Yemeni people to free their country from foreign intervention in the south" drew no response.[5] The Arab League meeting, which was convened on the initiative of the YAR, and which called for a freeze on relations between its members and the PDRY, was portrayed by Moscow as a continuation of the attempts of Egypt and Saudi Arabia to prevent the emergence of a united independent Yemen. (This, the first Soviet mention of Yemen unity in four years, was transparently a propaganda exercise, for the Soviets were secure in the knowledge that unity was not possible in the foreseeable future.) For their part the North Yemenis were also circumspect, confirming their verbal assaults to the Aden regime and not mentioning the Soviets.

This became the consistent pattern of each country's behavior toward the other. When the YAR's new president, Ali Abdullah Salih, conciliated the northern tribal leaders, moved even closer to Saudi Arabia, and attacked the NDF, Moscow made no comment. When the United States accelerated its arms shipments to the YAR, and then in September acceded to a further Yemeni request by promising $360 million in modern equipment equal in quality to what the Soviets were supplying to the PDRY (including 12 F-5 fighters, 50 M-60 tanks, and 100 armored personnel carriers), Moscow criticized Washington for its policy of penetrating the Red Sea to put pressure on the progressive countries and the national liberation movement. Nor, when anti-Aden groups (now bolstered by supporters of the late South Yemeni president) were allowed and encouraged to operate from YAR territory, did the Soviet media echo South Yemeni protests. Even the closure of the Soviet consulate in Taizz after a widespread but abortive coup (for which the Libyans and South Yemenis, not the Soviets, were blamed) did not provoke criticism.[6] Relations, however cool, were not to be allowed to disintegrate.

Indirectly, of course, the Soviets were working against the YAR regime, if only through their ever-tighter military and political relationship with the Ismail regime in Aden which was increasing its assistance to the NDF in the north. This assistance was generally clandestine, but began to be openly acknowledged at the founding conference of the Yemeni Socialist Party in October 1978, in which representatives of the NDF participated and publicly attacked the

North Yemen regime. The connection between the NDF and the regime in Aden was underlined at a mass rally in Aden at which the guests of honor were 2,000 North Yemeni tribesmen who had come to celebrate the October 14 anniversary. Ali Nasir Muhammad addressed them, claiming that only the NDF, not the Salih regime, would bring North Yemen into that long-sought goal, a unified Yemen state.[7] In November and December as clashes between the various 'liberation movements' and government forces became more frequent, both regimes began to name each other as the perpetrator of terrorists acts, and the NDF was heard more often on Aden radio announcing battles in the YAR.

Under extreme threat from the NDF and its patrons, Salih moved to consolidate his support within the country by further concessions to the northern tribes, and by appealing for external help. In December the North Yemeni president made quick visits to Riyadh (probably to discuss U.S. arms supplies, which because of Riyadh's second thoughts had not begun to arrive in the YAR), the UAE, and Oman. Finally, Salih turned to the Soviets, partly in hopes of their pressuring Ismail to reduce his assistance to the NDF, but partly also to send a warning to Riyadh and Washington. In November 1978 and January 1979, he and other North Yemeni officials held publicized talks with the Soviet Ambassador, discussing "ways to strengthen relations." At the end of January Salih declared that the United States had not supplied the YAR with the arms it needed. A few days later al-Asnaj, after holding talks with Oleg Grinevskiy (the head of the Soviet Foreign Ministry's Near Eastern Department), said that the YAR had no intention of becoming "the region's policeman against communism," and was not intending to decrease the size of the Soviet military mission.[8]

These developments were doubtless welcomed in Moscow, but the Soviets did not respond to them publicly; at the time they were engaged in one of those remarkable flirtations that seem to occur periodically between the USSR and Saudi Arabia. Soviet hopes were aroused by the Saudis' rejection of the Camp David agreements (September 1978) and its participation in the Baghdad Conference (November) to set an Arab strategy against Egypt. They were encouraged further by the visible irritation in Riyadh at Washington's inaction in the Horn of Africa (late 1977-early 1978) and in Iran as the Shah was forced to abdicate (January 1979). Statements by various Saudi princes at the end of 1978[9] seemed to provide the opening for a dialog, and the Soviets tried to respond.[10]

It is improbable that Salih took his moves toward Moscow seriously. He had already begun a desperate military drive against the NDF, and his main requirement was a rapid supply of arms, which the Soviets were not likely to provide. The moves stopped after U.S. Secretary of Defense Brown visited Riyadh in mid-February and signed an agreement with the Saudis on financing the arms supplies promised the previous September.

The North Yemeni drive against the NDF-held villages on the border with the PDRY provoked stiff resistance, and by February 24, 1979, South Yemen was drawn into the fight.[11] PDRY Foreign Minister Muti's presence in Riyadh arranging a visit by Ismail when the fighting broke out makes it unlikely that Aden intended a fight at that time. However, there was strong support in the regime (including Abd al-Fattah himself) for the NDF; these people would have been concerned to prevent an NDF defeat, and may also have seen the fight as a chance to deal Salih a defeat which might spark an internal revolt. On the other hand, there were also reports that North Yemeni forces had crossed into South Yemen and attacked several villages, and that PDRY forces struck back.[12] Within days the South Yemeni forces (already on alert at the border because of eight months of tension) had decisively demonstrated their superiority; by the time the fighting ended in mid-March they and the NDF occupied positions in a strip approximately 12 miles wide in some parts of the mountainous border territory.[13] North Yemen reports insisted that they intended to cut the Sanaa-Taizz road and take control of the whole southern section of the country, but there is no indication that they attempted to do this, or indeed intended to. Once in the war, their military objectives were limited, and these they probably achieved; their political hope (that Salih would fall) was unfulfilled, and when it became obvious that this was the case (particularly after the arrival of a sizable force of northern tribesmen), Aden acceded to heavy Arab pressure (and probably some Soviet pressure[14]) for a cease-fire and rapid troop withdrawal.

Moscow appeared to have been taken by surprise by the outbreak of war; the first reports, which merely repeated South Yemeni charges of YAR aggression and NDF claims to be acting on its own, did not appear until February 27. By then Soviet and Cuban advisers were involved in the war in various support functions in the PDRY; nevertheless, Soviet comment was very mild, almost noncommittal, welcoming the initiatives of the Arab League to end the war while insisting that Aden wanted only peaceful coexistence and non-interference in internal affairs.[15] It was only after Carter ordered the *Constellation* and its task force into the Arabian Sea (March 6) and invoked the 'emergency clause' to send the weapons and advisers already promised to the YAR before getting congressional approval (March 9) that the Soviet media began to show signs of disquiet.[16] By this time the South Yemeni and NDF forces had halted their advance, although fighting was still continuing in some areas.

The Soviets greeted the end of the war with relief. The war had proven South Yemen's military superiority in the southern part of the peninsula, over North Yemen, and probably over Saudi Arabia as well, since a Riyadh ultimatum was ignored with impunity. Saudi pretensions and prestige as a regional power, and U.S. expectations of it as a 'pillar' of U.S. interests, had been severely damaged. Continued fighting was not likely to lead to further South Yemeni gains; on the other hand, it might lead to greater U.S. intervention in the Red Sea and Arabian Sea and give Washington a chance to prove its reliability in defense of a friendly regime. Thus it ran counter to Soviet interests. The demonstrated weakness of North Yemen and Saudi Arabia had made both countries cautious, even conciliatory toward Moscow. North Yemen did not expel any Soviet personnel and was careful not to accuse Moscow of helping the South Yemeni forces. North Yemeni spokesmen were critical of high-profile U.S. actions like the *Constellation* mission even as the weapons for which they had pleaded were arriving. At the height of the fighting, Saudi Foreign Minister Saud al-Faisal told an interviewer that Saudi Arabia did not share Washington's fear that expanding Soviet influence in the Middle East would further destabilize the region, and expressed appreciation for the "positive policy adopted by the Soviet Union toward Arab issues."[17] However, the main reason the Soviets were relieved to see the fighting ended was that it was dividing the Arabs at the time of the Egyptian-Israeli negotiations toward a separate peace treaty. Both radical and moderate Arabs opposed this treaty, and it seemed to be the issue on which the Soviets' long-cherished dream of anti-imperialist Arab unity could be achieved.

The war ended (as usual for the Yemenis) in bizarre fashion; at a meeting in Kuwait on March 27, Presidents Salih and Ismail signed an agreement to have a constitution drafted within four months for a united Yemen. Ismail was reported to have agreed to

Salih's becoming President and Sanaa's being the capital. The constitutional committee began work three weeks later, and the old joint committees started to meet again. The Soviets did not comment on this unity agreement. It is likely that they did not approve, since it was still possible that a united Yemen would be dominated by North Yemeni numbers and Saudi money. It is more likely that they did not take it seriously. In the YAR, they knew, the northern tribes would not agree to unity. In the PDRY, the government did not go out of its way to moderate any policies to pave the way for unity, and insisted that a united Yemen must be "progressive" and "national democratic" in character. It ignored the clause in the armistice agreement binding it not to support the NDF; the latter organization continued to be active in the YAR, with its headquarters in Aden. The South Yemeni leadership also continued to take their country into closer relations with the USSR, which obliged it with a large resupply of modern weapons.

Moscow's tighter relations with Aden, and its preoccupation with crucial regional developments (the Egypt-Israel treaty and its effect on the Arab countries, the fall of the Shah, and U.S. naval build-up, and plans for a Rapid Deployment Force in the Indian Ocean) made it seem as if the Soviets paid little attention to the YAR in the summer of 1979. Nevertheless, Moscow recognized the difficulties that Salih was experiencing. Riyadh, in an attempt to keep control of the YAR's military development and to keep it from becoming too strong, slowed down the delivery of the weapons it was buying for the Yemeni armed forces. Irritated, Salih asked Washington for more arms, a large team of U.S. advisers to assist in training the Yemenis, and a direct supply relationship. The United States refused, still unwilling to deal with the YAR except in the context of its relations with Saudi Arabia. Ali Abdullah was also having great difficulty in balancing the northern tribes and the NDF (backed by their respective patrons). The NDF was trying to use its strong position in the south to gain legality and a place in the Sanaa government. In June Salih held talks with NDF representatives, who were reported to have demanded more democracy and less Saudi political and economic influence in Sanaa. Not surprisingly, this alarmed the tribes and the Saudis, and at the end of June there was an attempted coup and clashes between the army and the northern tribes. Salih's démarche with the NDF collapsed, and Riyadh announced that it would contribute $100 million to the North Yemen budget in 1979, as well as continue to fund many development projects; the announcement was accompanied by a pointed homily on the "importance of directing Yemeni efforts to deepen spiritual education and adherence to Arab and Islamic values."[18]

FROM THE AUTUMN OF 1979 TO NOVEMBER 1982

Within weeks of the attempted coup a Yemeni military mission travelled secretly to Moscow to discuss resumption of arms purchases. Salih, realizing that the United States would not provide the weapons he believed the YAR needed and that the Saudis intended to continue, even expand, their intrusive behavior, turned to the time-honored Yemeni balancing strategy and invited the Soviets back. (The move had the support of the armed forces, who were not enthusiastic about a complete change of weapons. It also raised the possibility of Soviet pressure on Aden to reduce its support for the NDF.) Moscow responded quickly and generously. By the beginning of September a large quantity of anti-tank and anti-aircraft missiles, light weapons, and ammunition had been delivered. By the end of September, 100 T-55 tanks had arrived, and 40 MiG-21s were on their way. Soviet military advisers accompanied the weapons; early in 1980 they numbered 200, an increase of about 50 percent over the year before. Approximately 200 Yemeni military trainees went to the USSR, a 40-fold increase over the previous year.[19] The package was said to be worth $700 million and some sources claimed that the Soviets actually charged one-tenth of that, with repayment on easy credit terms.[20]

In seizing the opportunity presented to them, the Soviets seemed to pay scant attention to some of their other interests in the area. The flirtation with Riyadh, which had continued through the summer, would cool. Washington was alarmed and would likely redouble its efforts to establish military facilities in the region. Most significant, the rapid strengthening of the YAR military would be a setback for the NDF and its supporters in Aden, especially Ismail. However, Moscow realized that friendly relations with the Saudis were not imminent (and might even be realized quicker with a Soviet presence on their borders). The Soviets also realized that the U.S. military build-up was a response to events in Iran and the Gulf, and would not be much affected by the North Yemeni situation.

Ismail's position in Aden was damaged, but Moscow moved to restore it with Kosygin's visit and the Treaty; the overall Soviet position in South Yemen was not affected. The NDF, however, was to be sacrificed if necessary (although there was never any indication that Moscow had agreed to induce Aden to restrict or cease its support); Soviet state interests were judged to demand closer Moscow-Sanaa relations. The Soviets, clearly, had seen in the PDRY military success in March and in the YAR's move away from Saudi Arabia in August, the possibility that unity might favor the South. Accordingly, on the September 26 anniversary, as a Soviet delegation watched Soviet and U.S. weapons parade through the streets of Sanaa, Moscow radio proclaimed the Soviets' "deep understanding at the aspirations of the Yemeni people for unity."[21] It appears that throughout the fall pressure was exerted on Ismail to declare himself for the peaceful development of relations between the Yemens, both by the Soviets and by the Muhammad faction in Aden.

Ali Abdullah Salih's aim was to gain some independence from Saudi Arabia, some freedom to maneuver. To a certain extent he succeeded. In October the YAR rejected Oman's plan for the security of the Straits of Hormuz, a plan which would have involved the United States. The YAR abstained on the United Nations vote to censure the USSR for its invasion of Afghanistan; Salih later declared that the YAR "refused to be pushed by anyone [i.e., Saudi Arabia, which exerted considerable pressure on Sanaa on this issue] in the game of international struggle to adopt stands in his interests."[22] On the other hand, true to its balancing game, the YAR did participate in the Islamic Conference at Islamabad which did condemn the invasion.

In internal affairs, Salih's desire for room to maneuver led him into negotiations with the NDF at the beginning of 1980, from which NDF leader Sultan Ahmad Umar reported an agreement to end the struggle and to include NDF politicians in the government. Although Salih never confirmed that an agreement had been reached, the process had gone too far, and the reaction set in. The northern tribes were already concerned at the USSR-PDRY Treaty, and at the growing YAR-Soviet military relations which were threatening to make the army superior to the tribal forces; they saw in the negotiations with the NDF the danger of a unity pact on a socialist basis, with themselves in a minority. The Saudis had been angered by Salih's arms deal with Moscow. They were concerned at the

USSR-PDRY Treaty and the invasion of Afghanistan, while the takeover of the Grand Mosque in November frightened them. When Salih appeared to be coming to terms with the NDF, they acted. Cutting off their annual $250 million subsidy, and stirring up the tribes, they demanded an end to the negotiations, a freeze on the number of Soviet military advisers in North Yemen, and their eventual expulsion. Salih at first refused, but Riyadh's economic weight was too great; the YAR could not meet its payroll. The negotiations with the NDF ended. The Saudis also believed that Sanaa had given a commitment to reject Soviet advisers, and resumed payment of the subsidy. However, Sanaa insisted that no promise had been made to reduce the number of Soviet advisers, and in fact arms shipments and advisers continued to increase.

The Saudis protested, but in the end did nothing more drastic to try to put an end to the relationship. It appears that they were immobilized by the danger of pushing the YAR into the arms of the PDRY and the Soviet Union if they pushed too hard; it is also likely that they were encouraged by the apparent deterioration in Soviet influence in the Middle East because of Afghanistan, and by South Yemen's overtures, particularly after Ali Nasir Muhammad deposed Ismail in April 1980. Most important, however, was the realization that came sometime in the spring that Salih was not seriously pursuing unity with South Yemen, nor was his rapprochement with the NDF more than a tactical political maneuver. Thus, while meetings of the unity committees continued, and South Yemeni officials made numerous trips to North Yemen (including three visits by Muhammad, in June, July, and September), there were few reciprocal visits, and little real progress could be observed. At the same time, Salih had embarked on a political initiative in the YAR to create a General People's Congress and a 'Unified Yemeni Organization,' which seemed to be an attempt to broaden his support; although these were supposed to encompass all 'national forces,' the prominence given to Islam as one of their main pillars indicated that they would be at odds with significant elements in the NDF and with Aden.[23] Riyadh could also take some comfort from the deterioration in Salih-NDF relations. Fighting escalated throughout the summer as the North Yemeni army, its weapons and training upgraded, became more aggressive; nevertheless, relations between the Yemens remained calm, since Muhammad was perceived as not assisting, indeed even as squeezing, the rebel group.

The Soviets paid little attention to the vagaries of YAR politics. Nor did they concern themselves about the faltering unity movement, or about Sanaa's open declaration of a policy of playing off the superpowers.[24] They were content, at least for the moment, to have reestablished good state-to-state relations, to receive occasional gestures of North Yemeni support (such as its attendance at the Islamic Conference at Tashkent in September), and especially to have reestablished contact with the North Yemeni military. Soviet arms continued to arrive throughout a campaign in the fall of 1980 in which the military, aided by northern tribal forces now grouped in the Islamic Front, gained the upper hand over the NDF in the central regions of the YAR. By March 1981 it was estimated that the Yemenis had received over $1 billion worth of military equipment, including more than 500 T55 tanks, 26 MiG-21s, and 14 SU-22s (with more planes promised). According to the U.S. State Department, there were 700 Soviet military advisers in the country, and another 700 Yemeni military men had gone to the Soviet Union for training.[25]

Salih then attempted to distance himself from Saudi Arabia. The North Yemenis were angered by their exclusion from the Gulf Cooperation Council (reportedly on the insistence of Saudi Arabia[26]), membership in which could have meant a significant broadening of its aid sources (and less dependence on Saudi Arabia), an increase in its stature, and tangible political support for its dealings with the PDRY. However, aside from arresting Abdullah al-Asnaj on a charge of working for Riyadh to undermine relations with the PDRY, Salih could do little. The North Yemeni government was becoming even more dependent on Saudi budgetary aid as remittances from Yemenis working abroad declined from their 1979 peak; Sanaa was also undoubtedly concerned over the PDRY-Ethiopian defense agreement. Thus, at the April 1981 meeting of the Saudi-YAR Coordination Committee, both sides projected a high degree of understanding and stressed their "deep conviction in Islam and Arabism"; Saudi Arabia pledged to maintain its budgetary support and project assistance.[27]

At the same time Salih began cautiously to expand his relations with the Soviets. At the end of March 1981, on the anniversary of the 1964 Soviet-YAR friendship and trade treaty, a delegation travelled to Moscow to solicit Soviet assistance in searching for oil, but also to arrange a visit by Salih in July. Moscow was keenly interested in expanding the exclusively military relationship into a broadly based political and economic one as well. Two long articles had signalled a positive attitude toward Sanaa at the time. One, in *Izvestiia* on November 21, 1980, had been complimentary (but not effusive) about the YAR, noting the points of agreement between its foreign policy and that of the Soviet Union, and approving the development of relations between the two Yemens which, it said, would promote the attainment of unity. In January 1981, an extensive (and rare) interview with the Soviet Ambassador to the YAR extolled Soviet disinterested aid and appeared to promise as much aid as Sanaa wanted in the political, economic, and military fields. The Ambassador discussed with unusual frankness the reason for Soviet interest in the YAR:

> ... it overlooks an area of extreme importance for the strategies of the major powers regarding both East Africa and the southern Arabian Peninsula. . . . (G)eographically and politically this area is very close to us and it is located in 'our belly.' We are very interested in knowing what happens in it and around it with regard to developments and changes so that we can reach conclusions which we incorporate in our calculations of our strategic dealings with the powers around us.[28]

In addition to its general wish to expand relations, Moscow hoped to receive Salih's support for Brezhnev's Persian Gulf proposal and to then enlist him in its campaign against the U.S. military access agreements in the region (a campaign which he supported in any case); it may also have wanted to try to encourage North Yemen to join the PDRY-Ethiopian agreement, or at least try to reassure Salih about it.

However, shortly after the visit was arranged renewed fighting with the NDF broke out. In view of the more militant stance adopted by Muhammad in the early months of 1981, it is likely that Salih suspected his hand in the latest round. Relations had not been very good since late fall, when Salih failed to show up for the PDRY's independence day celebrations to reciprocate Muhammad's attendance at the YAR's festivities. Although the unity committees continued to meet, no noticeable progress was made. The two countries were at odds on a number of issues, not least of which was the Iran-Iraq war, in which Aden was supporting Iran while Sanaa was selling Iraq some of the Soviet arms it had not been able to absorb. This led them into opposing stances in the Syria-Iraq dispute, and when Syria began to encourage and support the NDF, Salih had another reason to suspect Aden of involvement. The Soviet Union was, of course, a close friend of both Syria and the PDRY, and as the fighting grew more intense, Salih postponed his visit until August.

In early August Moscow sent Oleg Grinevskiy to Sanaa for five days of talks on bilateral relations, which the Soviets hoped would clear the way for Salih's visit. However, the creation of the Tripartite Alliance, which was seen in Sanaa as possibly intended to control the southern end of the Red Sea, alarmed Salih, especially after Qadhdhafi's reported promise of weapons and £500,000 to the NDF.[29] The appointment of a new South Yemeni Defense Minister (Salih Muslih Qasim) with close ties to both Libya and the NDF added to Salih's worries. He decided to meet this new danger by continuing to prosecute the war in the south, by warming up his relations with Riyadh, but also by moving toward Aden and Moscow. Muhammad visited North Yemen in mid-September, for the first time in a year. He was dealing from strength, with the Tripartite Alliance behind him and the NDF doing well in the south; however, he was not averse to undermining the NDF to bolster his own domestic position, and equally important, the Soviets were sympathetic to a more moderate approach. Thus, in return for indications of greater commitment to unity from Ali Abdullah, and for foreign policy declarations compatible with those of the PDRY,[30] he apparently undertook to curb the activities of the NDF.

Soviet-North Yemeni relations then began to expand with the despatch of an economic delegation for the September 26th anniversary and with a warm telegram from Brezhnev. The delegation signed an agreement granting a $15 million loan for water resources projects (the first Soviet development loan to the YAR for three years and, incidentally, the only new Soviet aid committed to Middle East countries in 1981[31]). Salih then went to Moscow at the end of October 1981, seeking: more economic aid; more weapons, to replace those lost, destroyed, or sold to Iraq; relief from repayment of debts (although the 1979 arms had been sold at rock-bottom prices, the YAR still owed money on arms and supplies bought in the late 1960s and 1970s, as well as on Soviet loans from that time); and Soviet good offices in solving the NDF problem. In these specific aims he was partly successful. The communiqué[32] indicated that the Soviets were willing to provide further economic and military aid; although no agreements were publicized, arms shipments in 1982 indicated that a further arms deal was signed. The Arab press reported that Moscow had cancelled $265 million in past arms debts. The communiqué was, however, noncommittal on the subject of the YAR internal problem. The Soviet side merely "expressed satisfaction with the development of fraternal relations between the YAR and the PDRY in the light of documents signed in Kuwait. . . ."; this could be taken as a hint that Moscow wanted to see more steps taken toward cooperation with the PDRY before it would make any moves regarding the NDF; on the other hand, the lack of mention in the communiqué or any of the speeches or publicity during the visit of a 'democratic' basis for unity meant that Moscow was not willing to push Salih to accommodate the NDF.

In general, the visit was a success for both sides. In addition to the gains mentioned above, Salih's reception increased his stature in the Arab world and at home. He was greeted by Brezhnev at the airport with full ceremony, had his picture published in *Pravda*, and had discussions with Brezhnev, Gromyko, and Ustinov. An "exchange of opinions" was said to have taken place in "an atmosphere of mutual understanding and friendship," terminology which indicated a reasonably friendly meeting, considering the state of relations between the two countries. Ali Abdullah was less than effusive in his praise of Soviet assistance to the YAR, but made up for it by lining up with the Soviets on all the major regional issues (including the Soviet call for an international conference on the Arab-Israeli struggle [something Muhammad had not yet supported] except Afghanistan, which was not mentioned.

On these issues, Salih was thus at odds, at least in emphasis, with Saudi Arabia. However, having demonstrated his freedom to maneuver and his nonalignment, Salih travelled immediately to Riyadh to assure the Saudis that his 'balance of patrons' was intact, and to seek more aid. He was reported to have asked not only for development aid, but also for money to purchase Soviet weapons;[33] not surprisingly, the Saudis turned down the latter request. Nevertheless, they did promise to increase financial and economic aid. In return, Salih endorsed the Fahd Plan for a Middle East peace settlement and a Red Sea security formulation which was marginally different from the "zone of peace" concept. He apparently gave adequate assurances of his reliability for the Saudis to accept a North Yemeni move toward reducing tension with South Yemen.

The timing seemed right. All countries in the region were concerned by the polarization which took place in 1981 and the danger of superpower involvement if the conflict on the Yemeni border should get out of hand as it had done in 1979. At the same time the Saudis and Soviets seemed closer to a rapprochement because of Moscow's interest in the Fahd Plan. For his part, Ali Nasir Muhammad seemed to want to improve relations both with the GCC countries because of their movement toward a common defense pact and their aid potential, and with the YAR to improve his position in the power struggle within the Aden regime. On November 23 the two Yemeni leaders arrived in Kuwait together with NDF leader Umar, and with the mediation of the Amir negotiated a ceasefire between the NDF and Sanaa. No details were revealed, but it appears that Salih did not have to make political concessions to the NDF. The price of the deal for him was a significant improvement in relations with the PDRY: on December 1 he visited Aden (the first visit by any YAR leader — al-Hamdi, it will be remembered, was about to visit when he was assassinated). After a tumultuous welcome and two days of discussions he signed a wide-ranging cooperation pact pledging the two governments to work closely on matters of the economy and foreign policy (but not on internal political matters). The two leaders formed themselves into a Yemeni Council which was to meet every six months, and established a Ministerial Council, which included the Prime Ministers and senior ministers of each Cabinet. In the foreign policy sphere the two states pledged to cooperate in procuring unconditional Arab economic aid and to follow a common policy which included support for radical Arab causes, opposition to the United States, and support for both Muhammad's summit conference proposal and for the Soviet Gulf and Indian Ocean initiatives.[34]

This was clearly a plan for closer cooperation, not unity. However, at the end of December the unity committee on the constitution reported agreement on a draft document. It indicated that both sides were anxious to report progress; Islam was to be the state religion and neither Marxism nor scientific socialism was mentioned; however, the state would be governed by the principles of "social justice" not the principles of Islam. There was to be a private sector and a public sector in the economy. It was to be a parliamentary democracy, which would mean that opposition parties would have to be allowed in South Yemen, but also that the NDF would have to be legalized in the North. It was clear that each side could draw what it wanted from the document to justify signing it, and equally clear that neither side expected it to produce a unified state in the near term.[35]

On the surface, unity prospects remained hostage to the activities of the NDF and to the power struggle in Aden. The NDF, apparently on the initiative of PDRY Defense Minister Qasim (for whom active support of the NDF was a tool in his struggle with Ali Nasir Muhammad), began to receive more sophisticated weapons from South Yemen, Libya, and Syria. After fighting flared up again in February 1982, NDF forces used (Soviet) surface-to-air missiles to bring down three YAR planes, including two (Soviet) SU-22s. The Saudis were reported to have instigated the northern tribes' proposal to create a 'people's army' under the slogan 'Defending Islam against the Communist Threat from Aden,' and PDRY forces were said to be mobilizing on the border. The danger subsided only after the flooding in South Yemen in early April required troops to be removed from the border, and Ali Nasir was able to curtail the flow of weapons to the NDF.

This gave Salih more room to maneuver. A high-level Saudi delegation, led by the Defense Minister, flew to Sanaa on April 7 for the annual meeting of the Joint Coordination Council, and promised not only continued economic and budgetary aid, but also $400 million of immediate military aid. The two sides, declared the communiqué, had "decided to confront anyone who tries to harm the territorial integrity, security or independence of either of them."[36] Shortly thereafter fierce fighting broke out as Salih's forces attacked. The NDF was pushed out of the central regions south of Sanaa to the border, and several thousand supporters in the cities were arrested. By the beginning of May it had conceded defeat for the present by withdrawing most of its fighters to the PDRY, and on May 5 Salih and Muhammad again met in Taizz. Salih was, for once, in a strong position, and the two leaders emphasized that "the achievement of security and stability is the most pressing demand of the masses."[37] The meeting apparently produced a commitment from Muhammad to limit South Yemen's support for the NDF, but relations between the two Yemens remained cool, and the unity committees did not resume their work. Salih could not be confident of Ali Nasir's moderation, especially as the NDF continued to be represented in the YSP Central Committee and could count on support within the Politbureau in Aden. Moreover, Salih had been forced to move much closer to Riyadh to weather the latest crisis.

The Soviets ignored the hostilities. Neither the NDF's victories nor its losses were allowed to spoil relations. Sanaa ignored in public the role that Soviet weapons were playing in its civil strife, accepting Soviet assurances that they had no contacts with the guerrillas.[38] Sanaa may also have been reassured by signs that Moscow supported Muhammad and not his more radical rivals. Nevertheless, YAR-Soviet relations were undoubtedly cooled by the tension between the two Yemens and the Soviets' close involvement in South Yemen. The number of delegations exchanged remained low. In April (just as the major offensive against the NDF began) a delegation from the YAR Moral Orientation Directorate visited Moscow for talks on political work in the military; there is no doubt that the Soviets would like to play a role in the political indoctrination of the North Yemeni military, but Sanaa did not invite a similar Soviet delegation to visit, either then or since. Also in April a Soviet Embassy official participated in a conference in Sanaa on the YAR's new Five-Year Plan; he gave general promises of aid, but no specifics. More important to Salih, however, military supplies continued to arrive (SU-22s, helicopters, and missiles), and Moscow promised to deliver MiG-23s. In early August a detachment of Soviet warships visited Hodaydah; while not unusual in itself, the visit was the first in over a decade to be publicized.

The Israeli invasion of Lebanon in the summer of 1982 gave the YAR more leeway to pursue its nonaligned course and even gave it (with the PDRY) a moment on center stage in Arab politics. In July Salih's adviser al-Hubayshi visited Moscow for talks centering on the Lebanese situation; however, he did not, as did Muhammad a short time later, criticize the critics of the Soviet response to the Israeli invasion. Then in early August Salih and Muhammad joined in a visit to Riyadh and Damascus (and sent their Foreign Ministers to other Middle East capitals) to urge an Arab summit to find a common policy on Lebanon; they had earned the right to a brief prominence by being the only Arab countries to send 'volunteers' to Beirut to fight alongside the PLO. When PLO fighters were evacuated, 800 members of Fatah went to the YAR [and 1,700 members of the Democratic Front for the Liberation of Palestine (DFLP), PFLP, and PFLP-General Command went to the PDRY].

These joint endeavors, and cooperation at the second Fez conference in September, warmed relations between the two; unity again began to be mentioned as a goal, and in November the secretariat of the Yemeni Council met for the first time since being established eleven months previously. However, this did not mean that unity was any closer, for in the meantime Salih had convened a General People's Conference which had approved a National Charter and elected him its General Secretary; these moves, on the surface the introduction of democracy to the YAR, seemed designed more to consolidate his position in the country[39] and at the same time to leave him in a stronger position to bargain with Muhammad. Perhaps recognizing this, and believing that unity could not for the moment take place on terms favorable to the PDRY, the Soviets ceased to refer to Yemeni unity (even when it was brought up by Ali Nasir Muhammad during his September visit), and concentrated on improving relations with Salih. They chose to ignore the exclusion of the NDF (as a party — several members of the NDF were chosen to sit as individual representatives) from the General People's Congress, and to regard it positively. On the 20th anniversary of the September 26th revolution, Brezhnev sent a warm telegram to Salih (who also replied warmly), and the Soviet media praised the YAR's foreign policy and Salih's leadership.[40]

THE ANDROPOV MONTHS (NOVEMBER 1982 TO FEBRUARY 1984)

Six weeks later Brezhnev was dead. Ali Abdullah Salih, accompanied by a small entourage, joined Ali Nasir Muhammad on a flight to Moscow for the funeral. His reception was correct, with no special touches. This was merely in keeping with the actual nature of the Soviet-North Yemeni relationship, and signified that Moscow wished to maintain it unchanged. When a strong earthquake shook the central regions of the YAR in mid-December, Moscow was quick to respond with emergency relief shipments. As with the flood aid to South Yemen the previous spring, these were not large, the Soviets preferring to leave it to the oil states to provide the bulk of the aid. Similarly, when YAR Deputy Prime Minister Makki visited Moscow immediately after this for talks on aid, he received only minor commitments, although he may also have been able to convince Moscow to reschedule Sanaa's military debt.

Other than this, the Soviets made no effort to advance the relationship during the first few months of Andropov's tenure. It was evident that there continued to be no enthusiasm in Moscow for Yemeni unity. Salih and Muhammad were scheduled to meet in January 1983 to discuss practical steps toward unity and to move the draft constitution toward popular ratification. The unexplained postponement of this meeting to March, and then to August, elicited no Soviet comment; nor, when the two leaders did finally meet, did Muhammad's call for a unified political organization and unity by peaceful and democratic means. This inattention was also due to the Kremlin's preoccupation with the Lebanese and Palestinian crises and the Iran-Iraq war during this period; South Arabia was not a region of high priority. Moreover, Moscow may have been hoping yet again for a breakthrough in its relations with Riyadh after Foreign Minister Saud al-Faisal's participation in the Arab states' delegation to Moscow in December 1982, and King Fahd's reported appeal to Andropov for help in bringing the Iran-Iraq war to an end.[41] If that were the case, the less obvious Soviet involvement with Sanaa, the better.

Moscow was, however, looking ahead to March 1984 when the little-noticed 20-year Treaty of Friendship was due for renewal. Articles began to appear rating highly recent North Yemeni economic and political progress and foreign policy. In March 1983, for only the second time, the Soviets commemorated the treaty's anniversary, in an obvious effort to ensure that it would be renewed. This may have been a factor in the increase in Soviet interest in the second half of 1983. Other factors may have been: the indications of closer Saudi-North Yemeni (and Saudi-South Yemeni) relations in the spring and summer, as Salih visited the kingdom twice; Salih's involvement in mediation between Arafat and Qadhdhafi and Arafat and his opponents in the PLO; and Sanaa's assurances that the USSR would remain the YAR's principal arms supplier.[42] Whatever the reason, there was a noticeable increase in the tempo of messages and visits. A Soviet military group visited in early June; no arms were promised, and shortly after it left Salih aimed an indirect appeal at Andropov for a "comprehensive development of all aspects of cooperation."[43] A Yemeni parliamentary delegation visited in late July, with considerable Soviet publicity. In August the Minister of Health met Politbureau member Gaidur Aliev and delivered a message to Andropov; the meeting was said to be "warm and friendly," but referred to an exchange of opinions on bilateral relations and the means of strengthening them,[44] probably over the Soviets' reluctance to provide new aid commitments. The following month Moscow sent a low-level delegation to the September 26 anniversary celebrations. This greater-than-usual attention continued in October as the Soviet leadership sent a cable on the 55th anniversary of the establishment of relations between the USSR and Yemen.

Nonetheless, relations did not improve, and Moscow may have been disturbed by the YAR's supporting the readmittance of Egypt to the Islamic Conference Organization, as well as by reports of increased tensions in south Arabia at the end of 1983.[45] At the end of January, Salih reportedly received a message from Andropov which included an invitation to visit Moscow. The intent of the Soviet leadership was probably to improve Soviet-Yemeni relations and to reap propaganda advantage from the renewal of the 20-year Friendship Treaty. However, two weeks later Andropov died, and in the ensuing succession process, the treaty was renewed automatically, without fanfare.

NOTES

1. Cf. *MECS 1977-78*, pp. 657-9, and *Arabia and the Gulf* 1 (October 24, 1977): 6.
2. *FBIS/USSR*, October 24, 1977, p. F1; *FBIS/USSR*, October 25, 1977, pp. F4-5; *FBIS/USSR*, October 27, 1977, p. F2.
3. A technical training agreement was signed in February, two U.S. delegations visited in the spring. However, an indication of Soviet feeling about the YAR could be seen in the inclusion in the curriculum of Soviet training camps for the PLO of a course entitled "The Reactionary Nature of North Yemen and Saudi Arabia." C. Sterling, *The Terror Network* (New York: Holt, Rinehart & Winston, 1981), p. 279.
4. In December 1977 the Saudis pledged $570 million toward the 5-year Development Plan (one-sixth of the total expected investment). In early 1978 they pledged $70 million in budget assistance and 50,000 tons of oil.
5. *FBIS/MENA*, July 3, 1978, p. A4.
6. However, the appearance of a brief announcement of the attempted coup in several Soviet newspapers was unusual, and may have indicated official unhappiness with Salih.
7. *FBIS/MENA*, October 26, 1978, pp. C5-6.
8. *FBIS/MENA*, January 30, 1979, p. C5. Grinevskiy had visited Kuwait to try to reassure Gulf rulers that Moscow had not been responsible for the turbulence in Iran; this may have been his task in Sanaa as well, but it is possible, since he visited Aden next, that he tried to mediate between the two Yemens.

9. N. Novik, *Between Two Yemens: Regional Dynamics and Superpower Conduct in Riyadh's 'Backyard'* (Tel Aviv: Center for Strategic Studies, 1980), p. 8; "Riyadh - Washington Axis in Jeopardy," *Middle East International*, no. 94 (March 2, 1979): 2.

10. There were many positive references to Saudi Arabia in the Soviet media between October 1978 and March 1979, the most noted being Igor Beliaev's article in *Literaturnaia Gazeta*, January 31, 1979, in which he suggested that it might be an opportune moment for the USSR and Saudi Arabia to improve their relations.

11. For an outline of the 1979 War and U.S. and Arab responses to it, cf. *Keesing's Contemporary Archives*, April 18, 1980, pp. 30197-98.

12. Not surprisingly, this was Aden's version of the start of the fighting. But some Western intelligence sources tentatively agree with the idea that Salih was trying to speed up U.S. arms shipments.

13. While many of the North Yemeni claims about the extent and ferocity of the fighting should be viewed skeptically, U.S. photographic intelligence showed that considerable territory had in fact been taken.

14. Fred Halliday has confirmed from a PDRY government source that the Soviets "held back" the South Yemenis when they were in an "advantageous position"; the timing of this move was not specified, but the wording indicates that it took place in the first week of the fighting. F. Halliday, *Threat from the East? Soviet Policy from Afghanistan and Iran to the Horn of Africa* (New York: Penguin Books, revised ed., 1982), p. 49.

15. *FBIS/USSR*, March 2, 1979, p. F2; *Pravda*, March 2, 1979.

16. *FBIS/USSR*, March 9, 1979, p. F8; *Pravda*, March 14, 1979.

17. S. Scarlis, "On the Eve of a New Saudi-Soviet Relationship?," *Radio Liberty Research Bulletin* #RL 163/79 (May 29, 1979).

18. *FBIS/MENA*, June 25, 1979, p. C1.

19. Compare figures in U.S., Central Intelligence Agency, *Communist Aid to the Less Developed Countries of the Free World 1977* (McLean, VA: CIA, 1978), p. 4; U.S., CIA, *Communist Aid Activities in Non-Communist Less Developed Countries 1978* (McLean, VA: CIA, 1979), p. 5; U.S., CIA, *Communist Aid Activities in Non-Communist Less Developed Countries 1979 and 1954-1979* (McLean, VA: CIA, 1980), p. 16.

20. The Economist, *Foreign Report*, September 19, 1979, p. 7; C. van Hollen, "North Yemen: A Dangerous Pentagonal Game," *The Washington Quarterly* 5 (Summer 1982): 140; C. Kutschera, "On the Brink of Stability," *The Middle East*, no. 75 (January 1981): 26.

21. *FBIS/USSR*, September 28, 1979, p. H7.

22. *Al-Khalij*, May 31, 1980, in *MECS 1980-81*, p. 834.

23. *MECS 1979-80*, p. 830.

24. *FBIS/MENA*, April 3, 1980, p. C7.

25. U.S. Arms Control & Disarmament Agency, *World Military Expenditures and Arms Transfers 1971-1980* (Washington, D.C.: ACDA, 1983), p. 115; U.S. Department of State, *Soviet and East European Aid to the Third World, 1981* (Washington, D.C.: Department of State, 1983), pp. 8, 15. The

U.S. military contingent had shrunk to six, and they were reported to be increasingly isolated.

26. *MECS 1980-81*, pp. 872-3.
27. *Ibid*, p. 270.
28. *FBIS/USSR*, January 15, 1981, pp. H4-7.
29. M. Adams, "Qadafi's Itchy Fingers," *Middle East International*, no. 164 (December 11, 1981): 7; *Al-Nahar al-Arabi wal-Duwali* 4 (September 21, 1981): 21.
30. *FBIS/MENA*, September 16, 1981, pp. C3-4.
31. U.S., Department of State, op. cit., p. 7.
32. The communiqué is found in *FBIS/USSR*, October 19, 1981, pp. H9-12.
33. A. Yodfat, *The Soviet Union and the Arabian Peninsula* (New York: St. Martin's Press, 1983), p. 161, fn. 70.
34. The text is in *FBIS/MENA*, December 4, 1981, pp. C3-7. The first test of this agreement came at the Fez Conference in mid-December, which was to discuss the Fahd Plan; the YAR did not line up with the Steadfastness Front's rejection of the plan, but it did not give Saudi Arabia its full support, either. *Plus ça change*, ...
35. As Mark Katz has pointed out, for Sanaa, "the primary value of efforts toward unity may be to broaden and strengthen those elements in Aden who support cooperative relations with the YAR," M.N. Katz, "North Yemen between East and West," *American-Arab Affairs*, no. 8 (Spring 1984): 106.
36. *FBIS/MENA*, April 9, 1982, pp. C14-16; *Defense & Foreign Affairs Daily* 11 (April 21, 1982). This interest in a militarily strong North Yemen should be seen in the context of the Saudi decision to export considerable amounts of oil via the Red Sea.
37. *FBIS/MENA*, May 6, 1982, p. C9; interestingly, Aden radio's account of the meeting did not mention security and stability, perhaps a sign that Ali Nasir's control was still incomplete.
38. It was said that in private the North Yemenis several times warned the Soviet Ambassador against Soviet interference in the YAR's internal affairs. *FBIS/MENA*, May 10, 1982, p. C9.
39. *MECS 1981-82*, p. 815.
40. *FBIS/MENA*, September 22, 1982, p. H12; *Izvestiia*, October 29, 1982.
41. *FBIS/MENA*, April 29, 1983, p. C2.
42. R. Dergham, "Blueprint for a United Yemen," *The Middle East*, no. 101 (March 1983): 30.
43. *FBIS/MENA*, June 20, 1983, p. C4.
44. *FBIS/USSR*, August 15, 1983, p. H5.
45. *Agence France Presse*, January 17, 1983 reported military clashes on the Saudi Arabia-South Yemeni border.

PART IV

CONCLUSION

8
CONCLUSION

It is clear from the foregoing that over the past 15 years the Soviets have moved from a peripheral position regarding southern Arabia to a central position from which, in a variety of ways, they can affect events and conditions both there and in adjacent territories and waters. This has largely been due to their decision in the 1960s to adopt a 'forward' policy in both political and military spheres, and to its subsequent implementation, in the Indian Ocean in 1968, in Somalia and the PDRY, and Ethiopia in 1977. These new capabilities, combined with U.S. policies and regional events, created new conditions in the region which limited the options open to the YAR (and to its aspiring patron, Saudi Arabia), not least because of their fear of a Soviet-armed, and presumably Soviet-inspired, PDRY. The options available to the PDRY, on the other hand, expanded somewhat with the strengthening of its presumed protector, but were still limited by the need for policies broadly acceptable to Moscow, and by the suspicions of its neighbors about Soviet goals in the region.

In the process of improving their regional positions, it is evident that the Soviets have developed the resources (in part economic, but mainly military) to persuade governments in the area to take actions to which the latter were predisposed anyway ('influence' in its broadest sense). It is less clear that the Soviets have the ability to affect *any or every* event that they wish, much less to achieve desirable outcomes for events consistently. And it is even less clear that they can at any given time persuade the governments in the area to take action which the latter perceive as inimical to their interests ('influence' in its strictest sense).

MOSCOW AND THE YEMEN ARAB REPUBLIC

Directly or indirectly, the Soviets played an important role in preserving the YAR in the 1960s. Yet they were never able to make an impact on the political, economic, or social fabric of the country. The dominant internal forces were, and largely remain, Islamic, tribal, and conservative, suspicious of radical change and communism. These have been buttressed by Saudi Arabia, which has drawn on its economic power to intrude into Yemeni political life and at times to exert direct influence on decisions. This situation has left Moscow in an outsider's position, able only to respond to local or regional events in hopes of affecting their outcomes. (This it has done with some success, witness the final collapse of the Red Sea security concept with Moscow's decisive entry into Ethiopia.)

Further compounding the Soviets' difficulty in developing an influence relationship with Sanaa are their very close ties with the PDRY. For the past 17 years relations with South Yemen have been a central concern in Sanaa's policies. For most of that period these relations have oscillated between 'poor' and 'hostile,' and Moscow's record of consistent support for Aden has inevitably made it suspect in Sanaa. It is never easy to back both sides in a dispute.

Nonetheless, there is a bright spot for Moscow in the picture, created by the very intrusiveness of Riyadh and dependence on Saudi financial aid that limit Soviet possibilities in the YAR. For these inevitably cause resentment in Sanaa, and Saudi heavy-handed interference reinforces an innate Yemeni desire to play off those who seek to influence. Thus Ali Abdullah Salih, defying what appeared in Western eyes to be the logic of the situation, invited the Soviets to play again the role of modernizing the North Yemeni armed forces. This is what the Soviets do best in the Third World, and they responded quickly and effectively. But an arms deal is not tantamount to the creation of influence. (Indeed, one might argue that it was the North Yemenis who exercised influence over the Soviets, for the upgrading of the YAR military was to the detriment of a Soviet client, the PDRY, and its clients, the NDF.)

Given the difficulties inherent for them in YAR-Saudi ties and YAR-PDRY relations (which were compounded by the PDRY-Soviet Treaty and by the Tripartite Alliance), the Soviets appear to be comfortable with the prospect of stable state-to-state relations in which they can expand their contacts with groups or individuals who are or may become politically important. By this is not meant the NDF; it is still a force in the southern YAR and may yet play a role in Yemeni politics, but Salih is obviously sensitive about it; the Soviets, if they have direct contacts with the NDF, are not admitting it. They have been cultivating students; currently there are over 1,000 in the USSR at any one time. This is of course no guarantee of future influence, since students are often anti-Soviet when they return, and thus far few have been given significant jobs. However, the latter condition may change. Far more important is the officer class, which already forms an important political group, and from which Salih's successor will probably come. Moscow is donating millions of dollars worth of military equipment (for the prospects of repayment of the military debt are slim) largely, it appears, for the chance to keep military advisers in the country, to train Yemeni officers in the socialist countries, and in general to try to cement ties with the officer class.

While this appears to be a very modest and tentative policy for expanding Soviet influence, it is evident that Soviet aims in the YAR are quite modest. There is little expectation that it will provide a gateway to Saudi Arabia (although Moscow would doubtless welcome and try to take advantage of any events in the YAR which promised to weaken Saudi antagonism and resistance to the USSR). Good, more secure, military facilities are available elsewhere in the vicinity. Moscow is definitely hostile to Yemen unity except under the circumstance of South Yemeni dominance; however, this is extremely unlikely, and no amount of Soviet influence could bring it about, or is necessary to prevent unity under adverse circumstances. Aside from that, Moscow at present seems to want only that the YAR not be actively hostile to South Yemen, that it be friendly toward the USSR and support some of its policies, and, most important, that it not move closer to Saudi Arabia or the United States. Sanaa has similar goals, given its fear of a too-tight embrace by Saudi Arabia, its resentment of Washington's ties with Israel, and the deep divisions in North Yemeni society; thus, even the low level of influence generated by Soviet arms aid is sufficient for the time being.

MOSCOW AND THE PEOPLE'S
DEMOCRATIC REPUBLIC OF YEMEN

Moscow was invited to play a role in the new republic of South Yemen in 1967 by a regime which was viscerally anti-Western and committed to revolution against the reactionary rulers on the Arabian Peninsula. After some hesitation, the Soviets agreed to do so, for reasons that were rooted in ideology, in the Sino-Soviet dispute, but mainly in the strategic location of South Yemen.

Once having grasped this opportunity, they and their East European and Cuban allies quickly became the main source of assistance to Aden. They provided essential help through advisers and training programs in building the Yemeni Socialist Party, a ruling party which espoused the cause of 'scientific socialism' and had very close ties to the CPSU. They worked to enhance the regime's legitimacy in the international arena through propaganda support and a stream of delegations to and from Aden. Their economic aid program, never very large in absolute terms, and increasingly ineffective, was nevertheless a significant factor in the country's survival in its early days. Of greatest importance, however, were their security assistance and military aid: relatively large amounts of modern weapons, military and security personnel, and training. The aid was absolutely vital to the survival of the regime in the early 1970s and to its revolutionary ambitions; it continues to be seen in Aden as an essential shield against the perceived threats of the 1980s. Thus the penetration into South Yemeni society of Soviet, Cuban, and East European advisers, and of institutions modelled on the institutions of these countries, has been widespread (although apparently not complete). One would assume, therefore, that Soviet influence in Aden has been extensive.

If 'influence' is defined in its broadest sense, this is certainly true. The South Yemeni rulers have by virtue of their ideology been predisposed to the USSR in the years under study; the PDRY became a 'country of socialist orientation,' an ally, often the Soviet Union's most loyal friend in the Middle East. By and large, their national and regional goals have parallelled Moscow's, and they have been willing to pay the price, in poor relations with the conservative oil states and lost economic aid, for cooperating in Soviet regional activities. (Their willingness, of course, has been accentuated by the actual and perceived threats to national and regime security from their neighbors and the 'imperialists,' and by the demonstrated commitment from the Soviets and their allies to the security of the country and the preservation of the regime.)

Thus since June 1969, Aden has willingly adopted Moscow's friends as its own and enthusiastically endorsed Soviet international and regional campaigns. It has been quick to leap to the defense of the USSR against its detractors. It has established training camps for Palestinian fighters and international terrorist groups which Moscow supports clandestinely.[1] It has furthered Soviet policy in the Middle East (and reduced its own isolation) through its participation in the Steadfastness Front. Most visibly it has provided access to its facilities in the port of Aden and has allowed the Soviets to build an airbase and other facilities near Aden, for use in support of the Soviet Navy's Indian Ocean activities, for maritime reconnaissance, and for staging flights to the Horn and beyond; the most spectacular example of Soviet-South Yemeni cooperation in this respect was of course the Soviet-Cuban operation in Ethiopia, in which South Yemenis also participated. (Again, this operation demonstrated the Soviets' ability to influence PDRY policies through its regional actions which create conditions limiting Aden's options.)

However, as the record shows, this is not the complete story. Although all the prominent members of the regime have been pro-Soviet and willing to endorse Soviet policy in general and to accept a strong commitment from Moscow to support them, not all have been willing to support all Soviet policies and activities. Thus in the early years the regime was far more enthusiastic than the Soviets about the prospects of revolution in the Gulf, ignoring Moscow's desire to develop good relations with the new states as the British withdrew. Then again, Aden in the 1970s refused to endorse Soviet proposals for a political solution to the Arab-Israeli conflict; for the South Yemeni leaders, this would have been a betrayal of their radical roots and of the Palestinian groups they supported, and would have isolated them from the Steadfastness Front countries. For reasons again of their self-image, the PDRY regime resisted early Soviet requests for more or different facilities in the highly visible port of Aden; the Soviet Navy does have easy access to the existing facilities but opinions differ as to whether it is free and automatic. (Moscow has not tried to establish a formal base in Aden because of the political costs in the region, and because their access is sufficient to their needs, when considered with the anchorages off Socotra and the facilities in the Dahlacs.)

Salim Rubay Ali's tenure demonstrated the limitations of Soviet influence in a Third World country with a charismatic leader whose sense of national interest diverges to some degree from Soviet interests. Although Moscow might have benefited from his policies, it was worried that the attraction of oil money might be too powerful, and that Rubay Ali might go too far. However, the Soviets found that they had little direct leverage over him. They had to wait until a combination of regional conditions (the failure of Saudi aid to materialize) and internal conditions (poor harvests, Rubay Ali's eccentricities, and Ismail's political maneuvering aided to some extent by the Soviets) weakened him to a point where a coup could be successful. The lesson that both Abd al-Fattah Ismail and Moscow learned from Rubay Ali's actions was that there must be a stronger party in charge in the PDRY and that it must forge close ties to the CPSU. This seemed to have been accomplished with the creation and development of the Yemeni Socialist Party. Nevertheless the vanguard party and close ties, even though reinforced by a Treaty of Friendship and Cooperation with the USSR, could not prevent the ouster of Ismail in April 1980, despite direct Soviet political intervention.

These episodes demonstrate the limitations on Soviet influence in the PDRY. Despite a high degree of penetration (direct and indirect) into South Yemeni society, despite consistent political and security support, and despite the fact that their arms supply relationship fulfills all but one of Leitenberg and Sheffer's criteria for maximized influence of the supplier,[2] Moscow has not been able to influence Aden's policies in the direction of its own interests when those interests are perceived by a major faction in the ruling group to be inconsistent with the PDRY's interests.[3] Moreover, as the communiqués and reports of visits show, the Soviets have never been able to accomplish even a surface illusion of complete agreement in the relationship. Furthermore, the Soviets have been unable to manipulate the PDRY's political system sufficiently to ensure that their favorite stays in power.

This is so primarily because of the strong factional nature of South Yemeni politics, evolving still around personalities, tribal affiliation, birthplace (South Yemeni vs. North Yemeni), and, to a lesser extent, ideology, all under the umbrella of the YSP. Strong opposing factions have existed in the ruling group since its formation in the 1960s; when one has become dominant, another has always arisen to challenge it. Inevitably, one of the factions has or claims closer ties to the Soviets (either causing the other to distance itself somewhat from Moscow, or resulting from that action); this brings the Soviets into the domestic struggle and reduces their ability to influence the other faction. Moreover, although the Soviets, Cubans, and East Europeans have a substantial presence in the PDRY, they do not station troops there in sufficient numbers to force or prevent changes.

The PDRY's involvement with the Dhofari rebels and its relations with Oman have demonstrated both the general convergence of the goals of Moscow and Aden and the difficulty that Moscow experiences when those goals diverge. The Soviets were slower than the South Yemenis to espouse the Dhofari cause; they began to provide some direct political support and more indirect military support through South Yemen only after local and regional conditions encouraged them. From that point their interests were parallel, though possibly never quite identical, the Soviets focussing more on the danger of a U.S. and/or Iranian military foothold in Oman from which to dominate the Persian Gulf/Indian Ocean region.

Since the mid-1970s, particularly since the fighting in Dhofar stopped, their interests have often diverged. The Soviets' focus remained unchanged; if anything, it sharpened after the fall of the Shah and their Afghan invasion brought increased U.S. activity. On the other hand, South Yemeni hostility toward the Sultan has waxed and waned primarily according to the progress of the various power struggles in Aden (but not exclusively, for South Yemeni leaders have also been concerned at U.S. activity). Most recently, Ali Nasir Muhammad's pursuit of normalization of PDRY-Omani relations as an earnest of his desire for rapprochement with the moderate states on the peninsula (and economic aid from the oil states), despite close U.S.-Omani ties, has been conducted in the face of many indications of Soviet disapproval. Nevertheless, it continues.

One should, however, guard against overstating the negative case. The predominant facts of the USSR-PDRY relationship have always been these: those in control in Aden since 1969, of whichever faction, have been committed to 'socialist principles'; they have favored (more or less) Soviet types of economic, social and political organization; they have seen their security (and advantage in their factional struggles) in military and militia forces armed with modern weapons by the Soviets and trained by Soviet and Cuban advisers; for the most part, they have agreed willingly with Soviet global and regional diplomatic and military policies and activities. Moscow appears not to have had to bring pressure or even much persuasion to bear.

The factional struggle, which has been mentioned as a liability to the Soviets, can of course also work to their advantage. There has always been a strong faction in Aden which has closely identified itself with Moscow; if it is in power, the relationship has tended to function more smoothly; if it is out of power, its strength has restrained the leader from straying beyond boundaries acceptable to it. This appears to be almost a self-regulating mechanism; however, it is likely that the Soviets succeed in manipulating it to some extent, and thus create influence or pressure. Nonetheless, they have been fairly subtle in this (with the exception of the spring of 1978, when Salim Rubay Ali's position had already been severely weakened), for they understand the danger of backlash.

Since 1967 the USSR has moved from being in an extremely weak position in southern Arabia to being the strongest outside power involved there. It has accomplished this mainly by responding to changing conditions, at first cautiously, but after the mid-1970s with increasing confidence and strength. It has used a wide variety of tools, of which economic aid has been least important (and perhaps has become almost counterproductive, because it is so much less than needed and because other donors are available), and military aid (weapons, advisers, and in Ethiopia, Cuban forces) the most important. In the process, the Soviets have utilized local conflicts effectively; in the case of the Yemeni war in 1979 they were able to tie South Yemen more closely through resupply and new weapons, while allowing the North Yemenis to think that if they had better relations with Moscow, the Soviets would restrain Aden.

Moscow's major aims during these 15 years have been to reduce U.S. and Western presence and influence in the region (which reduction, to the extent that it has occurred, has done so largely despite Soviet activity), and to increase Soviet presence and influence while gaining secure access to military facilities (especially airfields). As this study has shown, it has succeeded in establishing a strong presence in South Yemen with apparently secure access to facilities and a significant presence in North Yemen. Its military presence in the YAR has been marginally translated into influence, to the extent that it encourages Sanaa to follow policies which it favors and which the Soviets judge to be in their interests, such as limiting Saudi influence; Moscow's activities in South Yemen and elsewhere in the region are other factors promoting some degree of influence. However, Saudi wealth and the continuing conservative and fragmented state of North Yemeni society have prevented, and seem likely to continue to prevent for some time, the Soviets from attaining an influential position.

In the PDRY, Soviet actions and presence have been important in the creation and preservation of a ruling group whose goals are essentially similar to the Kremlin's; thus on most issues the Soviets have hardly needed to exert influence. However, where national interests have diverged, Aden has had the strength to resist. Moscow has accepted these stands (*zigzagy* on the complex path to socialism, acknowledged as inevitable by all Soviets writing about socialist orientation[4]), at the very least because they have not threatened its very considerable assets in the PDRY. One can only speculate as to what the Soviets would do if Aden adopted policies which did threaten those assets. However, given Soviet statements after the Afghanistan invasion about the preservation of socialist regimes,[5] and their assignment of "rather high priority" to "safeguarding the regime chosen by the people of the PDRY,"[6] it seems very likely that they would act, either through their friends in South Yemen or as a last resort through proxy forces from outside. Ali Nasir Muhammad, for one, recognizes this, and for all his search for aid, has consistently staked out the PDRY's position as the USSR's loyal ally.

NOTES

1. According to Western intelligence sources, Aden appears to have reduced its involvement with international terrorists, while its involvement with the Palestinians has grown.
2. M. Leitenberg and G. Sheffer (eds.), *Great Power Intervention in the Middle East* (New York: Pergamon Press, 1979), p. 111.
3. A possible exception might be the reported Soviet restraint of the PDRY in the March 1979 war with the YAR. However, without better

knowledge of Aden's aims in that fighting, it is difficult to be sure that influence was exercised.

    4.   Cf. K.N. Brutents, *Osvobodivshiesia strany v 70-e gody* (Moscow: Politizdat, 1979), p. 76.

    5.   Cf. E.M. Primakov, "The USSR and the Developing Countries," *Journal of International Affairs* 34 (Fall/Winter 1980/1): 270; *Soviet World Outlook* 5 (June 15, 1980): 4; V.V. Aspaturian, "Soviet Global Power and the Correlation of Forces," *Problems of Communism* 29 (May-June 1980): 17.

    6.   B. Shiburin (Deputy Head of the USSR Foreign Ministry's Middle East Department) to K. Dawisha, June 1982, as told to the author.

SELECTED BIBLIOGRAPHY

Abir, M. *Oil, Power and Politics: Conflict in Arabia, the Red Sea and the Gulf.* London: Frank Cass, 1974.

Aleksandrov, I.A. *Narodnaia Demokraticheskaia Respublika Iemen.* Moscow: Iz. Nauka, 1976.

Bell, J.B. *South Arabia: Violence and Revolt.* Conflict Studies No. 40. London: The Institute for the Study of Conflict, 1973.

Bidwell, R.L. *The Two Yemens.* Boulder: Westview Press, 1973.

Burmistrov, V.N. "NDRI: pervoe desiatiletia nezavizimogo razvitiia," in *Istoriia i ekonomika Arabskikh stran: sbornik statei*, edited by E.A. Lebedev, pp. 3-24. Moscow: Iz. Nauka, 1977.

Chaudhry, S.A. *The People's Democratic Republic of Yemen: Review of Economic and Social Development.* Washington, D.C.: The World Bank, 1979.

Chubin. S. *Soviet Policy toward Iran and the Persian Gulf.* Adelphi Paper, No. 157. London: The International Institute for Strategic Studies, 1980.

Dawisha, A.I. and K. Dawisha (eds.) *The Soviet Union in the Middle East: Policies and Perspectives.* London: Holmes & Meier, 1982.

Dismukes, B. and J.M. McConnell. *Soviet Naval Diplomacy.* New York: Pergamon Press, 1979.

Freedman, R.O. *Soviet Policy Toward the Middle East since 1970.* 3rd ed. New York: Praeger, 1982.

Gerasimov, O.G. *Iemenskaia revoliutsiia 1962-1975 gg.: problemy i suzhdeniia.* Moscow: Iz. Nauka, 1979.

Halliday, F. *Arabia without Sultans.* New York: Penguin Books, 1974.

—— *Threat from the East? Soviet Policy from Afghanistan and Iran to the Horn of Africa.* London: Penguin Books, 1982.

—— "Yemen's Unfinished Revolution: Socialism in the South." *MERIP Reports*, No. 81 (October 1979), pp. 3-20.

Haselkorn, A. *The Evolution of Soviet Security Strategy 1965-1975.* New York: Crane, Russak, 1978.

Hensel, H.M. "Soviet Policy toward the Rebellion in Dhofar." *Asian Affairs* 13 (June 1982): 183-207.

Hosmer, S.T. and T.W. Wolfe. *Soviet Policy and Practice toward Third World Conflicts.* Toronto: D.C. Heath, 1983.

Kaplan, S.S. et al. *Diplomacy of Power: Soviet Armed Forces as a Political Instrument.* Washington, D.C.: The Brookings Institution, 1981.

Kotlov, L.N. and L.V. Valkova. *Iuzhnii Iemen.* Moscow: Iz. Misl, 1973.

Legum, C., H. Shaked and D. Dishon (eds.) *Middle East Contemporary Survey.* 6 vols. New York: Holmes & Meier.

Lenczowski, G. *The Middle East in World Affairs.* 4th ed. Ithaca, N.Y.: Cornell University Press, 1980.

Melikhov, I.A. *Oman mezhdu proshlym i nastoiashchym.* Moscow: Iz. Znanie, 1979.

Mylroie, L. *Politics and the Soviet Presence in the People's Democratic Republic of Yemen: Internal Vulnerabilities and Regional Challenges.* Rand Note N-2052-AF Santa Monica: Rand, 1983.

Novik, N. *Between Two Yemens: Regional Dynamics and Superpower Conduct in Riyadh's 'Backyard'.* Tel Aviv: Center for Strategic Studies, 1980.

—— "On the Shores of Bab al-Mandab: Soviet Diplomacy and Regional Dynamics." *Crossroads*, no. 2 (Winter 1979), pp. 61-101.

Page, S. *The USSR and Arabia: The Development of Soviet Policies and Attitudes Toward the Countries of the Arabian Peninsula.* London: Central Asian Research Centre in association with the Canadian Institute of International Affairs, 1971.

Peterson, J.E. *Conflict in the Yemens and Superpower Involvement.* Washington, D.C.: Center for Contemporary Arab Studies, Georgetown University, 1981.

——— *Oman in the Twentieth Century: Political Foundations of an Emerging State.* London: Croom Helm, 1978.

——— *Yemen: The Search for a Modern State.* Baltimore, The Johns Hopkins University Press, 1982.

Price, D.L. *Oman: Insurgency and Development.* Conflict Studies No. 53, London: Institute for the Study of Conflict, 1975.

Rubinstein, A.Z. *Soviet Foreign Policy since World War II: Imperial and Global.* Cambridge, Mass.: Winthrop Publishers, 1981.

Stookey, R.W. *South Yemen: A Marxist Republic in Arabia.* Boulder: Westview Press, 1982.

——— *Yemen: The Politics of the Yemen Arab Republic.* Boulder: Westview Press, 1978.

U.S. Arms Control and Disarmament Agency. *World Military Expenditures and Arms Transfers 1971-1980.* Washington, D.C.: ACDA 1983.

U.S. Central Intelligence Agency. *Communist Aid Activities in Non-Communist Less Developed Countries 1979 and 1954-1979.* McLean, VA: CIA, 1980.

U.S. Congress, House Committee on Foreign Affairs, Subcommittee on Europe and the Middle East. *Proposed Arms Transfers to the Yemen Arab Republic.* 96th Cong. 1st Sess., 1979.

U.S. Department of State, Bureau of Intelligence & Research. *Soviet and East European Aid to the Third World, 1981.* Washington, D.C.: Department of State, 1983.

Vorobev, V.P. *Politicheskaia i gosudarstvennaia sistema Narodnoi Demokraticheskoi Respubliki Iemena.* Moscow: Iz. Nauka, 1978.

Watson, B.W. *Red Navy at Sea: Soviet Naval Operations on the High Seas 1956-1980.* Boulder, Westview Press, 1982.

Yodfat, A. *The Soviet Union and the Arabian Peninsula.* New York: St. Martin's Press, 1983.

Zabarah, M.A. *Yemen: Traditionalism vs. Modernity.* New York: Praeger, 1982.

INDEX

Abd al-Alim, Abdullan, 170; rebellion, 180
Aden: military facilities, 3, 8, 169 [Soviet use of, 21, 29, 72, 79-80, 97, 105, 209-10]; refinery, 64, 67, 111
Afro-Asian Peoples' Solidarity Organization, 128, 134, 140, 142
al-Ahmar, Abdullah, 166
Ali, Salim Rubay, 22, 26, 31, 34, 35, 36, 37, 52, 54, 57ff., 62, 63, 65, 68, 72, 76, 164, 172, 173, 181; Soviet reaction to moderate line, 51, 53, 54, 57-58, 60, 63, 65, 67, 133, 137; visits to USSR, 37-40, 130, 164; visit to Saudi Arabia, 66-68; execution, 77-78
al-Amri, Hasan, 6
Andropov, Iuri, 115, 116, 117, 198, 199
Antar, Ali, 69, 75, 76, 77, 91, 102, 105-06
Arab League: freeze on relations PDRY, 78, 87, 182
al-Asnaj, Abdullah, 160, 161, 180, 182, 183, 190
al-Ayni, Muhsin, 159, 161, 164, 165, 168; visit to USSR, 161-62

Bab al-Mandab, Straits of, 3, 49, 167
BaDhib, Abdullah, 44
BaDhib, Ali, 64, 77, 100
Barre, Siad, 24, 71, 174
al-Bayd, Ali Salim, 103, 105
Brezhnev, Leonid, 20, 30, 32-33, 39, 40, 42, 43, 51, 58, 65-66, 73, 93-94, 99, 100, 105, 112-13, 114, 193, 197
Brutents, Karen, 68, 71, 103, 110, 116, 118

China, and Oman: support for Dhofar rebellion, 125, 126, 127, 128; change of policy, 128, 129, 130, 138; and PDRY, 19, 23, 26, 29, 34, 35, 40, 75; and YAR, 5, 158, 160, 162, 172

Dahlac Islands, 80, 85fn, 105
Dhofar Liberation Front, 125
Dhofar War, 130, 131, 133, 134, 135, 138, 139, 140
Diego Garcia, 29, 50, 55, 59 128, 131, 134, 143

219

Egypt: involvement in the Yemens, 6, 17; relations with USSR, 30-31, 36, 57, 108, 158, 162-63, 170
Epishev, Alexei, 29, 90

Findley, Paul, 51, 69, 72

al-Ghashmi, Ahmad, 169, 170, 179, 180; assassination, 77, 181
Gorshkov, Sergei, 29, 64, 74, 116
Grechko, Andrei, 7, 16, 20, 29, 31, 42, 51
Gromyko, Andrei, 38, 51, 65, 69, 139, 193
Gulf Cooperation Council, 104, 105, 108, 143, 144, 149, 190; PDRY reaction to, 104, 105, 106, 107, 142, 143, 149; Soviet reaction to, 142, 143

al-Hajari, Abdullah, 165, 166
al-Hamdi, Ibrahim, 65, 167, 168, 170, 171, 172, 175; assassination, 70, 179 [Soviet reaction to, 179]
Hormuz, Straits of: security of, 140

Iran-Iraq War: PDRY and YAR reaction to, 192
al-Iryani, Abd al-Rahman, 160, 161, 164, 166; visit to USSR, 161-62
Ismail, Abd al-Fattah, 17, 18, 23, 27, 35, 36, 37, 42, 52, 55, 69, 70, 76, 77, 86, 87, 88, 90, 91, 92, 93, 95, 102, 186; ouster, 99 [Soviet reaction, 99]; responsibility for 1972 PDRY-YAR fighting, 37; role in al-Ghashmi assassination, 77, 181; visits to USSR, 25-26, 29, 30, 42-43, 51-52, 132, 58, 70-71, 93-95, 138, 141

Kamaran Island, 164, 165
Kirilenko, Andrei, 58, 71, 100
Kosygin, Aleksei, 7, 20, 30, 31, 32, 35, 38, 39, 53, 73, 74, 101, 162, 164; visit to PDRY, 91-92, 141
Kutakhov, Pavel, 103, 108
Kuwait: mediation between PDRY and Oman, 140, 142, 144, 145, 146; mediation between PDRY and YAR, 186, 194

Masirah Island, 134, 136, 142
Mecca, Grand Mosque of: occupation of, 95, 120fn. 27
Muhammad, Ali Nasir, 26, 31, 37, 40, 52, 58, 69, 77, 79, 88, 91, 92, 98, 99, 100, 102, 105, 107, 109-10, 115, 116, 118, 142, 143; policy of accommodation with conservative Arab states, 99-100, 102-03, 110, 112, 114, 116, 145, 146, 149, 192, 194, [Soviet reaction, 102, 104, 108, 114, 118, 147, 148, 192]; visit to China, 75; visits to USSR, 29, 31-33, 42, 53, 67, 91, 101-02, 105,
112-14, 115-16, 117-18, 129, 138, 147, 149, 162
Muti, Muhammad Salih, 35, 54, 58, 66, 69, 75, 77, 79, 105, 133, 184; visit to USSR, 65-66, 137, 174

National Democratic Front, 171, 172, 175, 186, 188, 189, 192, 193, 194, 197; struggle with YAR Government, 110, 182, 184, 190, 191-92, 195-96; ties to PDRY, 107, 110, 171, 180-81, 182, 184, 186, 190, 192, 195, 196
National Front, 41-42; Congresses, 18, 55 [Soviet reaction, 34; factional infighting in, 16, 17-18, 19, 22, 36, 52; Higher Party School, 26 (*see also* United Political Organization-National Front; Yemeni Socialist Party)

October War 1973: consequences for PDRY, 49-50; impact on USSR-YAR relations, 166-67
Oman, and Great Britain, 129, 131; and Iran, 131, 135, 138, 140 (*see also* China; PDRY; Saudi Arabia; USSR; U.S.)

People's Democratic Republic of Yemen (PDRY): celebration of Lenin anniversary, 25; flood disaster, 110, 145; membership in CMEA, 91, 94; 1970 Constitution, 27; strategic location, 9; threat from émigré forces, 19, 24, 29, 31, 33, 35, 73, 78; and Cuba, 36,

43, 71, 76, 78, 130; and Dhofar, 125-46; Salim Rubay Ali's policy, 131-32, 133, 135, 136, 137, 138; Abd al-Fattah Ismail's policy, 133, 136, 137, 138, 140, 141 [Soviet reaction, 139, 141]; Ali Nasir Muhammad's policy, 138, 139, 141, 143, 145; and Ethiopia, 64, 66, 68, 69, 70, 73, 75; and GDR, 20, 23, 25, 27, 77; and Iran, 133, 136, 138; and Iraq, 35, 91-92, 98, 108, 109; and Oman, 91, 101, 102, 106, 109, 114, 116-17, 129, 130, 136, 137ff.; Soviet reaction, 114, 116, 129, 140, 146, 147, 149; agreement 1982, 147 [Soviet reaction, 148]; and Palestinians, 24, 43, 112, 116; and Persian Gulf states, 33, 52, 55, 58, 66, 75, 96, 100, 109, 111, 117, 145; and YAR, 36, 100, 109, 165, 168, 172, 173 [Soviet reaction, 146, 163]; 1972 War and results, 163-64 [Soviet reaction, 37, 38, 164-65]; 1979 War and results, 89, 140, 184-85 [Soviet reaction, 184-85; U.S. reaction, 184]; tensions, 35, 78, 157, 158, 160, 161, 163, 165, 182, 191, 194-95 [Soviet reaction, 181-82, 196]; and USSR re. Dhofar, 53, 73, 90, 126, 129, 130-31, 133-34, 135, 136, 138, 140-42; need for Soviet support, 19, 22, 23-24, 29, 31, 33, 35, 39, 52, 71, 77-78, 87-88; re. Oman, 137, 138, 142-45, 147-48; reaction to USSR's claim to Islamic legitimacy, 90, 96; reaction to Soviet policy in the Middle East, 24, 31, 32, 39, 66, 73, 101, 104, 106, 112, 123 fn. 91; Soviet interests in, 9-10, 15, 22-23, 31, 39-40, 71, 89, 119; support for Soviet invasion of Afghanistan, 95, 96, 100, 101, 105; Treaty of Friendship and Cooperation, 93-95, 99, 141 (*see also* National Front; United Political Organization-National Front; Yemeni Socialist Party; Saudi Arabia; USSR; U.S.; Yemeni unity)

People's Vanguard Party, 25, 56

Persian Gulf security, 136, 144, 149

Podgornyy, Nikolai, 16, 20, 22, 25, 51, 163

Ponomarev, Boris, 25, 38, 58, 64, 68, 71, 100, 103

Popular Democratic Union, 17, 25, 55

Popular Front for the Liberation of the Occupied Arab Gulf, 125, 128; visit to

USSR, 128
Popular Front for the Liberation of Oman, 132-36, 138-39, 140, 141, 142, 144, 146, 148; visits to USSR, 134, 140, 143
Popular Front for the Liberation of Oman and the Arab Gulf, 128, 130, 132; 2nd Congress, 132; visits to USSR, 130

Qabus bin Said, 127, 134, 136, 138, 139, 140, 141, 142, 144; visits to U.S., 134, 138, 148
Qadhdhafi, Muammar, 140, 192
Qasim, Salih Muslih, 68, 75, 107, 117, 192, 195

Red Sea security, 64, 66, 68, 79, 169, 171, 173-74, 193 [Soviet reaction, 66]; Taizz Conference, 65, 137, 173

Salih, Ali Abdullah, 182, 183, 186-89, 190-92, 194, 196-97, 199; visit to PDRY, 194; visit to USSR, 192-93
Saudi Arabia, and Oman, 128, 138; and PDRY, 19, 28, 29, 31, 50, 52, 55, 58, 60, 63-64, 66-68, 70, 71, 73, 76, 78, 83 fn. 66, 88, 96, 100, 102, 104, 114, 117, 133, 138, 180; aid, 57, 59, 61, 64, 66, 68, 71, 115, 116, 118, 149 [tied to PDRY policy toward Oman, 132, 135]; diplomatic relations, 56 [Soviet reaction, 57]; and YAR, 7, 53, 70, 157, 160, 162, 165, 166, 168, 171, 173, 179, 182, 190, 193-94, 195, 198; economic and military aid, 160, 166, 167, 169, 171, 173, 180, 186, 190, 195
as-Shaabi, Qahtan, 15, 17, 18, 22, 127; visit to USSR, 20-22, 127
Skachkov, Semen, 53, 65, 67
Sokolov, Sergei, 64, 106
'state of socialist orientation', 86-87, 119 fn. 3
Suslov, Mikhail, 30, 51, 58

Tripartite Pact, 107, 144, 192

Umar, Sultan Ahmad, 194
USSR: Indian Ocean policies, 32, 50, 55, 60, 66, 71, 73, 76, 89; naval activities

in Indian Ocean, 19-20, 22, 95, 97, 115; Red Sea policies, 31, 49, 59, 66, 158, 162-63, 170, 173, 174; 24th CPSU Congress, 30; and Dhofar, 126-30, 132, 134-35, 136, 137, 138, 139, 140, 142, 146; and Horn of Africa, 64, 67, 69, 71, 137, 279-80; and Iran, 126, 129, 131, 132; and Kuwait, 108, 140; and Oman, 92, 102, 127-28, 129, 134, 137, 138, 139, 140, 142, 144, 145, 146, 147, 148, 149; and PDRY: economic aid, 17, 19, 20, 21, 22, 23, 25, 27, 29, 31-32, 36, 39, 40-41, 44, 51, 56, 60-61, 64, 74, 79, 88, 91, 92, 97-98, 101, 111, 113-14, 116 [quality of, 61, 91, 97, 111]; hesitation before commitment, 15-19, 24; military aid, 16, 17, 20, 23, 26, 29, 32, 33, 36, 41, 42, 43, 51, 60, 64, 71-72, 74, 78, 88, 89, 97, 106, 110; naval visits to, 19-20, 34, 50, 58, 78-79, 89, 90, 106, 144; political aid, 25, 61, 74, 77, 87; reported strategic agreement, 72, 75; results of aid programs, 62; use of PDRY military facilities, 29, 41, 43-44, 62, 71, 72, 74, 79, 97, 109, 119; and Persian Gulf states, 126, 128-30; and Saudi Arabia, 53, 57, 60, 66, 77, 87, 88, 89, 92, 96, 108, 139, 140, 174, 183-84, 185, 194, 198; and Somalia, 24, 56, 60, 62; Treaty of Friendship and Cooperation, 51, 71; and YAR: pre-1962, 4-5; 1962-70, 5-7, 198-99; post-1970, 108, 157-58, 159-64, 166-68, 169, 175, 191, 207; aid, 159, 162, 164, 170, 172, 175, 180, 190, 191, 192, 196, 197-98; arms deal 1979, 93, 186-88 (*see also* Aden; PDRY)

United Political Organization-National Front: factional infighting in, 56, 63, 66, 67, 68, 69-70, 73, 75, 76ff., 79; founding conference, 56 [Soviet reaction, 56] (*see also* National Front; Yemeni Socialist Party)

United States: naval activities in Indian Ocean, 24, 29, 32, 49, 55, 89, 93, 95, 97, 128, 131, 134, 136, 140, 141, 143; Rapid Deployment Force, 97, 140, 141; and Oman, 60, 81 fn. 32, 89, 93, 95, 102, 107-08, 116, 129, 134, 140, 141,

142, 148 [PDRY reaction, 93, 102, 107-08, 116, 142; Soviet reaction, 142-43]; cooperation in military maneuvers, 143, 144, 147-48 [PDRY reaction, 144, 147-48; Soviet reaction, 145, 147, 148, 149] PDRY, 19, 51, 55, 68, 72, 77, 79; and YAR, 36, 89, 162, 169, 180; military aid, 170, 171, 182, 184, 186

Ustinov, Dmitri, 67, 73, 102, 116, 193

Vasilev, A., 127, 128, 150 fn. 4

Yemen Arab Republic: conservatism after 1970, 157, 158, 160, 165, 168; instability, 171; strategic location, 9, 11; tribal power in, 157, 165, 166, 168, 171, 172, 175, 179, 183, 186, 188 (*see also* National Democratic Front; PDRY; Saudi Arabia; USSR; United States)

Yemeni Socialist Party: factional infighting in, 91, 96-98, 102, 103, 105-06, 107, 109, 110, 112, 118, 194, 195, 210 [effects on PDRY policy re. Oman, 145-46, 148; effects on PDRY policy re. Dhofar, 133, 135, 136, 137-39, 140, 142]; 1st Congress, 86, 139 [Soviet reaction, 86-87] (*see also* National Front; United Political Organization-National Front)

Yemeni unity, 158, 159-60, 164-65, 170, 172-73, 174-75, 186, 189, 192, 194-95, 196-97 [Soviet reaction to, 159, 162, 168, 173, 182, 186, 188, 190, 197, 198, 207]; draft Constitution, 194; significance of, 158 (*see also* PDRY)

ABOUT THE AUTHOR

STEPHEN PAGE teaches International Relations at Sheridan College in Brampton, Ontario, Canada. He is the author of *The USSR and Arabia: The Development of Soviet Policies and Attitudes Toward the Countries of the Arabian Peninsula* (London: Central Asian Research Centre, 1971).

Dr. Page holds a B.A. from the University of Western Ontario, an M.A. from American University, and a Ph.D. from the University of Reading.

STUDIES OF INFLUENCE IN INTERNATIONAL RELATIONS

Alvin Z. Rubinstein, *General Editor*

SOUTH AFRICA AND THE UNITED STATES
The Erosion of an Influence Relationship
Richard E. Bissell

SOVIET-INDIAN RELATIONS
Issues and Influence
Robert C. Horn

SOVIET INFLUENCE IN EASTERN EUROPE
Political Autonomy and the Warsaw Pact
Christopher D. Jones

U.S. POLICY TOWARD JAPAN AND KOREA
A Changing Influence
Chae-Jin Lee and Hideo Sato

SOVIET AND AMERICAN INFLUENCE IN THE HORN OF AFRICA
Marina S. Ottaway

THE UNITED STATES AND IRAN
The Patterns of Influence
R. K. Ramazani

SOVIET POLICY TOWARD TURKEY, IRAN AND AFGHANISTAN
The Dynamics of Influence
Alvin Z. Rubinstein

THE UNITED STATES AND PAKISTAN
The Evolution of an Influence Relationship
Shirin Tahir-Kheli

THE UNITED STATES AND BRAZIL
Limits of Influence
Robert Wesson

THE UNITED STATES, GREECE AND TURKEY
The Troubled Triangle
Theodore A. Couloumbis

THE UNITED STATES AND MEXICO
Patterns of Influence
George W. Grayson

THE SOVIET UNION AND CUBA
Interests and Influence
W. Raymond Duncan